c|net Do-It-Yourself PC UPGRADE PROJECTS

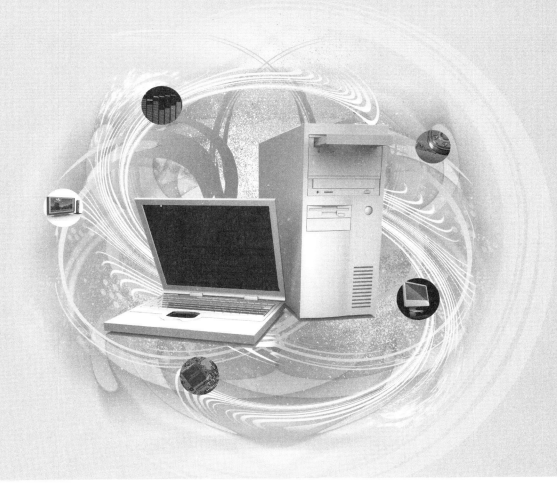

About the Author

Guy Hart-Davis is the author of more than 40 computer books, including *CNET Do-It-Yourself iPod Projects, How to Do Everything with Microsoft Office Word 2007*, and *How to Do Everything with Microsoft Office Excel 2007*.

c|net Do-It-Yourself PC UPGRADE PROJECTS

24 cool things you didn't know you could do!

Guy Hart-Davis

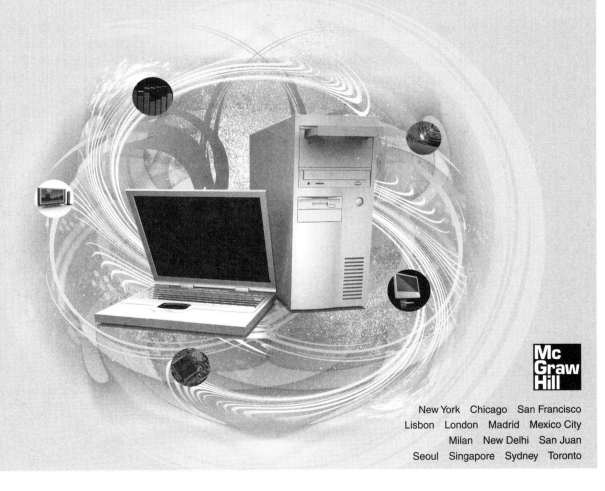

Mc Graw Hill

New York   Chicago   San Francisco
Lisbon   London   Madrid   Mexico City
Milan   New Delhi   San Juan
Seoul   Singapore   Sydney   Toronto

The **McGraw·Hill** Companies

Cataloging-in-Publication Data is on file with the Library of Congress

McGraw-Hill books are available at special quantity discounts to use as premiums and sales promotions, or for use in corporate training programs. To contact a special sales representative, please visit the Contact Us page at www.mhprofessional.com.

CNET Do-It-Yourself PC Upgrade Projects:
24 cool things you didn't know you could do!

1234567890   QPD QPD   0198

ISBN   978-0-07-149628-5
MHID   0-07-149628-9

Sponsoring Editor
Roger Stewart

Editorial Supervisor
Janet Walden

Project Manager
Vasundhara Sawhney,
International Typesetting
and Composition

Acquisitions Coordinator
Carly Stapleton

Technical Editor
Jennifer Ackerman Kettell

Copy Editor
Bill McManus

Proofreader
Divya Kapoor

Indexer
WordCo Indexing Services

Production Supervisor
Jean Bodeaux

Composition
International Typesetting
and Composition

Illustration
International Typesetting
and Composition

Art Director, Cover
Jeff Weeks

This book is dedicated to my parents.

Contents

Part III   Advanced

Foreword

The days of tinkering with our cars are largely over, but we wouldn't have time anyway—the PC takes up our tinker time now! Instead of shade-tree mechanics, we are now a nation of computer upgraders. Beefing up hard drives, RAM, and video cards has replaced carburetor tweaks and oil changes. (And we're a less greasy nation for it!)

McGraw-Hill and CNET have compiled the most asked-for upgrades in this very clear set of projects. This may be one of the most essential titles in our series because it's still a tricky world inside your PC case and, unlike working on a '69 Ford, you can't just figure out PC upgrades by looking at the parts.

Some of this book's projects are classic hardware jobs, like drive and memory upgrades or dual-monitor setups. Others are more software oriented, like setting up your PC as an IP phone or a living-room media center. And some projects are almost more of a user upgrade—the project on good practices and technology for backups fits that category!

You may also want to enjoy the hottest project in PCs today: virtualization. The idea of running more than one operating system on a single computer has been catching on in a big way. Macs and PCs now run on the same CPUs, Linux operating systems are desktop-friendly, and a certain détente has been reached that admits some operating systems are just better at some tasks than others. Now the question, "Mac, Linux, or PC?" can often be answered, "Yes."

One thing hasn't changed and that's the sharp metal edges inside your PC's case! So put on some gloves, open your machine, thumb ahead in this book, and get ready to create a new PC out of your old one. We promise, your nails will still be clean when you're done.

Brian Cooley
CNET Editor-at-Large

Acknowledgments

I'd like to thank the following people for their help with this book:

- Roger Stewart for developing the book and making it happen
- Carly Stapleton for handling the acquisitions end of the book
- Jennifer Kettell for reviewing the manuscript for technical accuracy and contributing many helpful suggestions
- Bill McManus for editing the manuscript
- Vasundhara Sawhney, Jean Bodeaux, and Janet Walden for coordinating the production of the book
- International Typesetting and Composition for laying out the pages
- WordCo Indexing Services for writing the index

Introduction

PCs are amazing. Every year, they become faster and their capabilities increase—yet the prices keep coming down. These days, most PCs come so loaded with features that many people never come to grips with some of the most useful ones.

This book shows you how to make the most of your PC's built-in features, from telephony to television, from networking to unbreakable encryption—and how to go far beyond them by adding further hardware and software to your PC.

What Does This Book Cover?

This book contains three sections of projects. Roughly speaking, the early projects are easy, and the later projects are harder.

Some of the early projects are general and form a good basis for the other projects. For example, the first two projects—increasing your PC's memory, and getting the fastest possible affordable Internet connection—are ones you may want to tackle before progressing to the other projects. But if your PC is already fully loaded and hooked up to a blazingly fast Internet connection, you'll already be set to dive into the other projects.

Most of the projects are independent, so you can tackle the projects that interest you in any order. However, some of the projects depend on other projects. For example, Project 14 shows you how to set up your PC for recording live audio (such as music you play), and Project 15 shows you how to perform the recording. So if you want to work through Project 15, you'll normally want to work through Project 14 first.

Here's a breakdown of the projects.

Easy Projects

Project 1, "Max Out Your Memory and Turbo-Charge It with ReadyBoost," shows you how to increase the amount of RAM in your PC to the max—and then add an extra kick by using Windows Vista rather than Windows XP, add an extra kick by using the ReadyBoost feature. For most PCs, memory is the least expensive and most effective way of making Windows run faster, so unless your PC is already stuffed to the gills with memory, you'll probably want to start here.

Project 2, "Get the Fastest Possible Internet Connection," explains your various options for Internet connections—depending on where you live and on how friendly your local utility companies choose to be. If you've already got the fastest Internet connection available, skip this project. Otherwise, upgrade your Internet connection, and you'll upgrade your entire computing experience.

Project 3, "Turn Your PC into a Free Phone," demonstrates how to install the Skype software and use it to make free phone calls (you'll need a headset, or speakers and a microphone). You'll find Skype easy to use and an easy way to save money on phone bills.

Project 4, "Turn Your PC into a Video Phone," shows you how to use Windows Live Messenger to make video calls on your PC. As you'd imagine, you need a video camera and a broadband Internet connection to make calls. Whoever you're calling needs the same.

Intermediate Projects

Project 5, "Turn Your PC into a Media Center," explains how to add a TV tuner to your PC so that you can use the Windows Media Center program included with Windows Vista Home Premium Edition and Windows Vista Ultimate Edition.

Project 6, "Learn to Work with Your PC's BIOS," gets you started making changes to the Basic Input/Output System that makes your PC tick. The project walks you through booting your PC from the optical drive (as you'll need to do for some of the other projects) and applying a BIOS password to protect your PC. The essentials you learn in this project will enable you to make other BIOS changes when you need to.

Project 7, "Replace Your Hard Disk—or Add Another Hard Disk," covers the ways in which you can increase the amount of hard disk space on your PC. If your PC can contain only a single disk drive (as is the case with most laptops), you will need to replace the drive and install the operating system. But if your PC can contain multiple hard drives, you can simply add one or more extra drives to supplement your existing drive.

Project 8, "Set Up a Multimonitor Monster," shows you how to increase the amount of screen real estate you have available for work or play. Almost any PC—laptop or desktop—can run two monitors out of the box. But if you need even more space to spread out your documents, read this project's advice for ways to connect the maximum possible number of monitors.

Project 9, "Build a Wired Network in Your Home," explains how to choose networking materials and tools, and then build a cabled network that connects all your PCs so that you can share data, devices, and your Internet connection. Building a wired network throughout a home can be a major undertaking—but you will reap the benefits of the network for years.

Project 10, "Recover from Windows Disasters with Knoppix," teaches you to use the "live" Linux distribution called Knoppix to fix problems that prevent your PC from booting Windows successfully. "Live" means that Knoppix boots and runs from your PC's optical drive, which gives you a platform to attack problems on the hard drive that you wouldn't otherwise be able to reach once problems have arisen.

Project 11, "Modify Your PC's Case," gets you acquainted with the tools you need if you're planning to cut, gouge, or otherwise alter your PC's case. This project gives you two examples of case-mod tasks, one practical and the other esthetic.

Project 12, "Use Your PC as Your Home Theater," shows you how to connect a Media Center PC to a TV or projector so that you can enjoy your media files on a wider screen, with others, or both.

Project 13, "Share Your Household's Music and Movies Easily and Effectively," explains the best ways of sharing music and movies among the PCs in your household. You'll learn how to share files via Windows Media Player and via iTunes—and even how to set up a media server for your household.

Project 14, "Turn Your PC into a Recording Studio," shows you how to set up your PC as a recording studio for your home. You'll learn how to prepare a room for recording and how to install and configure the software you need. This project works with Project 15, so you'll probably want to go through the two in turn.

Project 15, "Record Music on Your PC," carries on from Project 14. Now that you've set up your PC as a recording studio, it's time to start recording audio. This project shows you essential recording maneuvers, from laying down tracks to mixing them together and exporting a finished file, and gives you tips about achieving a polished and pleasing result.

Project 16, "Back Up and Restore Your Computer," shows you how to use the über-backup features included in Windows Vista Business Edition and Windows Vista Ultimate Edition to create a backup of either a full drive or your PC's entire contents so that you can restore everything at once if things go wrong.

Project 17, "Create a Wireless Network," teaches you how to set up a wireless network based around an access point—the kind of wireless network you'll want to create for long-term use. You'll learn about the various competing standards for wireless networks, choose suitable equipment for your needs, and then set up the network.

Project 18, "Create an Ad Hoc Wireless Network," shows you how to set up a computer-to-computer wireless network that you can use to share files, devices, or your Internet connection temporarily. If your PCs already have wireless network adapters built in, you're all ready to set up a network; if not, you'll need to add a wireless network adapter before you can begin.

Project 19, "Digitize Your Paper Documents," suggests strategies for getting rid of the heaps of paper that threaten to derail even the most determined digital lifestyle. You'll need a scanner to scan your documents, and perhaps a shredder to dispose securely of those you no longer want. Beyond that, you'll need a system for managing your documents so that you can easily locate the ones you need. This project provides approaches that work for light numbers of documents, moderate numbers of documents, and stacks-of-boxes-full quantities.

Advanced Projects

Project 20, "Seal Your Private Data in an Uncrackable Virtual Locker," explains how to use the encryption features built into Windows Vista Ultimate Edition to protect your important files against intrusion—even if someone else manages to get direct access to your PC's hard drive. This project also steers you toward free encryption software you can use with versions of Windows that don't have built-in encryption.

Project 21, "Stream TV to Your PC or Handheld Device Anywhere," covers getting a Slingbox and setting it up to stream the signal from your TV to either a PC or a handheld device. You can even access the Slingbox remotely over the Internet, which lets you watch your home TV signal from pretty much anywhere.

Project 22, "Silence Your PC or Build an Ultra-Quiet PC," walks you through the process of eliminating as much noise from your PC as possible by silencing each of the noisy components in turn. And if you want a totally silent PC, you can have one—as long as you're willing to pay the price.

Project 23, "Run Other Operating Systems on Top of Windows," explains how to use virtual-machine software such as Microsoft's Virtual PC to install another operating system right on top of Windows. You can then run that operating system, and the programs you install on it, while Windows is running. For example, you may want to install an older version of Windows so that you can use some ancient but still vital software or play an older game that's incompatible with Windows Vista or Windows XP.

Project 24, "Install Another Operating System Alongside Windows," shows you how to set up a dual-boot or multiboot configuration on your PC so that you can start either Windows or another operating system. For example, you may want to switch between Windows Vista and Windows XP, or between Windows Vista and Linux.

Conventions Used in This Book

To make its meaning clear concisely, this book uses a number of conventions, three of which are worth mentioning here:

- Note, Tip, and Caution paragraphs highlight information to draw it to your notice.

- The pipe character or vertical bar denotes choosing an item from a menu. For example, "choose File | Open" means that you should pull down the File menu and select the Open item on it. Use the keyboard, mouse, or a combination of the two as you wish.

- Most check boxes have two states: *selected* (with a check mark in them) and *cleared* (without a check mark in them). This book tells you to *select* a check box or *clear* a check box rather than "click to place a check mark in the box" or "click to remove the check mark from the box." (Often, you'll be verifying the state of the check box, so it may already have the required setting—in which case, you don't need to click at all.) Some check boxes have a third state as well, in which they're selected but dimmed and unavailable. This state is usually used for options that apply to only part of the current situation.

c|net   Visit this book's web page at http://diyupgrades.cnet.com to see related videos.

Max Out Your Memory and Turbo-Charge It with ReadyBoost

What You'll Need

- Hardware: New RAM modules; USB memory stick
- Software: CPU-Z
- Cost: $50–250 U.S.

Ever feel like you're losing your memory and could use a boost? If so, chances are you're not alone. Three-to-one odds says your PC gets that feeling too as you open ever more applications and documents at the same time. When your PC runs low on memory, it starts using hard disk space as virtual memory, and your PC slows down more than enough for you to notice.

This project shows you how to find out how much memory your PC currently has and how much it can have, find suitable memory, and install it. If you're using Windows Vista, you can also use a USB memory stick as virtual RAM, which can give your computer a kick. Microsoft calls this feature ReadyBoost. You can use ReadyBoost either, as well as, or instead of adding RAM.

Max Out Your PC's Memory

Your first task is to find out how much RAM your PC has and how much it can contain. If it can take more memory, you can then decide whether you want to add more memory. If it can't, or if you decide the cost is too high, you may be able to improve your PC's performance by using a USB memory stick to provide ReadyBoost memory. See "Turbo Charge Your PC with ReadyBoost" later in this project for details.

How Much Memory Do You Need?

Windows Vista needs at least 512MB RAM to run well, and Windows XP needs at least 128MB RAM. But both operating systems run much better, and feel far more responsive, if your PC has much more RAM than this. Your PC needs RAM to run the operating system (Windows itself)—in fact, that's what the minimum RAM figures in the first sentence are for. But each application you run requires RAM too. And if you run two or more user sessions at the same time, by using Windows' Fast User Switching feature, you'll need enough RAM for all the applications and documents each user has opened.

Here are memory recommendations for good performance:

- **Single user, few applications**   If you're the only user of your PC, and you run only a few applications (say Internet Explorer and Windows Mail), 1GB RAM should be enough for Windows Vista and 512MB should be plenty for Windows XP.

- **Single user, many or large applications**   If you're the only user but you run large applications, aim for 2GB for Windows Vista or 1GB for Windows XP.

- **Several concurrent users, several applications each**   If you share your PC with several others and use Fast User Switching, aim for 2GB for Windows Vista or 1GB for Windows XP.

- **Several concurrent users, many or large applications**   Get the maximum amount of memory your PC can hold—anywhere from 2GB to 4GB, depending on the model.

Memory generally comes in modules of 128MB, 256MB, 512MB, 1GB, and 2GB. At this writing, 512MB memory modules are the best value for most upgrades, with 1GB modules costing a little more per megabyte but still affordable. 2GB modules are significantly more expensive, but prices are gradually coming down.

4GB is the maximum amount of memory that 32-bit PCs can use. If you have a 64-bit PC (for example, one with an Athlon64 processor) and a 64-bit version of Windows, you should be able to use far more RAM. In theory, a 64-bit computer can use up to 16 exabytes (16 billion gigabytes) of RAM, although current hardware makes 32GB a practical maximum for any computer that's still recognizable as a PC.

Step 1: Find Out How Much Memory Your PC Has

To find out how much memory your PC has, what type it is, and how it is configured, download and install the CPU-Z program, and then run it.

note *If you simply want to find out how much memory your PC has, press WINDOWS KEY–BREAK. On Windows Vista, this key combination displays the System window; look at the Memory (RAM) readout, and then click Close (the × button) to close the window. On Windows XP, this key combination displays the General tab of the System Properties dialog box; look at the readout near the bottom that gives the processor speed and the amount of RAM, and then click OK to close the dialog box.*

Download and Install CPU-Z

1. Open your web browser (for example, choose Start | Internet) and navigate to the CPUID web site, www.cpuid.com.

2. Click the link to download the latest version of the CPU-Z application. The download link is usually on the CPUID home page.

3. If Windows displays the File Download dialog box, prompting you to decide whether to open the file or save it, click Save, and then choose the folder in which to save it. For example, on Windows Vista, you might save the file in the Downloads folder in your user account.

4. When Windows has finished downloading the file, it displays the Download Complete dialog box. Click Open.

5. If Windows displays an Internet Explorer Security dialog box, warning you that "A website wants to open web content using this program on your computer," click Allow. This dialog box appears because CPU-Z is distributed in a zip file, and Windows Explorer needs to unzip it.

6. Follow through the process of unzipping the file to a folder of your choosing. If Windows opens a Windows Explorer window showing you the folder's contents, keep that window open for the next section.

Run CPU-Z and Find Out about Your PC's Memory

To use CPU-Z, follow these steps:

1. In the Windows Explorer window showing the unzipped files, double-click the cpuz.exe file to launch CPU-Z.

2. If Windows displays the Open File – Security Warning dialog box, warning you that "The publisher could not be verified," click Run, and then authenticate yourself to User Account Control. The CPU-Z window then appears.

note *If you have set Windows to hide file extensions, you'll see two files named cpuz in the folder to which you've extracted the zip file's contents. One is the application file, the other a text file containing configuration settings. The file you want is the application file, which is much larger than the text file. (It's no big deal if you double-click the wrong file—you'll just see a text document in Notepad.)*

3. Click the Memory tab (see the left screen in Figure 1-1), and then look at the Size readout in the General group box at the top. This is the total amount of RAM—in the figure, 2048MB, or 2GB. (1GB equals 1024MB.)

Figure 1-1

The Size readout shows the total amount of RAM installed in your PC. The SPD tab lets you examine the size and type of each memory module. Use the Memory Slot Selection drop-down list to select the module you want to view.

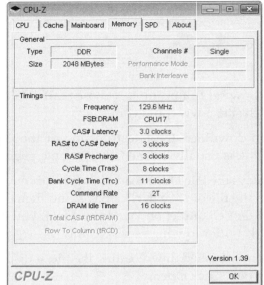
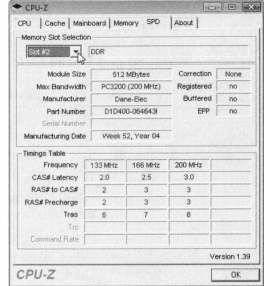

4. In the upper-left corner of the General group box, check whether the Channels readout says Single or Dual:

    ● **Single**   If your PC uses single-channel memory, you can safely put different-sized memory modules in different slots. Provided that the memory is compatible, the only issue is the total amount of memory installed.

    ● **Double**   If your PC uses dual-channel memory, you may need to install identical memory modules in each pair of memory slots to get the best performance. If your PC has four memory slots, you can have different-capacity memory modules in each pair—for example, 512MB modules in one pair, and 1GB modules in the other pair.

5. Click the SPD tab (see the right screen in Figure 1-1). The Memory Slot Selection drop-down list should show the first memory slot that contains memory. Note the details of the memory module:

    ● **Module Size**   Shows the size of the memory module—for example, 512 MBytes (512MB) or 1024 MBytes (1GB).

    ● **Max Bandwidth**   Shows the memory's speed and its "PC" rating—for example, PC3200 or PC5300. This is one of the terms you'll use when searching for memory.

note   *Depending on your PC's configuration, CPU-Z may not be able to detect any memory information on the SPD tab except the module size.*

- **Manufacturer**   Shows the name of the memory manufacturer. You may need this information to identify the type of memory your PC needs.

- **Part Number**   Shows the part number of the memory. You may need this information when searching for more memory.

6. In the Memory Slot Selection drop-down list, select the next memory slot, and then note the details of the memory module. Repeat the process for each of the memory slots.

note *Most laptops have two memory slots, while most desktops have two, three, or four memory slots.*

Use Other Information Sources if Necessary

If CPU-Z can't tell you which type of memory your PC needs, use one of these two approaches:

- Consult your PC's documentation. This will tell you both the type of memory and the PC's maximum capacity. If you've lost the documentation, search the manufacturer's web site for it.

- Use a tool such as those provided by Micron Technology, Inc.'s Crucial memory division:

  1. Open your web browser and go to www.crucial.com.

  2. To find out which memory type is installed on your PC, click Scan My System, and then agree to the terms and conditions. The Crucial System Scanner displays a recommendation of compatible upgrades together with details of your current memory and configuration.

Figure 1-2 shows an example of the Crucial System Scanner's output. While the scanner has read the PC's memory accurately and provides useful information (the PC takes DDR2 PC2-5300 memory and has two memory slots), the upgrade recommendation is not a good choice—a cost of $599 for a 1GB memory module that provides only a 512MB increase (because it involves removing a 512MB module) is not worthwhile.

Figure Out Your Memory Options

From what you've learned in the previous sections, figure out whether your PC can contain more memory. Here are examples of two configurations you may run into.

Laptop PC, Two Slots, 512MB RAM in One Slot   Say you have a laptop PC with two memory slots, one of which currently contains a 512MB memory module. You have three choices for increasing the memory:

- **Add 512MB to the second slot**   By installing a 512MB memory module in the second slot, you get 1GB RAM. This is an inexpensive upgrade that will improve your PC's performance significantly.

Figure 1-2

The Crucial System Scanner can tell you your PC's memory configuration and recommend compatible memory. Evaluate its recommendations carefully before implementing them.

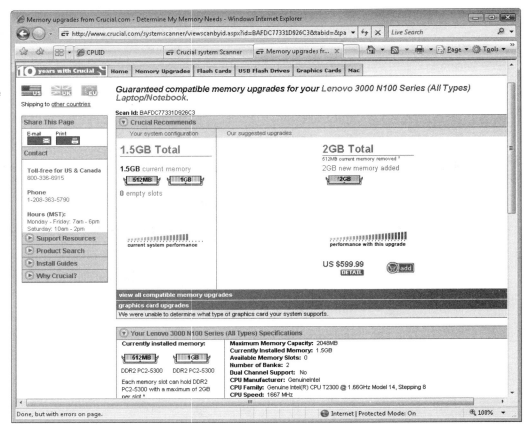

- **Add 1GB to the second slot**   By installing a 1GB memory module in the second slot, you get 1.5GB RAM. This upgrade is more expensive than the preceding option, but you'll be able to run even more programs.

- **Switch to two 1GB modules**   To get the most RAM, you must remove the 512MB memory module and install a 1GB memory module in each slot. This upgrade gives you the best possible performance but is also the most expensive. Treat the surplus memory module gently, and you may be able to sell it on eBay.

note   *Another option is to buy 2GB modules. These tend to be expensive, and some laptops don't support them—so verify that your laptop does before you buy them.*

Desktop PC, Three Slots, 512MB in Each of Two Slots   Say you have a desktop PC with three memory slots, two of which contain a 512MB memory module each. The third memory slot is empty. Again, you have three main choices for increasing the memory—but there's an extra option in this case:

- **Add 512MB to the third slot**   By installing a 512MB memory module in the third slot, you get 1.5GB RAM. This is an inexpensive upgrade that will give your PC an appreciable performance boost—but you may well want more.

● **Add 1GB to the third slot**   By installing a 1GB memory module in the third slot, you double the memory to 2GB. This is an affordable upgrade that will make a big difference without you needing to discard any of the existing memory.

● **Add 1GB to the third slot and replace one or two of the 512MB modules**
If 2GB memory isn't enough, you'll need to not only add a 1GB memory module to the third slot but also replace either one or both of the 512MB memory modules. You can go to 2.5GB or 3GB total. Again, you may be able to sell the memory modules you remove—or, better, use them in another of your PCs.

note   *Another option is to buy one or more 2GB modules. These are available for most desktop PCs, but they tend to be more than twice as expensive as 1GB modules. There's also another problem you need to know about: most normal PCs can have a maximum of 4GB of memory. This is enough for all conventional computing needs, but because of hardware limitations in the ways PCs are designed, the PC cannot actually use the full amount of memory. If you install 4GB of memory, typically between 3GB and 3.5GB will actually be available.*

Step 2: Buy the Memory

Armed with the information you've gathered so far, you're ready to buy the memory for your PC. Your local computer store probably has suitable memory, but you'll almost certainly find a wider selection—and perhaps better prices—online, either from a major online retailer such as CDW (www.cdw.com) or PC Connection (www .pcconnection.com) or directly from a memory company such as Crucial (www.crucial .com) or Kingston Technology Company (www.kingston.com).

Get the Most Bang for Your Memory Buck

Here are two strategies for getting the maximum amount of memory for the money you pay:

● **Max out the memory when you buy**   If you have enough money, get the maximum amount of memory installed when you buy the PC. This way, you'll enjoy the best possible performance from the start, and you can be sure that you'll never need to discard memory modules in order to upgrade.

● **Leave some memory slots free**   If you can't max out the memory when you buy your PC, don't fill up the memory slots with low-capacity modules. Instead, put higher-capacity modules in one or more of the slots, and leave the remaining slots empty until you can afford to stuff high-capacity modules into them. For example, if you buy a laptop that has two memory slots, it's better to buy a 1GB module for one slot (and then be able to upgrade to 2GB by adding another 1GB module) than to reach 1GB by putting 512MB in each of the slots and needing to discard one or both modules when you upgrade.

Step 3: Install the Memory

With the memory in hand, you're ready to install it:

● **Desktop PC**   The installation process is usually straightforward, as shown in the first example that follows. However, if you have a small or specially shaped PC, you may have to remove some components in order to access the RAM.

● **Laptop PC**   Laptops have widely varying designs. If you're lucky, your laptop's memory is in an easily accessible location—for example, under a screwed-down hatch on the bottom of the laptop, as in the following second example. If you're unlucky, you may have to partly disassemble the PC to install the memory—for example, flipping back the keyboard and then removing components under it. Consult your PC's manual to learn the details.

Install the Memory in a Desktop PC

To install the memory in a desktop PC, follow these general steps:

1. Shut down Windows, turn off your PC, and disconnect all the cables.

2. Put your PC on a table or other suitable surface.

3. Open the side opposite the motherboard. For example, you may need to undo a latch, unscrew a couple of thumb-screws (the knurled kind you turn with your fingers), or unscrew case screws with a screwdriver.

4. Touch a metal part of the PC's case to discharge any static from your body.

5. If you need to remove one of the existing memory modules:

   ● Lay down a sheet of paper or an antistatic bag (the kind computer components come in) so that you have somewhere to put the module.

   ● Press down and out with a thumb on each of the spring clips at the ends of the socket, as shown in Figure 1-3. When the clips release, they push the memory module up and out.

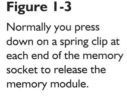

Figure 1-3

Normally you press down on a spring clip at each end of the memory socket to release the memory module.

- Remove the module using your fingers, and then put it on the bag or sheet of paper. Avoid touching the contacts on the module—they're sensitive.

6. Insert the new memory module:

- Remove the memory module from its protective bag.

- Align the memory module with the memory slot, making sure the notch in the module matches the break in the socket, as shown in Figure 1-4.

Figure 1-4

Place the memory module's corners in the guides in the spring clips so that you can press it down into place.

- Press the memory module down gently but firmly, so that it slides into the socket and the spring clips engage.

7. Close the PC, restore it to its normal place, and then reconnect the cables.

 While your PC is open, you might want to give it a quick spring clean—especially if the fan is as dusty as the fan in the sample PC is.

Install the Memory in a Laptop PC

To install the memory in a laptop PC, follow these general steps:

1. Shut down Windows, turn off your PC, and disconnect any cables.

2. Remove the battery.

3. Touch a metal object to discharge any static from your body.

4. Following the instructions in the PC's documentation, open the memory area.

5. If you need to remove one of the existing memory modules:

- Lay down a sheet of paper or an antistatic bag (the kind computer components come in) so that you have somewhere to put the module.

- Press out with a thumb or finger on each of the spring clips at the ends of the socket. (If the space is confined enough to make using your hands awkward, use the eraser ends of a couple of eraser-tipped pencils.) When the clips release, they push the memory module up and out.

- Remove the module using your fingers, and then put it on the bag or sheet of paper.

6. Insert the new memory module:

   - Remove the memory module from its protective bag.

   - Align the memory module with the memory slot, making sure the notch in the module matches the break in the socket. For many laptop memory slots, you need to insert the memory module at an angle, as shown in Figure 1-5.

Figure 1-5

Insert the memory module carefully. Usually it goes in at an angle, like this.

   - Press the memory module down gently but firmly, so that the spring clips engage. Figure 1-6 shows an example.

7. Close the laptop, replace the battery, and then reconnect any cables needed.

Step 4: Restart Your PC and Verify It Recognizes the Memory

Restart your PC and verify that it recognizes the memory you have added. The easiest way to do this is to run CPU-Z again after Windows has loaded.

note *If your PC doesn't recognize the memory, consult the documentation to learn whether you must make a change in the BIOS to tell the PC to find the memory. (Project 6 discusses what the BIOS is and how to access it.) Failing that, you may need to open your PC again to make sure the memory is properly seated in its socket.*

Figure 1-6

Press the memory module into place. The spring clips are the shiny metal pieces just above each fingernail.

Spring clip   Spring clip

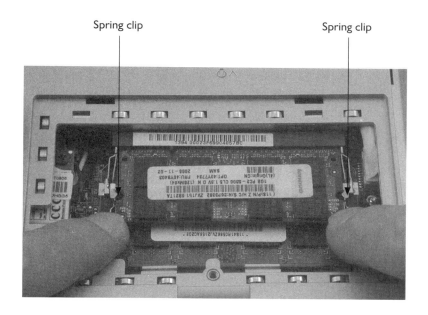

Turbo Charge Your PC with ReadyBoost

Apart from RAM, Windows Vista provides a second way that you can add memory to your PC: ReadyBoost.

Step 1: Understand What ReadyBoost Is and How It Can Help

ReadyBoost is a new memory technology that Microsoft introduced in Windows Vista. Earlier versions of Windows cannot use ReadyBoost; nor can other operating systems (for example, Mac OS X or Linux). ReadyBoost allows you to plug a USB memory stick or similar memory device into your PC and assign it for use as extra memory. (You can use only one memory device for ReadyBoost at a time.) Windows stores small chunks of frequently needed data on the ReadyBoost device, from which Windows can retrieve the data more quickly than if the data were stored on the hard disk.

Step 2: Decide Whether to Use ReadyBoost

Look to use ReadyBoost in any of the following situations:

- You've already installed the maximum amount of RAM that your PC can have, and performance is still disappointing.

- Your PC doesn't have its maximum amount of RAM, but to increase the RAM, you would need to replace some or all of the existing memory modules.

note   *If you can easily add RAM to your PC, do so before trying ReadyBoost. RAM will give you a far greater performance improvement. However, ReadyBoost is well worth trying, especially if you already have a spare memory device you can use.*

- You've borrowed someone's PC and find performance lacking.

Step 3: Find Memory That Will Work for ReadyBoost

ReadyBoost requires memory that can store and return data quickly enough to supplement RAM effectively. Many USB 2.0 memory devices *are* fast enough to use for ReadyBoost, but others are not, including some that claim to be very fast. The problem is that ReadyBoost requires all the memory in the memory device to be consistently fast, while some devices use a special high-speed memory gateway to get better performance out of a larger bank of slower memory. Such an arrangement doesn't work for ReadyBoost.

Some companies market memory devices as being suitable for ReadyBoost. With such devices, you're on safe ground—although the prices tend to be higher than for regular memory devices. If a device isn't marked as being suitable for ReadyBoost, make sure all its memory can provide at least 1.75 megabytes per second (Mbps) for 512KB random writes, and 2.5 Mbps for 4KB random reads. Finding out this information usually involves reading the manufacturer's specification sheet.

If you already have a USB 2.0 memory stick, it'll cost you nothing to find out whether it works for ReadyBoost.

Step 4: Configure ReadyBoost on Your PC

Once you've chosen your device, configure ReadyBoost on your PC. Follow these steps:

1. Plug the drive into a USB port on your PC. (You can also use a USB hub, but plugging it directly into a port usually gives more consistent results.) Windows displays the AutoPlay dialog box for the drive.

note *If Windows doesn't display the AutoPlay dialog box for the drive, choose Start | Computer to open a Computer window. Right-click the icon for the USB drive and choose Properties. Windows displays the Removable Disk Properties dialog box. Click the ReadyBoost tab.*

2. Click the Speed Up My System Using Windows ReadyBoost link. Windows displays the ReadyBoost tab of the Removable Disk Properties dialog box.

   ● If you're lucky, the ReadyBoost tab will look like the one shown on the left in Figure 1-7.

   ● If the ReadyBoost tab looks like the one shown on the right in Figure 1-7, bearing the message "This device does not have the required performance characteristics for use in speeding up your system," click the Test Again button once or twice. Windows seems to find some USB devices marginally too slow on the first or second read, but passes them on a retest. If Windows gives you this message persistently, try a different device.

Figure 1-7

If the ReadyBoost tab looks like the left screen here, you're ready to proceed. If it looks like the screen on the right, try testing the USB device again.

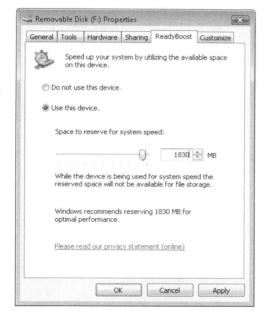

3. Select the Use This Device option button.

4. If you want to adjust the amount of space that Windows uses on the drive, drag the Space To Reserve For System Speed slider or change the value in the text box. Windows recommends setting ReadyBoost to a value between 1× and 2.5× the amount of RAM in your PC—the higher the value, the more performance boost you should get. For example, if your PC has 1GB RAM, you might set anywhere from 1024MB to 2536MB of ReadyBoost memory.

note *The biggest ReadyBoost value you can set is 4096MB (4GB), assuming your USB memory device is capacious enough. The smallest is 256MB.*

5. Click OK. Windows closes the Removable Disk Properties dialog box and starts using the drive for ReadyBoost.

You should now see a performance improvement, especially during long computing sessions or when you have many applications and documents open. However, the difference may not be dramatic.

Step 5: Remove a ReadyBoost Device

For best effect, you should leave the memory device attached all the time you use your PC. This is easy to do with a desktop PC, where you can plug in a USB memory stick and simply leave it, but having a memory stick protruding from a laptop PC tends to be awkward—so you'll probably want to remove it.

To remove the memory device, follow these steps:

1. Click the Safely Remove Hardware icon in the notification area (the icon with the green circle containing a white check mark).

2. On the menu that appears, click the Safely Remove USB Mass Storage Device item for the drive.

3. When Windows displays the Safe To Remove Hardware dialog box, click OK, and then unplug the device.

Windows mirrors all the data that's stored on the ReadyBoost device in a file on your hard disk, so removing your ReadyBoost device doesn't have any bad effects—Windows simply retrieves the data it needs from the hard disk rather than from the ReadyBoost device.

Now that you've maxed out your memory, and maybe turbocharged performance using ReadyBoost, your PC should be running well. It's time to turn your attention to your Internet connection—is it fast enough, and if not, could it be faster?

Get the Fastest Possible Internet Connection

What You'll Need

- Hardware: Modem, router, or satellite dish
- Software: None
- Cost: $10–50 U.S. per month

To get the most use and enjoyment out of your PC these days, you'll want to connect it to the Internet. And not just with any old connection—preferably with the fastest connection possible.

This project discusses your options for choosing a fast Internet connection and shows you how to proceed.

Step 1: Find Out How Fast Your Internet Connection Is

First, find out how fast your Internet connection is—if you haven't already checked. You can find various utilities and sites on the Internet for checking connection speed and throughput. Here, we'll use one of the easiest sites, the CNET Bandwidth Meter. To use the Bandwidth Meter, follow these steps:

1. Launch your web browser and go to http://reviews.cnet.com/7004-7254_7-0.html (see Figure 2-1).

2. Type your area code in the Area Code text box.

3. In the Choose Your Current Connection Type area, select the appropriate option button.

4. In the Select Your ISP drop-down list, choose your current ISP. This step is optional but may enable the Bandwidth Meter to make better recommendations of Internet connection upgrades available to you.

Figure 2-1

The CNET Bandwidth Meter Speed Test lets you check your Internet connection's throughput via a web page.

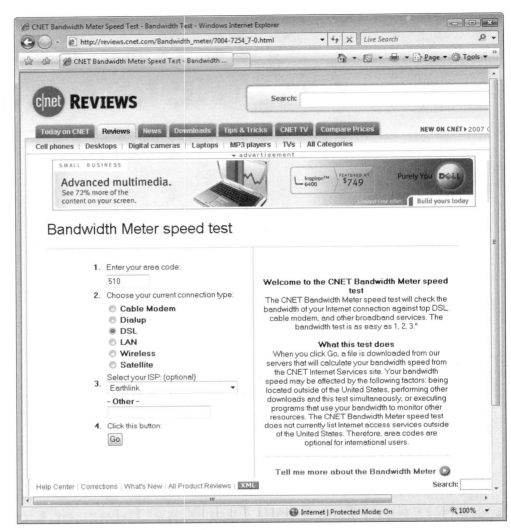

5. Click Go. The Bandwidth Meter runs the test, during which it displays an information screen, and then displays the results page. Figure 2-2 shows an example.

6. If you want, click one of the Find ISP or ISP name links in the Faster Providers column to find out about faster connections. But before you do, it may be a good idea to assess the different types of Internet connection available and decide which would suit you best—assuming it's available.

Step 2: Assess Your Options for a Faster Connection

In the beginning was the modem—and for many people, that's still as far as Internet connectivity has progressed. But in most places you can get a much faster connection, even if it costs more than you would like to pay. This section walks you through

Figure 2-2

The Bandwidth Meter results page shows you an estimate of your current connection speed, together with faster options and providers.

the commonly available Internet connection technologies, starting with the slowest and speeding up to the fastest. Once you know your options, you'll be able to decide which connection type makes sense for you.

Table 2-1 provides a generalized summary of widely available connection options in descending order of preference—in other words, with the best connections first.

Dial-Up Connections

A dial-up connection using a modem is normally the slowest form of Internet connection, but it works almost anywhere you can find a phone line and is usually reliable. On the downside, a dial-up connection is not only slow at transferring data but also slow to connect, typically taking 10–30 seconds to establish a connection.

Location	Connection types
Urban or suburban	1. Fiber 2. DSL or cable 3. Wireless 4. Satellite 5. ISDN 6. Dial-up
Rural	1. DSL (if near to a substation) 2. Satellite 3. ISDN 4. Dial-up

Table 2-1   Typical Connection Options in Descending Order of Preference

These days, a dial-up connection is practical for e-mail or text-only instant messaging, but for most other Internet activities you will find its limitations difficult. See the sidebar "Get the Most Out of a Dial-up Connection" for suggestions on maximizing the use of a dial-up connection while minimizing the irritation its slowness can cause.

The fastest dial-up connection you can get is 53.6 Kbps using a 56 Kbps modem. However, even this speed requires a good-quality telephone line and suitable equipment at the exchange. In practice, speeds of 33.6 to 48 Kbps are normal. The longer the distance from your modem to the ISP, and the greater the number of devices between the two, the slower the connection is likely to be.

Get the Most Out of a Dial-Up Connection

If you're stuck with a dial-up connection, first make sure that your connection is working as well as possible. Here are three suggestions:

- **Keep your connection open**   Get a flat-rate ("all you can eat") connection from your ISP and telephone provider. Configure Windows never to drop the connection and to redial if the connection does get dropped (for example, if the ISP drops it or if there's a problem on the phone line). Turn off call waiting so that incoming calls don't knock you offline. You'll need a second phone line or a cell phone if you want to be able to make phone calls as well.

- **Ensure your modem is tuned correctly**   Type **modem tune-up** into your favorite search engine to find recommendations for configuring a modem manually or modem-boosting utilities that do the tweaking for you.

● **Bond two or more modems together**   If you'll be using dial-up long-term and you have (or can get) two or more phone lines, consider bonding two or more modems together to form a single faster connection. There's some overhead on such connections, so you don't get the full bandwidth of the first modem plus the full bandwidth of each other modem—but you should see a considerable improvement. (For example, bonding two modems each capable of a 48 Kbps connection might yield a 90 Kbps connection.) Your operating system, your modems, and your ISP all need to support modem bonding.

Next, make sure your Internet applications are using your meager bandwidth sensibly. Here are four suggestions:

● **Web browser**   Turn off as much multimedia—pictures, sounds, and videos—as you can bear. For example, in Internet Explorer 7, follow these steps:

1. Choose Tools | Internet Options. Internet Explorer displays the Internet Options dialog box.

2. Click the Advanced tab, and then scroll down to the Multimedia section (about halfway down).

3. Clear the Play Animations In Webpages check box if you can dispense with animations.

4. Clear the Play Sounds In Webpages check box if you can do without sounds.

5. Select the Show Image Download Placeholders check box to make Internet Explorer display placeholders for images.

6. Clear the Show Pictures check box if you can dispense with pictures. (You can display a picture by right-clicking its placeholder and choosing Show Picture.)

7. Click OK. Internet Explorer closes the Internet Options dialog box.

8. If you cleared the Play Animations In Webpages check box in step 3, close and restart Internet Explorer.

● **E-mail**   If possible, set up your e-mail program so that it consults you before downloading attachments greater than a certain size (for example, 50KB). You can then decide whether to download the latest picture of your aunt's dog rather than have it hog your Internet connection when you need to retrieve time-critical messages. Some e-mail programs offer this option, while others do not. Depending on your e-mail service provider, you may also be able to read your e-mail on the Web. This allows you to choose which e-mail headers to open and avoid downloading all the spam along with genuine messages.

(Continued)

● **Queue your downloads** Rather than downloading files while you're performing other activities online, schedule your downloads for a time when you won't be using the computer—for example, in the early hours of the morning. Some web browsers provide download managers. Alternatively, use a third-party download manager such as GetRight (www.getright.com).

● **Close Internet applications you're not using** If you're not using an Internet program, close it to make sure it's not using your bandwidth surreptitiously. For example, IM clients such as Windows Live Messenger tend to lurk in the background, checking in to the IM server to see if there's anything new for you.

ISDN Connections

ISDN, which stands for Integrated Services Digital Network but is usually referred to by its abbreviation, is a digital telephone line that provides modest speeds but greater range than DSL (discussed later in this section) from the telephone exchange.

A normal consumer-grade ISDN line provides two 64 Kbps bearer channels and a delta channel that's used mostly for signaling. Depending on your ISP and phone company, you can use one bearer channel, use both bearer channels (giving 128 Kbps), or use the first bearer channel and add the second bearer channel on the fly when the first channel becomes busy.

Because the phone line is digital, connections take only moments to set up—so even if you do not keep the line open, you can establish a connection much faster than with a modem. If you do keep one channel open all the time (as you will probably want to do if you're paying a flat rate for the ISDN connection), you will find that even though 64 Kbps sounds slow, it is adequate for e-mail and web browsing. However, downloading large files will be slow, even if you add the second channel for the duration of the download.

Consider ISDN only if you can't get a faster type of connection.

DSL Connections

DSL, which stands for Digital Subscriber Line but is also usually referred to by its abbreviation, is a digital telephone line. DSL comes in various implementations, but most consumer ones are variations of ADSL—asymmetrical DSL—in which download (or *downstream*) speeds are much higher than upload (or *upstream*) speeds.

A typical DSL implementation splits off a part of the analog telephone line for digital use, leaving the still-analog part of the phone line for voice use—so with DSL, you don't need to get a second phone line. However, DSL works only within a certain distance of the telephone exchange (the exact distance depends on the implementation), so DSL is not usually available in rural areas.

DSL speeds vary depending on the implementation, with downstream speeds of 384 Kbps to 6 Mbps being common. High-speed DSL, which typically is available only in cities, can provide up to 24 Mbps. Most DSL connections are "always-on"—once you've configured and powered up the DSL router (often referred to as a "DSL modem"), it maintains the Internet connection permanently or until a problem occurs.

DSL can be great for home connections and small offices, because there is enough bandwidth to have multiple computers accessing the Internet at the same time. In many cases, your main choice will be between DSL and a cable connection.

Cable Connections

If you have cable television (or can get it), you can probably get cable Internet as well from your cable provider. Cable connection speeds vary depending on the cable company and its hardware and how far your house is from the cable connection point. But in general, speeds are comparable with DSL—for example, from 512 Kbps up to several megabits per second.

Like DSL connections, cable connections are always-on and provide a good solution for home connections and small offices, with enough bandwidth for multiple computers to connect to the Internet simultaneously.

Wireless Connections

Wireless Internet connections are very convenient, especially if you need to be able to connect from any point within the area covered by the wireless network. At this writing, many coffee shops, libraries, and similar institutions provide wireless Internet access for their patrons, but few wide-area wireless Internet connections are available.

In 2006, Google launched the first citywide wireless network in the United States, in Mountain View, California. Google and other companies are looking to create citywide wireless networks in other cities as well.

Satellite Connections

Satellite tends to be the most expensive form of Internet connection, but it is worth considering if you are in a rural area where the only alternatives are ISDN and dial-up—or perhaps only dial-up. For example:

- StarBand (www.starband.com) offers a 512 Kbps service for $49.99 a month and a 1 Mbps service for $129.99 a month—after you've paid $299 for the satellite dish that's needed.

- HughesNet (www.hughesnet.com) offers a service of up to 1.5 Mbps for $99.99 a month with no upfront fee, but you'll need to commit to a two-year contract.

Fiber-Optic Connections

If your building or street is wired for fiber-optic connections, you should jump at the chance to get one. This is the fastest form of connection, providing bandwidth of 100 Mbps or so. You'll probably be sharing the circuit with your neighbors, but even so, you'll get great performance.

The drawback to fiber-optic connections is that they are normally available only in new communities or refitted buildings (for example, apartment blocks). However, they are gradually becoming more widespread.

Step 3: Order and Install Your Faster Connection

Once you've decided which Internet connection type will suit you best, research Internet service providers (ISPs) who offer that connection type where you live. Here are some pointers:

- To find out which broadband technologies are available where you live, put your area code into a broadband search engine. For example, click one of the Find ISP links or ISP name links in the CNET Bandwidth Meter (discussed earlier in "Step 1: Find Out How Fast Your Internet Connection Is").

- Consult your neighbors, colleagues, or friends about what Internet connection type they have, how well it works, and whether they're happy with it.

- If you've decided to get a cable connection, you may find that your only choice is your existing cable company—in which case, the decision-making process shouldn't take long.

After selecting a provider, order the service and either install it yourself or have it installed (depending on the technology).

Step 4: Find Out How Fast Your New Connection Is

After establishing your Internet connection, run the CNET Bandwidth Meter again to check how fast your connection is. If you've upgraded from a slow connection (such as dial-up) to a broadband connection, you should be able to see the difference easily without measuring the speed.

Your fast Internet connection is just crying out to be used—and use it you will. The next project shows you how to turn your PC into a free VoIP phone, and the project after that shows you how to use your PC for videoconferencing over the Internet.

Project 3

Turn Your PC into a Free Phone

What You'll Need

- Hardware: Broadband Internet connection; headset or speakers and microphone; webcam (optional)
- Software: Skype
- Cost: Free to $75 U.S.

Having a broadband Internet connection opens up all sorts of possibilities to you. Not only can you download massive files in minutes and upload files at a respectable speed, but you can also make phone calls over the Internet. This project shows you how to make Internet phone calls by using the Skype software and service. Skype uses a data-transfer called Voice Over Internet Protocol, or VoIP for short, so you'll often see the term VoIP in connection with Internet phone calls.

Step 1: Line Up Your Audio Hardware

If you're considering this project, you'll need a fast Internet connection. If you don't yet have one, go straight to Project 2 to find out your options.

Next, you need audio hardware—either speakers and a microphone or a headset that includes a microphone. If you plan to make family calls, speakers and a microphone can be a good solution. Otherwise, a headset is normally a better choice, as it lets anyone nearby overhear only the half of the conversation that you control.

If you decide to buy a headset, your main choice is between wired and wireless models. Go with wireless (for example, Bluetooth) if you may feel the need to leave your PC and gesticulate wildly during calls. If you're content to remain tethered, a wired headset should do fine. Using a USB connection is normally easier than using audio jacks—but if you already have a headset that uses audio jacks, it should work fine.

Whichever type of audio hardware you choose, plug it in and install it. As an added bonus, Windows Vista identifies most current USB headsets correctly and installs them automatically, although for some headsets you may need to provide a software driver manually.

Step 2: Download and Install the Skype Software

Next, download and install the Skype software. Follow these steps:

1. Open your web browser. For example, choose Start | Internet.

2. Click in the Address bar, type **www.skype.com**, and then press ENTER or click Go.

3. Click the Download Skype button, and then follow the directions to start the download. Internet Explorer then displays a File Download – Security Warning dialog box.sss

4. Click the Run button. Internet Explorer may display the Internet Explorer – Security Warning dialog box, telling you that "The publisher could not be verified."

5. Click the Run button. Windows displays a User Account Control dialog box warning you that "A program needs your permission to continue."

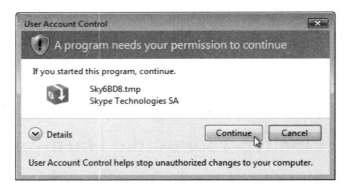

 note *If you've turned off User Account Control, you won't see the User Account Control dialog box—but be warned that turning off User Account Control removes one of Windows Vista's main layers of defense against malware (malicious software). No matter how annoying you find User Account Control's constant naggings for reassurance that you're the one running potentially dangerous software, keeping User Account Control on is a good idea.*

6. Click the Continue button. The Skype Install routine launches and displays the first screen.

7. In the Select Your Language drop-down list, choose you language. Click the links to read the End User License Agreement and the Skype Privacy Statement, and then select the Yes, I Have Read And Accept check box.

8. Click the Options button. The Skype Install routine displays the Options screen.

9. The Select Where Skype Should Be Installed text box shows the default installation folder for Skype—in a \Skype\Phone folder inside your Program Files folder. For most computers, this is a good choice. However, if you want to use a different folder, click the Browse button, use the Browse For Folder dialog box to select the folder, and then click the OK button.

10. Select the check boxes for the options you want:

    ● **Create A Desktop Icon**   Select this check box if you want an icon for Skype on your Desktop. Having the icon there is handy if you want to be able to launch Skype directly from your Desktop rather than using the Start menu.

    ● **Start Skype When The Computer Starts**   Select this check box if you want Windows to launch Skype automatically whenever you log on. This setting is handy if you intend to use Skype in every Windows session. If you plan to use Skype less frequently, clear this check box.

    ● **Install Skype Extras Manager**   Select this check box if you want to install the Skype Extras Manager, a feature for using additional Skype features (such as games).

11. Click the Install button. The Skype Install routine installs the features you chose and then displays the Thank You For Installing Skype screen.

12. If you want to use the Skype add-on for Internet Explorer, which allows you to use Skype to easily call the phone numbers shown on websites using Skype, leave the Also Install The Skype Add-On For Internet Explorer check box selected. Otherwise, clear this check box.

13. Click the Start Skype button. Windows launches Skype. Go straight to the next step.

Step 3: Set Up Your Skype Account

The first time you run Skype, you need to create a Skype account (unless you have one already) and then configure Skype to use that account. Follow these steps:

1. If you're continuing directly from the previous step, you should have Skype open with the Skype – Create Account Wizard running and the first Create A New Skype Account screen displayed. If not, double-click the Skype icon on your Desktop or choose Start | All Programs | Skype | Skype to launch Skype.

2. Click the Skype End User License Agreement link, the Skype Terms Of Service link, and the Skype Privacy Statement link, and then read each in turn. If you can accept the terms, continue with this list. If not, click the Cancel button to stop installing Skype.

3. Type your name in the Full Name text box. This is optional, but it'll help identify you to the people you call.

4. In the Choose Skype Name text box, type the Skype username you want to request. The name you want may well be taken already, so it's a good idea to think of several alternatives before you start.

5. Type the password you will use for Skype in the Password text box and in the Repeat Password text box (to make sure you get it right). The password must be at least four characters long, but you'll get much greater security if you use six characters or more.

6. Select the Yes, I Have Read And I Accept check box for all the items you read in step 2, and then click the Next button. The wizard displays the second Create A New Skype Account screen.

7. Type an e-mail address in the E-mail text box. You're required to enter an address here; and if you want to be able to retrieve your password, you need to use a real address.

8. Clear the Yes, Send Me Skype News And Special Offers check box unless you want to receive e-mail news and offers.

9. Optionally, choose your country or region in the Country/Region drop-down list, and enter your city in the City text box.

10. Select the Sign Me In When Skype Starts check box if you want Skype to sign you into the service automatically as soon as you launch Skype. If you want people to be able to contact you easily, signing in automatically is a good idea.

11. Click the Sign In button. If Windows Vista displays a Windows Security Alert dialog box, to tell you that "Windows Firewall has blocked some features of this program," verify that the name is Skype, and then click the Unblock button and authenticate yourself to User Account Control.

12. If the wizard displays a screen telling you that "The Skype name you chose is already taken," select the option button for one of the alternative names offered, or select the last option button and type a different username that you want to try. Click the Sign In button.

13. When you've chosen an unused name, Skype registers that name for you, and then displays the Skype – Getting Started tutorial. Go through it as described in the next section.

Step 4: Make Sure Your Sound Equipment Works with Skype

To make those calls, you need to make sure your headset, or your speakers and microphone, work with Skype. Follow these steps:

1. If you're following on directly from the previous section, you should have the Skype – Getting Started Wizard running and showing its Hello screen. If not, choose Help | Getting Started from the main Skype window to launch the wizard.

2. Select the Do Not Show This Guide At Startup check box to prevent the wizard from running again automatically, and then click the Start button. The wizard displays the Check That Your Sound Works In Skype screen:

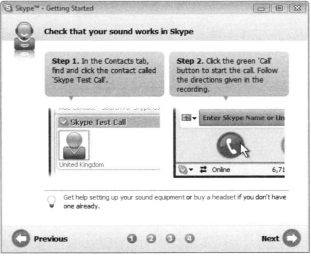

3. Arrange the window so that you can see both the Skype window and the wizard, and then follow the instructions. Click the Call Me To Test Your Sound item in your Contacts. Skype displays the Profile For Skype Test Call window:

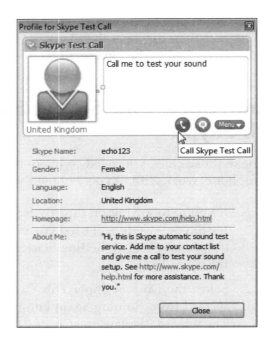

4. Click the Call Skype Test Call button. Skype opens the call window:

5. Click the Call button to place the test call. Listen to the audio message (change the volume if necessary), record a message of your own after the tone, and verify that the audio volume and quality are acceptable when Skype plays the message back to you.

6. Click the Hang Up button to end the call.

You're now ready to make some calls—as soon as you have some people to call.

tip   *If you don't want the Skype Test Call contact to appear in your Contacts list, click it, click the Menu button, and choose Remove From Contacts. Alternatively, leave the test contact in place in case you need to check your Skype setup again.*

Step 5: Add Contacts to Skype

The easy way to make calls with Skype is to create a *contact* (an entry in the address book) for each person you want to call. To create a contact, follow these steps:

1. In the main Skype window, click the Contacts tab if it's not already displayed.

2. Click the Add Contact button. Skype launches the Add A Contact Wizard, shown in Figure 3-1, after a successful search.

Figure 3-1

Searching by a person's "real" name may turn up 24 or more aliases.

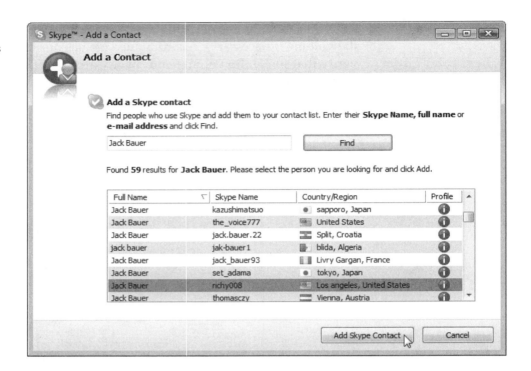

3. Type the person's Skype name, full name, or e-mail address in the text box, and then click the Find button. Skype searches its user list and displays matches.

4. Select the right person, and then click the Add Skype Contact button. The wizard displays the Say Hello! dialog box:

5. Type a message to the contact in the text box.

6. If you want to prevent the contact from seeing your contact details, click the Show Options button, and then select the Do Not Share Your Contact Details With Them option button instead of the Share Your Contact Details With Them option button. Normally, you'll want to share your own details with your contacts so that they can be clear on who you are.

7. Click the OK button. Skype sends the message to the contact and returns you to the wizard.

8. Add further contacts as necessary, and then click the Close button to close the wizard.

Step 6: Call a Contact

To call a contact, follow these steps:

1. In the main Skype window, click the Contacts tab if it's not already displayed.

2. Click the contact you want to call. Skype displays the contact's details:

3. Click the Call button in the contact's details. Skype places the call.

4. If the contact answers the call, you can start talking. The Call Duration read-out shows the length of the call so far:

5. Click the Hang Up button when you want to end the call.

Step 7: Receive a Call

When someone calls you, Skype displays a pop-up window showing who is calling. Click the Answer button if you want to answer the call. Skype then establishes the call, and you can start talking.

Step 8: Make Calls to Conventional Phones

Internet telephony can be wonderful, but you'll probably sometimes need to call standard phones, be they landlines or mobiles. To do so, you can use Skype's SkypeOut feature. Unless you're calling a free phone number (for example, an 800 number), you must first buy Skype Credit. Choose File | Skype Account | Go To Account Page, and then follow through the procedure for buying credit. Once you have credit, to make a call to a conventional phone, follow these steps:

1. In the main Skype window, click the Call Phones tab to display its contents.

2. In the Select The Country/Region You Are Dialing drop-down list, choose your country or region—for example, United States.

3. In the Enter [Country/Region] Phone Number (With Area Code) text box, type the phone number.

4. Click the Call button. Skype places the call.

VoIP phone calls are great—but what if you want to be able to see the person into whose ear you're whispering sweet somethings? Your PC can help you out here as well. Turn the page to find out how.

Turn Your PC into a Video Phone

What You'll Need

- Hardware: Video camera with microphone, broadband Internet connection
- Software: Windows Live Messenger
- Cost: $50 U.S.

Turning your PC into a free phone, as described in the previous project, is great. But what if you want to catch the wave of the eternal future, the video phone? Various programs let you use your webcam, microphone, PC, and Internet connection to do this. This project shows you how to get, install, and use Windows Live Messenger, one of the easiest of these programs—and one that doesn't cost you a cent. You'll need a broadband Internet connection to be able to enjoy video phone calls. If you're still mulling broadband, read Project 2 to learn about your options.

Step 1: Get a Suitable Video Camera and Microphone

If your computer came with a video camera and microphone, you're all set. These days, most laptops have a built-in microphone, and increasing numbers of laptops have a basic video camera built in as well. Many desktop computer bundles include a webcam and a microphone, so you may not have to buy anything.

note *Having a webcam built into a laptop is handy, because you won't forget to take the webcam with you, and Windows should already have configured the camera, so that you don't need to configure it manually. However, having the webcam fixed like this means you can't change its placement in order to give your best profile to the person at the other end of the connection.*

If you need to buy a camera, you'll find a wide variety of options available. Use the following points as a brief shopping list:

- **Resolution**   640×480 resolution is adequate for Internet telephony; unless you have a fast connection, 320×240 resolution may be enough. Some as web-cams go up to 1600×1200 resolution, but you will not normally be able to transmit this much data at a reasonable frame rate.

- **USB connection**   USB is the best way to connect a webcam to a PC. You can get other connection types (for example, FireWire), but your first choice should be USB.

- **Stand or monitor clip**   Some webcams clip onto a laptop's lid or a flat-panel monitor. Others include stands or have a tripod thread that lets you mount them on a standard tripod.

- **Microphone**   Many webcams include a built-in microphone. These can be useful for simplicity, but you will get better audio quality from either a head-set microphone or a microphone that you can position freely.

- **Windows Vista or Windows XP compatibility**   Most webcams sold nowa-days include drivers for both Windows Vista and Windows XP, so compatibility is seldom a concern. However, if you dig up an old webcam designed for Windows 9x, you may have a hard time finding a driver for it. The main thing to avoid is buying a webcam designed specifically for Mac OS X.

note   *If you don't already have audio hardware, see "Step 1: Line Up Your Audio Hardware" in Project 3 for suggestions on choosing suitable audio hardware for making audio calls from your PC.*

Step 2: Download and Install Windows Live Messenger

Your computer's manufacturer may have included Windows Live Messenger with Windows on your computer, so have a quick look on the Start menu before you download and install it. Choose Start | All Programs, and then look for a Windows Live Messenger item. If you don't see one, you need to download and install Windows Live Messenger. Follow these steps:

1. Choose Start | Internet, and then go to the Windows Live Messenger website (http://get.live.com/messenger/overview).

2. Find the link to download Windows Live Messenger, and then click it. Internet Explorer displays the File Download – Security Warning dialog box.

3. Click the Run button. Internet Explorer downloads the Windows Live Messenger installation file, and then starts to run it. Internet Explorer then displays a Security Warning dialog box.

4. Click the Run button, and then follow through the installation process. Read the license agreement, and make sure that you are prepared to comply with its many stipulations before you agree to it. For example, the agreement makes you state that you will not use Windows Live Messenger to share other people's intellectual property without authorization, and that Microsoft may monitor your communications to verify that you're being a good citizen and

may disclose any evidence against you to the appropriate authorities. (I paraphrase lightly here, but in truth, you're agreeing to a lot—so you should read the license agreement.)

5. Apart from the license agreement, the part of the installation where you should pay attention is the Choose Additional Features And Settings screen. Windows Live Messenger usually tries to install several features that you may well prefer not to have. Here's what you need to know:

- **Windows Live Messenger Shortcuts**   You can launch Windows Live Messenger from the Start menu the way you would any other program. But if you leave this check box selected, you also get a Windows Live Messenger shortcut on the Desktop (which you probably won't need) and one on the Quick Launch toolbar (which is usually a useful way of launching Windows Live Messenger).

- **Windows Live Sign-in Assistant**   This feature is confusing at first, but it can be very helpful. What the Assistant does is allow you to use multiple Windows Live IDs from the same user account in Windows, rather than requiring you to keep one Windows Live ID associated with a single user account. For example, you may have one Windows Live ID for business and another for personal, but use them both from the same Windows user account. The Assistant lets you save the password for each Windows Live ID inside the user account. (This may not sound like a big deal, but it is much better than the arrangement that earlier versions of Messenger used.)

- **MSN Home**   Clear this check box unless you want the installation routine to change your existing home page in Internet Explorer to the MSN Home page.

- **Windows Live Toolbar**   Select this check box only if you want to install the Windows Live Toolbar, which offers instant searching, newsfeeds, course charting, and more. See the Windows Live Toolbar Features page (http://toolbar.live.com/features.aspx) for details to help you decide whether to install Windows Live Toolbar.

6. Click the Close button when the installation routine has finished. The installer then launches Windows Live Messenger. Go to the next step.

Step 3: Run and Configure Windows Live Messenger

At the end of the installation process, the installer opens Windows Live Messenger automatically. After that, you can open Windows Live Messenger in any of these ways:

- **Start menu**   Choose Start | All Programs | Windows Live Messenger.

- **Quick Launch toolbar**   Click the icon (if you let the installer create it).

- **Desktop**   Double-click the icon (again, if you let the installer create it).

Whichever way you start Windows Live Messenger, you see the main Windows Live Messenger window (see Figure 4-1). Windows Live Messenger uses separate windows for conversations with other users, as you'll see in a minute.

Figure 4-1

The main Windows Live Messenger window appears like this the first time you run Windows Live Messenger.

Create a Windows Live ID

To use Windows Live Messenger, you need a Windows Live ID, an electronic identifier with Microsoft's Windows Live service. Windows Live ID is the new name for the electronic ID that started life as Microsoft Passport and then became Microsoft .NET Passport.

If you have created a Hotmail account or an MSN (Microsoft Network) account, you do not need to create a Windows Live ID, because you already have one. Otherwise, follow these steps to create a Windows Live ID:

1. Click the Sign Up For A Windows Live ID link near the bottom of the main Windows Live Messenger window. Messenger opens an Internet Explorer window to the Windows Live ID sign-up page.

2. Click the Sign Up button, and then follow through the process of creating an account.

Sign Into Windows Live Messenger

Once you have a Windows Live ID, you can sign into Windows Live Messenger:

1. Type your Windows Live ID name in the E-mail Address text box.

2. Type your password in the Password text box.

3. Normally, you'll want to make Windows Live Messenger remember your Windows Live ID, so select the Remember Me check box. That'll save you having to type the Windows Live ID name into Messenger in the future.

4. If you want to be able to log onto Messenger quickly and easily, and you're not worried about security, select the Remember My Password check box.

 Saving your password compromises your security, because if someone else can access your Windows user account, they can log onto Messenger using your ID and impersonate you. If you're the only person who has access to your PC, or if you protect your user account with a hard-to-break password, someone else accessing your user account may not be a concern.

5. If you want Messenger to sign you in automatically each time you log onto Windows, select the Sign Me In Automatically check box. If you prefer to sign in manually, make sure this check box is cleared.

6. Click the Sign In button. Messenger signs you in, and then displays a Welcome window, as shown in Figure 4-2.

Figure 4-2

Messenger displays a Welcome window when you sign in.

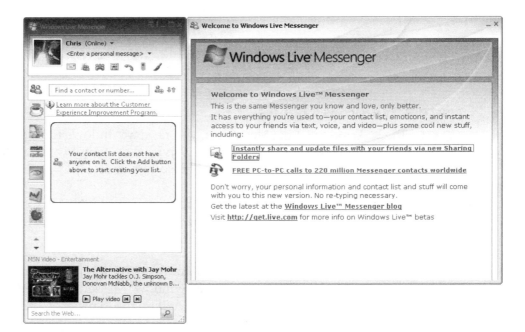

On subsequent logins, Messenger displays the Windows Live Today window, which provides quick access to news headlines and Hotmail e-mail. You may find the Windows Live Today window helpful, but you can also access Hotmail from Messenger itself, so you don't need to keep the window open just for Hotmail.

Configure Windows Live Messenger for Audio and Video

You can use Messenger for text-only chat, but this project assumes that you want to use its audio and video capabilities. To set them up, follow these steps:

1. In the main Messenger window, click the Show Menu button (the button to the left of the Minimize button on the title bar), and then choose Tools | Audio And Video Setup to launch the Audio And Video Setup Wizard.

2. Close all audio and video programs. For example, close Windows Media Player if you're listening to music.

3. Make sure your webcam, microphone, and speakers are connected.

4. Click the Next button. The wizard displays the Speaker Setup screen.

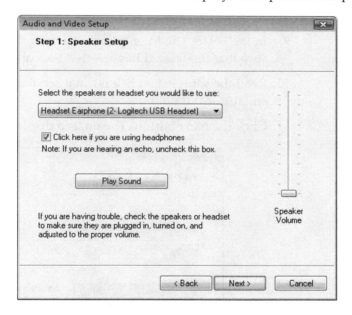

5. In the Select The Speakers Or Headset You Would Like To Use drop-down list, make sure that the wizard has selected your speakers or headset. (If you have only speakers, there's a good chance that the wizard will have made the right choice.)

6. If you're using headphones, select the Click Here If You Are Using Headphones check box.

7. Click the Play Sound button to start playing a sample sound, and then drag the Speaker Volume slider to set the volume to a reasonable level.

8. Click the Next button. The wizard displays the Microphone Setup screen.

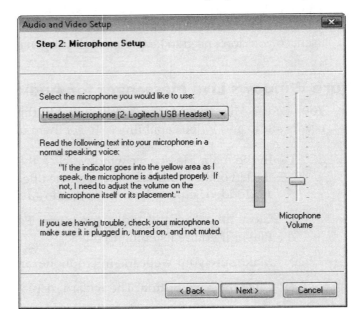

9. In the Select The Microphone You Would Like To Use drop-down list, make sure that the wizard has selected the correct microphone.

10. Read the sample text in a normal speaking voice to allow the wizard to set a suitable input volume.

11. Click the Next button. The wizard displays the Webcam Setup screen.

12. In the Select The Webcam You Would Like To Use drop-down list, make sure that the wizard has selected the correct webcam.

13. Check that the webcam preview is showing you as you want it to. If the webcam is movable, you may want to move it; if it's fixed to your laptop, you may want to move the laptop or move yourself.

14. Click the Options button, and then use the Properties dialog box to apply any options you want. Click the OK button when you're content with the choices. The contents of the Properties dialog box vary depending on your webcam's capabilities (Figure 4-3 shows examples of two tabs), but you may be able to make changes such as these:

    ● Flip the image or mirror it.

Figure 4-3

Your webcam may let you change the color balance or lighting—or distort your face in assorted ways.

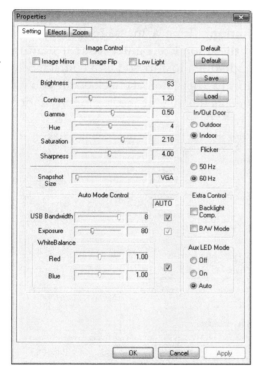 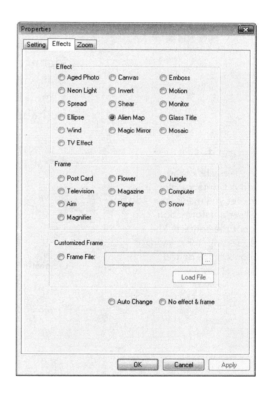

note To see the effects of the changes you're making, drag the Properties dialog box so that you can see the Webcam Setup page of the wizard.

    ● Change the brightness, contrast, or gamma correction.

    ● Apply effects such as making the picture look like an aged photo or making you look like an alien.

    ● Zoom in or out, or apply face tracking.

15. Click the Finish button to close the wizard and to apply the settings you chose.

Step 4: Add Contacts

You're all set to make a call—but you don't have any contacts to call. In order to call someone using Messenger, you need to add a contact for them:

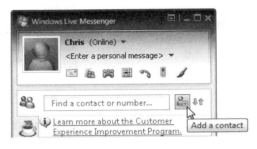

1. Click the Add A Contact button, shown here, to display the Add A Contact dialog box (see Figure 4-4).

2. On the General tab, type the essential information for the contact:

   - **Instant Messaging Address** You need this address to reach the contact.

   - **Personal Invitation** Type a message that will enable the contact to identify you if they don't recognize your instant-messaging name and that will persuade them to add you as a contact. Select the Also Send An E-mail Invitation To This Contact check box if you want to send an e-mail invitation as well as the instant-messaging invitation.

Figure 4-4

The five tabs of the Add A Contact dialog box let you maintain a full set of information about the contact. The key settings for creating a contact are on the General tab.

- **Nickname**   Type the name by which you want to refer to the contact.

- **Group**   Choose the group to which you want to assign the contact.

3. If you want to add further information, click one of the other four tabs, and then type the information you want. For example, you may want to click the Contact tab so that you can enter the contact's first, middle, and last names.

4. When you've entered all the information you want to enter now (you can enter more information about the contact later if you want), click the Add Contact button. Messenger closes the Add A Contact dialog box and adds the contact to the main Messenger window.

Step 5: Make a Video Call to a Contact

To make a video call, follow these steps:

1. Right-click the contact's name in the main Messenger window and choose Video | Start A Video Call. Messenger opens a Conversation window and displays advertisements at you until your contact accepts the call.

2. When your contact accepts the call, the video of him or her appears in place of the advertisements (see Figure 4-5). You can then start talking, smiling, gesticulating—whatever you need to convey your meaning.

Figure 4-5

Once Messenger establishes the connection, you see your contact's video feed.

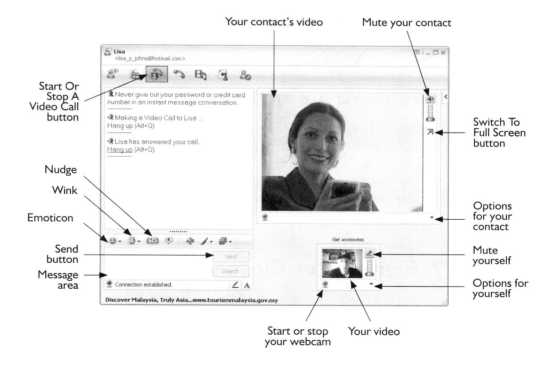

3. If you want to send a text message, type it in the message area, and then press ENTER or click the Send button. You can also send an emoticon (for example, a smiley) by clicking the Emoticon button or send a wink by clicking the Wink button. Some winks are free, while others cost you dearly.

 You can also click the Nudge button to send a nudge—which makes the Messenger window bounce gently on the recipient's screen—if you think you've lost someone's attention. Nudges can be useful (if annoying) for text chat. If you've established a video call with someone, you should be able to tell whether they're ignoring you.

4. If you want to change the size of your contact's video panel, click the Options button next to their picture, highlight Size on the menu, and then choose Small, Medium, or Large.

5. If you want to change the size of your video panel, click the Options button next to your video picture, highlight Size on the menu, and then choose Small, Medium, or Large.

6. If you want to give your contact your undivided attention, click the Switch To Full Screen button. To return the call to a window, click the Switch To Window button in the lower-left corner of the full screen.

7. To end the call, click the Hang Up link in the Conversation window, press ALT-Q, or click the Start Or Stop A Video Call button on the toolbar.

If you're not certain that your contact has a webcam or a fast enough Internet connection for a video conversation, start a text conversation, and then add video if the contact thinks it's a good idea. To start a text conversation, simply double-click the contact's name in the main Messenger window.

Step 6: Receive an Incoming Call

When one of your contacts calls you, Messenger displays a pop-up message above the notification area, as shown here, and flashes a Taskbar button for the Conversation window. Click the Answer button if you want to take the call.

Step 7: Sign Out or Close Windows Live Messenger

Even when you close the main Messenger window by clicking its Close button (the × button), Messenger keeps running so that you can receive incoming calls. If you don't want to receive any calls, sign out by right-clicking the Windows Live Messenger icon in the notification area and then choosing Sign Out. To close Messenger fully, right-click the Windows Live Messenger icon in the notification area and then choose Exit.

Turn Your PC into a Media Center

What You'll Need

- Hardware: TV tuner (if your PC doesn't have one)
- Software: Windows Vista Home Premium Edition or Windows Vista Ultimate Edition
- Cost: $100–300 U.S.

If your computer is running Windows Vista Home Premium Edition or Windows Vista Ultimate Edition, you've got all the software you need to watch and record TV right on your PC. If your PC included a TV tuner board, Windows Vista probably came configured to use it—in which case, you can simply run Windows Media Center without further ado. (If you haven't already set up Windows Media Center, see "Step 3: Set Up Windows Media Center.")

But TV tuners don't come free, so it's perhaps more likely that your PC doesn't have a TV tuner even if it has Vista Home Premium or Vista Ultimate. This project shows you how to add a TV tuner to your PC so that you can enjoy Windows Media Center.

If your computer has any other version of Windows Vista, you need to upgrade to Home Premium (from Home Basic) or to Ultimate (from Business) if you want to run Windows Media Center. Upgrading is simple, as you need only buy a new product key and then apply it to unlock the hidden depths of your current installation of Windows Vista, but you may find the price too high. To learn what an upgrade will cost, press WINDOWS KEY–BREAK, and then click the Upgrade Windows Vista link near the top of the System window.

note *Windows XP Media Center Edition has many of the same Media Center capabilities as Windows Vista Home Premium Edition and Windows Vista Ultimate Edition—so if your PC is running Windows XP Media Center Edition, you can largely follow the advice in this project to add a TV tuner (if needed) and set up and use Windows Media Center. However, this project concentrates on Windows Vista, as this is the version of Windows on which you will most likely want to watch TV at this writing.*

Step 1: Choose a TV Tuner

Your first step is to add a TV tuner to your PC if it currently lacks one. Your nearest electronics paradise should offer you plenty of options, but if you want to see the full range of what's available, visit one of the major retailers on the Web—for example, Amazon.com (www.amazon.com) or CDW (www.cdw.com).

Your first decision when buying a TV tuner is which connection type to use:

- In many cases, the best type of TV tuner is one that connects via USB, because you can quickly and easily disconnect it from one PC and connect it to another.

- For a desktop PC, the alternative to USB is to insert a PCI TV card in a PCI slot on the motherboard. This involves opening your PC's case, but, assuming you install the card successfully, you shouldn't need to open the case again. Having the card inside the case like this makes for a neat solution, as you don't have the USB device outside the PC's case.

- For a laptop PC, the alternative to USB is to use a PC Card or ExpressCard TV Card. However, given that most laptops have far more USB ports than PC Card or ExpressCard slots, and given that there is a far wider choice of USB TV devices, USB is usually a better choice.

Apart from the connection type, the following are the main considerations when you're choosing among TV cards:

- **How many tuners do you need?**   The most basic tuners come with a single TV tuner, letting you watch or record a single channel at a time, or record a show on one channel while playing back a show you've recorded earlier. Dual tuners give you far more flexibility but increase the cost.

- **Which kind of signal do you need the tuner to handle?**   To receive standard TV signals over the air, you need an analog tuner. To receive high-definition TV signals over the air, you need a TV tuner capable of receiving digital signals. To receive cable, both your cable system and the tuner card must support QAM (quadrature amplitude modulation, a kind of digital cable tuner).

- **Which forms of video input do you need?**   Most TV tuners accept standard forms of input such as S-Video and composite video, but it's wise to verify that the tuner has a connector for the type of input you're planning to use.

- **Do you need a remote control?**   Many TV tuners come with a remote control for controlling playback from across the room. A remote control is especially important if you plan to watch the TV shows on your TV rather than on your PC, as described in Project 12.

caution *You can install two or more TV tuners in the same PC, and you can have both standard tuners and digital tuners. However, you cannot install a digital cable tuner and a standard TV tuner at the same time. If you have a standard TV tuner and want to upgrade to a digital cable tuner, you must remove the standard TV tuner first.*

You must also make sure the TV tuner supports Windows Media Center in Windows Vista. Before buying a bargain TV tuner designed for Windows XP Media Center Edition, make sure that a Windows Vista driver is available.

> **tip** *As with much technology, you don't necessarily need to buy the latest and greatest TV tuner—which will usually be the most expensive—to get good results. You can save money without sacrificing quality by buying a short way behind the cutting edge.*

Step 2: Install a TV Tuner

Once you've got your TV tuner, the next step is to install it:

- **USB**   With Windows still running, plug the TV tuner into a spare USB port. Some tuners plug in directly; others connect via a cable; and others yet give you the choice of plugging in directly or using a cable if the area around the USB port is too crowded to let the tuner plug in directly.

- **PC Card or ExpressCard**   With Windows still running, plug the card into the slot.

- **PCI card**   Shut down Windows before you install the card:

  1. Unplug the power cable and other cables.

  2. Put the PC on a work surface.

  3. Open the case.

  4. Touch a part of the metal chassis to discharge any static electricity that you have accumulated.

  5. Locate an unused PCI slot, and then unscrew or remove the tab that closes the slot's opening on the outside of the case.

  6. Insert the tuner card, and then screw in the retaining screw.

  7. Close the case, reconnect the cables, and then restart Windows.

For any type of TV tuner, connect its cables. For example:

- If your building has an existing antenna, connect that to the TV tuner. If the tuner came with its own antenna, you can use that instead, but reception will be weaker.

- Connect any other TV source that you will be using via the appropriate type of cable—for example, S-Video or composite. (If you're not clear on cable types, see Step 1 in Project 12 for a quick reference.)

- If the TV tuner has an infrared extender for controlling an input source, connect that cable and position the extender within striking distance of the input source's infrared receiver.

When Windows Vista notices the TV tuner, it launches the Found New Hardware Wizard. Click the Locate And Install Driver Software button, go through User Account Control for the Device Driver Software Installation feature (unless you've turned User Account Control off), and then follow through the procedure of identifying and installing the driver for the TV tuner.

If the TV tuner included a CD containing drivers for Windows Vista, insert the CD in your computer's optical drive. Otherwise, allow the wizard to search Windows Update for the drivers, download them, and then install them.

note *In some cases, you may need to download the drivers manually from the TV tuner manufacturer's web site, unzip them, and then tell the wizard where to find them.*

When the wizard has finished installing the software, click the Close button. If Windows prompts you to restart your PC, do so.

Step 3: Set Up Windows Media Center

Now that you've installed your TV tuner, you're ready to set up Windows Media Center. This takes a while because of the many different options, but Windows Media Center makes the process as straightforward and painless as possible. The following instructions outline the key steps:

1. **Launch Windows Media Center** Choose Start | All Programs | Windows Media Center. The first time you launch Windows Media Center, the application displays the first Welcome screen.

2. **Choose between Express Setup and Custom Setup** Express Setup signs you up automatically for the Customer Experience Improvement Program, which allows Windows Media Center to share your data anonymously with Microsoft. If you're not comfortable with this, choose Custom Setup, which lets you decide whether to join the Customer Experience Improvement Program. With either setup type, click the OK button. Windows Media Center verifies that you have a functioning Internet connection, and then (provided you do) downloads the latest configuration and programming information.

3. **Decide whether to use enhanced playback** On the Enhanced Playback screen, decide whether to allow Windows Media Center to connect to the Internet periodically to download TV program guides, music and movie information, and cover art for CDs and DVDs. Doing so greatly improves your experience of Windows Media Center at a minimal cost to your privacy. Click the Next button.

4. **Configure your tuner, signal, and Guide** On the Optional Setup screen (see Figure 5-1), select the Configure Tuners, TV Signal, And Guide option button, and then click the Next button. On the TV Signal: Confirm Your Region screen, verify that Windows Media Center has chosen the correct region—for example, United States. If not, select the No, I Want To Select A Different Region option button, click the Next button, and then choose

Figure 5-1

On the Optional Setup screen, you'll normally want to go through the Configure Tuners, TV Signal, And Guide process.

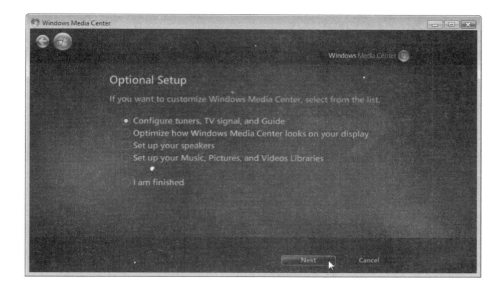

the region on the Select Your Region screen. Windows Media Center then downloads the latest TV setup options for your region.

5. **Choose whether to use the Guide**   On the Guide Privacy screen, choose whether to use the Guide, which provides TV program listings. Normally, you'll want to select the Yes option button here and then agree to the Guide Terms Of Service, but you should be aware that when you use the Guide, Windows Media Center sends anonymous information to Microsoft about your use of the service (so that Microsoft can improve the service). If this reporting bothers you, select the No option button.

6. **Identify the television service type, and then scan for services**   Windows Media Center walks you through the process of choosing the type of television service the tuner will receive, and then scans for services you can receive. The scan may take a while, but when it is complete, click the Next button, and then click the Finish button. Windows Media Center returns you to the Home screen, the screen with a vertical scrolling menu of major categories (such as Music, TV + Movies, and Sports) and a horizontal scrolling menu of choices within those categories.

Step 4: Watch TV

After you finish setting up Windows Media Center, you should be ready to watch TV. Follow these steps:

1. From the vertical scrolling menu, select the TV + Movies item.

2. From the horizontal scrolling menu, select the Live TV item. Windows Media Center starts showing a TV picture.

3. Change to the channel you want by using the controls displayed on the window.

Step 5: Record TV

You can start to record a TV show that you're watching by simply clicking the Record button, but what you'll probably want to do is schedule recordings to record your favorite TV shows that are on at times that aren't convenient for you to watch TV.

Choose Suitable Recording Settings

Before you do much recording, it's a good idea to check that Windows Media Center's recording settings are suitable for you. To do so, follow these steps:

1. From the vertical scrolling menu on the Home screen, select and click the Tasks item.

2. From the horizontal scrolling menu, select and click the Settings item.

3. On the next menu, select and click the TV item.

4. On the TV menu, select and click the Recorder item.

5. On the Recorder menu, select and click the Recorder Storage item to display the Recorder Storage screen (see Figure 5-2).

Figure 5-2

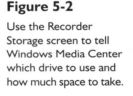

Use the Recorder Storage screen to tell Windows Media Center which drive to use and how much space to take.

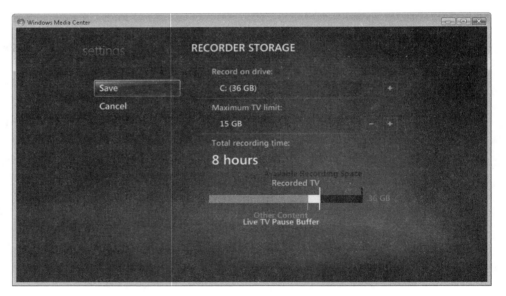

6. Use the Record On Drive control to pick the drive on which you want Windows Media Center to save recorded TV files.

7. Use the Maximum TV Limit control to specify how much of the drive you want to devote to recorded TV.

8. Click the Save button to apply your choices and to return to the Recorder menu.

9. Select and click the Recording Defaults item to display the Recording Defaults screen. Figure 5-3 shows the top part of this screen. (You click the down-arrow button in the lower-right corner to move to the settings lower down the screen.)

Figure 5-3

The Recording Defaults screen lets you choose when to start and stop recordings—and control how long Windows Media Center keeps them.

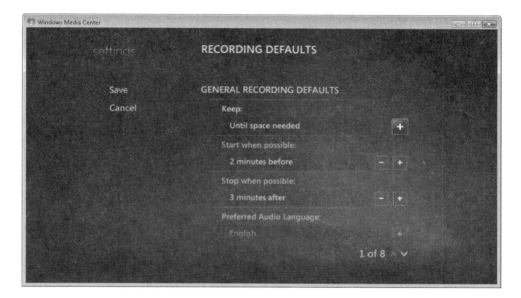

10. Choose settings for recording. The key settings are Start When Possible and Stop When Possible, which let you specify how much extra recording time to allow at the beginning and end of shows in case the timings are not accurate. For example, you may choose to start recording 4 minutes before the scheduled beginning of the show when possible. (An early start or late finish may not be possible when you're recording on other channels around the same time.) You can also choose settings for recording series and decide how long to keep shows.

11. Click the Save button to apply your choices and to return to the Recorder menu.

12. Click the Back button in the upper-left corner three times to return to the Home screen.

Record a Show from the Guide

To record a show from the Guide, follow these steps:

1. From the vertical scrolling menu on the Home screen, select the TV + Movies item.

2. From the horizontal scrolling menu, select the Guide item.

3. Move to the show you want to record.

4. Right-click the show, and then choose Record.

Record a TV Show by Time and Channel

To record a TV program by time and channel, follow these steps:

1. From the vertical scrolling menu on the Home screen, select and click the TV + Movies item.

2. From the horizontal scrolling menu, select and click the Recorded TV item.

3. Select and click the Add Recording button to display the Add Recording screen.

4. Select and click the Channel And Time button to display the Manual Record screen.

5. Choose the channel, date, start time and stop time, and frequency of recording.

6. Click the Record button.

7. Click the Back button to return to the Home screen.

Watch Recorded TV

To watch recorded TV on your Media Center PC, follow these steps:

1. From the vertical scrolling menu on the Home screen, select the TV + Movies item.

2. From the horizontal scrolling menu, select the Recorded TV item.

3. Click the item you want to view. Windows Media Center starts playing it.

You should now be set to watch, record, and maybe enjoy TV on your PC. But if you find family members or friends crowding around jockeying for viewing positions, you may need to switch to a bigger screen. See Project 12 for advice on doing so.

Learn to Work with Your PC's BIOS

What You'll Need

- Hardware: None
- Software: None
- Cost: Free

This project shows you how to work with your PC's BIOS—the essential software that makes the hardware usable. PC BIOSes are complex (more on this shortly), but the underlying principles tend to be the same. This project shows you how to make two simple changes on the two most widely used types of BIOSes: First, boot your PC from the optical drive (as you'll need to do in Project 10), and second, apply a BIOS password to protect your PC.

If you work through these examples—without actually applying the changes if you don't want to—you will be in good shape for making other BIOS changes as needed. For example, you may need to adjust specific BIOS settings in order to troubleshoot certain problems on a particular type of PC—or to achieve special effects.

Step 1: Understand What the BIOS Is and Why You Should Treat It Gently

The BIOS (pronounced "buy-oss") is the Basic Input/Output System of the PC. Briefly, the BIOS is data stored in chips on the motherboard that enables the operating system (for example, Windows) to communicate with the PC's hardware.

When you start the PC, the BIOS springs into action. First, the BIOS checks that it itself is intact and hasn't been attacked by a virus. Then, it sees whether the hardware components it's expecting to be available are actually present and correct, and counts the RAM. Around this point, before it actually starts to boot the PC from the boot device (for example, the hard drive), the BIOS gives you a chance to interrupt the boot process so that you can access the BIOS's settings. If you don't interrupt the boot process, the BIOS locates the boot device, and your operating system starts.

Know Where Most PC BIOSes Come From

At this writing, the two predominant manufacturers of BIOSes for PCs are

- **Phoenix Technologies Ltd**   Produces the PhoenixBIOS
- **American Megatrends Inc. (AMI)**   Produces the AMIBIOS

Understand How Your PC's BIOS May Vary from the Examples Shown Here

This project shows examples using a PhoenixBIOS and an AMIBIOS, as the chances are pretty good that your PC's BIOS will be based on one or the other.

Wait a minute… "based on"?

That's right—and it makes the topic of dealing with BIOSes more complicated than would be ideal. A PC's BIOS is actually specific to the PC's motherboard, because different motherboards have different capabilities. This specificity means that even closely related models of PCs from the same manufacturer may have different BIOS setups, because the computers have different motherboards. So you'll always need to keep your wits about you while making changes in your PC's BIOS.

Even if your PC has a PhoenixBIOS or an AMIBIOS, use the examples in this project as a means of getting an idea of what you need to do, not as specific instructions to follow. And if the PC has a BIOS from a different manufacturer, use these examples simply as an idea of what you'll need to look for in that BIOS.

note   *To balance that bad news about the BIOS being specific to the motherboard, there's some good news: Many modern computers have far fewer options in the BIOS than older computers had, because manufacturers have whittled down the amount of hardware on the motherboard. This is especially true of laptops, which typically are less expandable than desktops. For example, the BIOS of a laptop designed to have only one hard drive and one optical drive doesn't suffer the configuration anxieties that plague the BIOSes of most desktop computers, so the laptop BIOS tends to have fewer options. On the downside, the laptop is less configurable—but you knew that when you bought it. On the upside, it's much easier to find those settings that you're actually allowed to adjust.*

Treat Your PC's BIOS Gently

Without the BIOS, your PC is a collection of (usually ugly) parts that do nothing. With the BIOS correctly configured, your PC is a silver machine that zips you along the information superhighway or conjures up hordes of detailed and vicious mutants for you to annihilate. And with the BIOS incorrectly configured, your PC may be a mess—unstable, balky, and with key components not functioning as they should.

If your PC is working correctly, you should make BIOS changes only with caution and only when necessary. Before making a change, write down the current settings so that you can restore them if the changes have any unfortunate effects.

tip *If you've made a change to the BIOS that seems to have caused trouble, and you've lost your notes about how the settings were beforehand, you may need to load the BIOS's default settings to recover. These settings may not be exactly what you had before you made changes, but they should provide a stable and functional configuration. To load the default settings, look for an option such as Setup Defaults or Load Setup Defaults in the BIOS, and then execute it.*

Step 2: Reach Your PC's BIOS

To reach your PC's BIOS, you typically have to press a designated key during startup. Which key that is depends on the BIOS, but many BIOSes use one of these keys:

- DELETE
- F2
- F10
- ESC
- ALT, F1
- ESC, F1

To find out which key to use, boot your PC and watch the messages that appear on the screen. If you're lucky, you'll see a message such as the AMIBIOS message shown at the top of Figure 6-1 or the PhoenixBIOS message shown below it.

Figure 6-1

Watch the beginning of the boot process like a hawk to learn which key to press to access the BIOS—and then strike that key like a snake.

```
AMIBIOS(C)2001 American Megatrends, Inc.
BIOS Date: 02/22/06 20:54:49  Ver: 08.00.02

Press DEL to run Setup
Checking NVRAM..

512MB OK
Auto-Detecting Pri Channel (0)...IDE Hard Disk
Auto-Detecting Pri Channel (1)...Not Detected
Auto-Detecting Sec Channel (0)...CDROM
Auto-Detecting Sec Channel (1)...
```

```
Starting
        Press F2 to enter SETUP, F12 for Network Boot, ESC for Boot Menu
```

In some PCs, the BIOS may load so quickly that you can't catch the message. Other PCs may have a "quiet boot" option that suppresses messages, including the message that tells you which key to press. If your PC seems not to tell you which key to press, either consult the documentation (what, you've lost it?), try the keys in the previous list one at a time, or search the Web for advice on your model of PC.

Figure 6-2

The opening screen of
a typical PhoenixBIOS
shows you an overview
of the system settings,
including the memory.

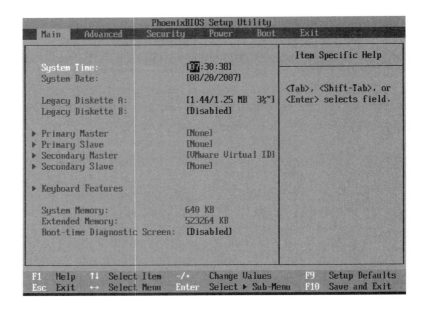

If you hit the magic key (or key sequence) before the boot process moves along,
the BIOS screen appears after a moment. Figure 6-2 shows an example of what you
see first when you access a PhoenixBIOS. Figure 6-3 shows an example of what you
see first when you access an AMIBIOS. As you can see, a typical BIOS screen presents
several categories of settings and requires you to navigate using the keyboard rather
than the mouse.

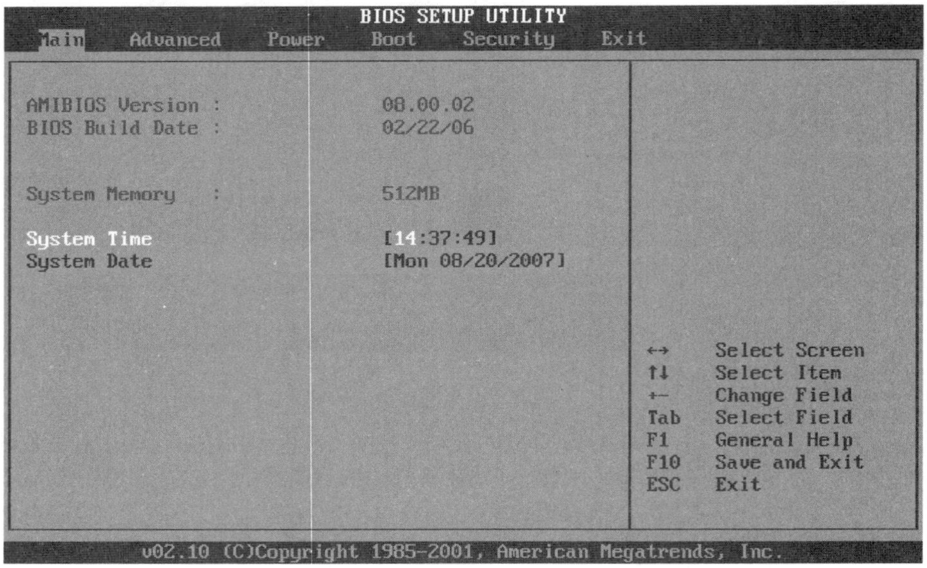

Figure 6-3

The opening screen
of a typical AMIBIOS
includes the version,
the build date, the
system memory,
and the system time
and date.

Step 3: Navigate the BIOS Screens

Nowadays, you can find BIOSes that let you navigate with a mouse, but most BIOSes still insist you use the keyboard. Using the keyboard tends to feel clumsy at first, but you'll get the hang of it quickly if you practice.

In a typical BIOS, you use the following keys to navigate:

To Do This	In PhoenixBIOS, Press	In AMIBIOS, Press
Move left by one screen or tab	LEFT ARROW	LEFT ARROW
Move right by one screen or tab	RIGHT ARROW	RIGHT ARROW
Move the selection down	DOWN ARROW	TAB
Move the selection up	UP ARROW	SHIFT-TAB
Expand the current selection or open a selection window	ENTER	ENTER
Collapse the current selection or return to the previous screen	ESC	ESC
Change the current setting	+ or – F5 or F6 PAGE UP or PAGE DOWN	+ or –
Get help	F1	F1
Exit the BIOS, saving changes	F10	F10

That may look complicated, but it's easy enough when you try it out. (Even if you don't want to make the changes described in the examples, work through the moves for practice—and then don't save the changes.) Besides, enough people have gotten stuck in BIOSes so that most screens include a quick reference chart of keys you can press from wherever you are.

tip *If you do get stuck on a BIOS screen, try pressing ESC to collapse the current selection or to go back to the previous screen. If you're at the top level of an AMIBIOS, pressing ESC typically causes the BIOS to prompt you to decide whether to discard changes and exit the BIOS. If you get this prompt unintentionally, simply press ESC again to get rid of it.*

Step 4: Boot Your PC from the Optical Drive

Under normal circumstances, your PC *boots*, or starts, from its hard drive, loading Windows (or another operating system) from there. Once Windows starts, you can log in, and then you're computing as usual.

But sometimes you may need to boot your PC from a different drive. For example, you may need to boot from the optical drive (the CD, DVD, or similar drive) in order to troubleshoot your PC or to install another operating system, or you may need to boot from a USB device in order to run another operating system.

To set your PC to boot from the optical drive, you usually need to change boot settings in the BIOS. The examples in this section show you how to make this change using a typical PhoenixBIOS and a typical AMIBIOS. Depending on the specific BIOS your PC uses, you may need to take somewhat different steps—even if the BIOS is one of these types.

Set a PhoenixBIOS PC to Boot from the Optical Drive

To set a PhoenixBIOS-based PC to boot from the optical drive, follow these steps:

1. Access the BIOS. For example, start your PC, and then press F2 when prompted. The PhoenixBIOS Setup Utility screen appears, as shown in Figure 6-3 (earlier in this project).

2. Press RIGHT ARROW four times (moving the gray highlight along the top row under "PhoenixBIOS Setup Utility") to select the Boot tab:

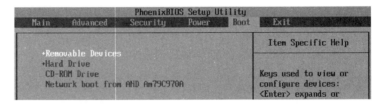

3. Examine the order in which the devices appear. In the preceding illustration, the devices appear in the following order:

  - **Removable Devices**   These are devices such as floppy disks. Booting from a floppy disk used to be a handy fallback in the old days, but now, few operating systems can boot from a floppy disk. (Worse, more and more new PCs come without a floppy drive.)

> **note**   *If a removable device or an optical drive doesn't contain a bootable disk, the BIOS continues to the next device. For example, in the setup shown here, the PC boots from the hard drive unless a removable device such as the floppy drive contains a bootable disk. A bootable disk is one that contains instructions for starting the PC.*

  - **Hard Drive**   The hard drive is the device from which the PC usually boots. Right now, though, you want to tell the BIOS to boot the PC from the optical drive rather than the hard drive if the optical drive contains a disk.

  - **CD-ROM Drive**   Despite its name, this category describes both standard CD-ROM drives (and burners) and DVD drives (and burners), so it refers to the optical drive on your PC. To make the PC boot from this drive, you must insert a bootable CD or DVD in it.

  - **Network Boot From [Device Name]**   Many PCs are designed so that they can boot from a network device. This capability is very useful in managed networks, such as a corporate network, but you probably won't want to use it at home.

4. Move the CD-ROM Drive item up to the top of the list. Follow these steps:

   ● Press DOWN ARROW twice to move the highlight down to the CD-ROM Drive item.

   ● Press + twice to move the CD-ROM Drive item up to the top of the list, as shown here:

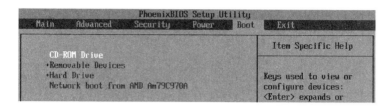

5. Press F10 to invoke the Save And Exit command. The BIOS displays this Setup Confirmation screen.

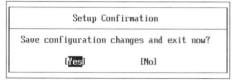

6. Make sure the black highlight is on the Yes button. (It should be there by default.) If not, press TAB to move it there.

7. Press ENTER to "click" the Yes button. Your PC restarts. This time, it boots from the optical drive if that drive contains a bootable disk.

Set an AMIBIOS PC to Boot from the Optical Drive

To set an AMIBIOS-based PC to boot from the optical drive, follow these steps:

1. Access the BIOS. For example, start your PC, and then press DELETE when the BIOS prompts you. The BIOS Setup Utility screen appears, as shown in Figure 6-3 (earlier in this project).

2. Press RIGHT ARROW three times (moving the gray highlight along the top row under "BIOS Setup Utility") to select the Boot tab:

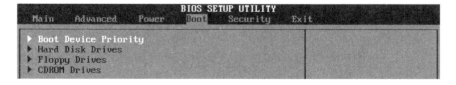

3. With the Boot Device Priority item selected, press ENTER to open the Boot screen.

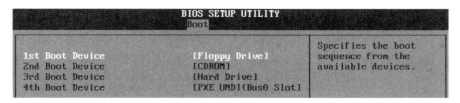

4. With the 1st Boot Device item selected, press ENTER to open the menu of boot devices:

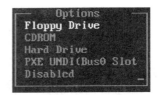

5. Press DOWN ARROW to select the CDROM item, and then press ENTER to make that item the 1st Boot Device and to close the menu. The BIOS moves the Floppy Drive item down the list to the 2nd Boot Device:

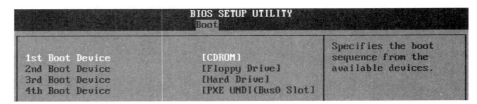

6. Press F10 to invoke the Save And Exit command. The BIOS displays the Save Configuration Changes And Exit Now screen:

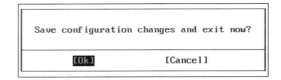

7. Make sure the black highlight is on the OK button. (It should be there by default.) If not, press TAB to move it there.

8. Press ENTER to "click" the Yes button. Your PC restarts. This time, it boots from the optical drive if that drive contains a bootable disk.

Step 5: Set a Supervisor Password and User Password

To prevent other people from making changes to the PC's BIOS without your permission, you can set a supervisor password and make the BIOS challenge anyone who tries to access the BIOS. You can also set a user password that allows the user to access the BIOS but gives the user limited access, so that the user can see BIOS settings but not change them. (This can be useful if you need the user to be able to report BIOS settings to a remote help desk.) The steps for setting a supervisor password and user password are similar on the PhoenixBIOS and the AMIBIOS. The first section shows the PhoenixBIOS, and the second shows the AMIBIOS.

Set a Supervisor Password on a PhoenixBIOS PC

On a PhoenixBIOS-based PC, you can set two passwords:

- **Supervisor password** This password is required to access the BIOS and make changes.

- **User password** This password is required to view the BIOS.

You can also set the BIOS to require a password before anyone—whether supervisor or user—can use the PC at all.

To set a supervisor password on a PC that has a PhoenixBIOS, follow these steps:

1. Access the main BIOS screen as usual.

2. Press RIGHT ARROW twice to display the Security tab, shown here. The BIOS selects the Set Supervisor Password item at first, because this is the master setting.

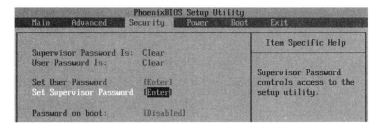

3. To set the supervisor password, follow these steps:

- Press ENTER to display the Set Supervisor Password screen:

- Type the password in the Enter New Password field (where the cursor appears at first). Press ENTER to move the cursor to the Confirm New Password field, type the password again, and then press ENTER again. The BIOS displays the Setup Notice message box.

- Press ENTER to dismiss the Setup Notice message box. The Security tab now shows Supervisor Password Is: Set at the top to indicate that you've set a supervisor password.

4. If you want to set the user password, follow these steps:

- Press UP ARROW to select the Set User Password item.

- Press ENTER to display the Set User Password screen, shown here.

- Type the password in the Enter New Password field (where the cursor appears at first). Press ENTER to move the cursor to the Confirm New Password field, type the password again, and then press ENTER again. The BIOS displays the Setup Notice message box.

- Press ENTER to dismiss the Setup Notice message box. The Security tab now shows User Password Is: Set at the top to indicate that you've set a user password.

5. If you want to set the BIOS to require a password when the PC is booted, follow these steps:

   - Press DOWN ARROW once or twice (as needed) to select the Password On Boot item.

   - Press ENTER to display the available values.

   - Press DOWN ARROW to select the Enabled item.

   - Press ENTER to apply the change.

6. Press F10 to invoke the Save And Exit command. The BIOS displays this Setup Confirmation screen.

   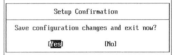

7. Make sure the black highlight is on the Yes button. (It should be there by default.) If not, press TAB to move it there.

8. Press ENTER to "click" the Yes button. Your PC restarts, with the password protection in place.

Set a Supervisor Password on an AMIBIOS PC

On an AMIBIOS-based PC, you can set two passwords:

- **Supervisor password**   This password is required to access the BIOS as a supervisor. The supervisor has the freedom to make changes.

- **User password**   This password is required to log on or access the BIOS as a user. The supervisor can permit the user to have different levels of access to the BIOS—for example, only being able to view the BIOS but not make changes, being able to make limited changes, or having full access.

You can also set the BIOS to require a password before anyone—whether supervisor or user—can use the PC at all.

To set a supervisor password on a PC that has an AMIBIOS, follow these steps:

1. Access the main BIOS screen as usual.

2. Press RIGHT ARROW four times to display the Security tab, shown here. The BIOS selects the Change Supervisor Password item automatically if no password is currently applied.

3. To set the supervisor password, follow these steps:

   ● Press ENTER to display the Enter New Password screen, shown here.

   ● Type the password, and then press ENTER. The BIOS displays the Confirm New Password screen:

   ● Type the password again, and then press ENTER once more. The BIOS displays the Password Installed message box.

   ● Press ENTER to dismiss the message box.

4. If you want to set a user access level and password, follow these steps:

   ● Press DOWN ARROW to select the User Access Level item.

   ● Press ENTER to display the Options list:

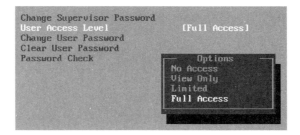

   ● Choose the option you want: No Access to prevent the user from accessing the BIOS at all, View Only to allow the user to view the BIOS but not make changes, Limited to allow the user to view the BIOS and change largely innocuous settings such as the time and date but not settings that affect the PC's operation, or Full Access to allow the user to change the BIOS freely.

- Press ENTER to apply the selection.

- Press DOWN ARROW to select the Change User Password item.

- Press ENTER to display the Enter New Password screen.

- Type the password, and then press ENTER. The BIOS displays the Confirm New Password screen.

- Type the password again, and then press ENTER once more. The BIOS displays the Password Installed message box. Press ENTER to dismiss the message box.

5. To specify when the BIOS should check the password, follow these steps:

- Press DOWN ARROW as many times as needed to select the Password Check item.

- Press ENTER to display the Options list:

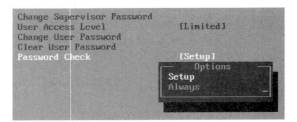

- Select Setup if you want the BIOS to demand a password when the user tries to enter the BIOS Setup program. Select Always if you want the BIOS to require the password each time someone tries to start the PC.

- Press ENTER to apply your choice.

6. Press F10 to invoke the Save And Exit command. The BIOS displays the Save Configuration Changes And Exit Now screen.

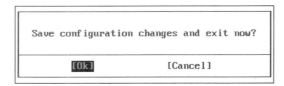

7. Make sure the black highlight is on the OK button. (It should be there by default.) If not, press TAB to move it there.

8. Press ENTER to "click" the Yes button. Your PC restarts, with the security options now in place.

After working your way through the examples in this project, you should have developed the skills you need to apply any specific BIOS changes your PC needs—no matter exactly which BIOS your PC is using.

Replace Your Hard Disk—or Add Another Hard Disk

What You'll Need

- Hardware: New hard disk, USB hard disk enclosure, USB cable, Philips screwdriver, Torx wrenches
- Software: Windows Vista DVD or Norton Save & Restore
- Cost: $50–150 U.S.

Chances are that all too soon you'll find yourself running out of space on your PC. When this happens, you can attach an external hard disk via USB easily enough, but in many cases a better solution is to add a new internal hard disk to your PC.

If your PC can contain only one hard disk, you'll need to replace the existing disk—and then either reinstall Windows on the new disk or clone your existing operating system installation to the new disk. But if you can add a hard disk to your existing disk, the upgrade is faster and more convenient, and you'll end up with even more hard disk space.

Step 1: Check How Many Hard Disks Your PC Has—and How Many It Can Have

Your first step is to check how many hard disks your PC currently has—and how many disks it can hold. If you have a laptop, you can probably skip this step, because almost all laptops contain only a single hard disk. If you have one of the monster laptops that can contain two or more hard disks, you probably are well aware of the fact because the manufacturer likely trumpeted it to the skies—and that may even be one of the reasons you decided to buy this particular laptop.

Similarly, if you have a standard model of desktop PC, most likely it has a single disk. But if you're not sure, or if you want to make sure that the hard disk doesn't contain unused space on which you could create another drive, follow these steps:

1. Press WINDOWS KEY–R. Windows displays the Run dialog box.

2. Type **diskmgmt.msc** and press ENTER or click the OK button. On Windows XP, you'll see the Disk Management window immediately. On Windows Vista, when the User Account Control dialog box appears (unless you've turned off User Account Control), make sure the component mentioned is Microsoft Management Console, and then click the Continue button. Windows displays the Disk Management window. Figure 7-1 shows an example.

Figure 7-1

The Disk Management window lets you see both, how many hard disks (and other types of disks) are installed on your PC, and how they are partitioned.

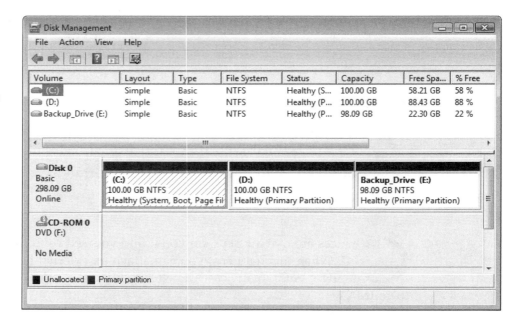

3. In the lower part of the window, look at each Disk readout. The figure shows one disk, called Disk 0 (because computer counting starts at zero rather than one), which is divided into three drives (100GB, 100GB, and 98.09GB). There's also a drive called CD-ROM 0, which is the first optical drive on the system. As the DVD designation indicates, this optical drive is actually a DVD drive rather than a CD drive.

4. Click the Close button (the × button) or choose File | Exit to close the Disk Management window.

Okay, that's how many disks your PC currently holds. But how many *can* it hold? At this point, we're probably talking about a desktop rather than a laptop. If you have the PC's documentation on hand (or if you can locate it on the Web), look up the number of disks. Otherwise, shut down Windows, turn the PC off and disconnect the cables, open the case, and take a look. Figure 7-2 shows an example of what you may see in a sparsely populated case.

Figure 7-2

Most tower-style PCs offer you the choice of 3.5-inch bays for hard disks or 5.25-inch bays that can contain optical drives, hard disks, or other components.

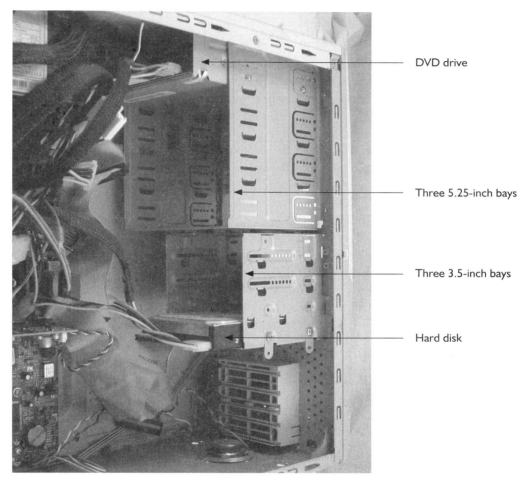

DVD drive

Three 5.25-inch bays

Three 3.5-inch bays

Hard disk

Look for three things here:

● **An empty drive bay**   It may be either 3.5 inches wide (the width of most desktop hard disks) or 5.25 inches, the width of optical drives and some heavyweight hard disks. It's easiest to mount a 3.5-inch disk in a 3.5-inch bay, but you can also mount it in a 5.25-inch bay if you buy mounting rails.

● **A power connector**   Unless your PC is loaded with drives and extras, you'll probably find several power connectors available, though they may be wrapped up in a tight bundle with a plastic tie. This illustration shows a power connector.

● **A drive cable with a free connector**   Drive cables are the flat, wide ribbons that go from the hard drive and optical drive to the motherboard. Usually, you'll find a connector free.

Replacing a Laptop's Hard Disk Can Be a Nightmare

Before you commit to replacing the hard disk on a laptop, it's a good idea to check how serious an operation the disk replacement is. Some laptops are designed to be easy to maintain and upgrade, but others are designed to be opened only by trained technicians armed with special tools. You can get the special tools yourself, but buying them increases the total cost of the upgrade. And if you end up wrecking your PC, the cost becomes far too high.

So consult your laptop's user manual and find out exactly what is involved. If you see the magical words "field replaceable unit" or "FRU" describing the hard disk, that's great news. If not, carefully review the steps involved in opening the PC.

If you find that you have to remove several internal components before you can even access the hard disk, you may want to save the time and effort and solve your disk-space problem another way. For example, you can archive older files or move seldom-used files to an external hard disk to make more space on the internal hard disk so that you do not need to replace it.

Step 2: Decide Whether to Add a Disk or Replace the Disk

By this point, you should be in a position to decide whether you're adding a hard disk to your PC or replacing the existing hard disk. (If your PC can contain only one hard disk, you have had no choice all along.) If you haven't yet decided, you're probably better off adding a disk, because you don't need to reinstall Windows or transfer your data—you simply get the extra storage space that the new disk provides.

Step 3: Buy the Hardware

Buy a suitable hard disk for your PC. Make sure it has the right physical size, enough capacity for your needs, and a fast enough rotational speed, as explained next.

Choose the Disk's Physical Size

Most laptop PCs use 2.5-inch disks. You'll find a wide variety of these at a good computer store. Some subnotebooks use 1.8-inch disks. The selection of these tends to be smaller; capacities tend to be lower; and prices tend to be higher.

For a laptop, you must also check the disk height. Some slim-line laptops can use disks only up to 9mm high, while others accept 12mm disks. You can use a 9mm disk in a 12mm space easily enough, but the other way around doesn't fit.

Most desktop PCs can use either 3.5-inch disks or 5.25-inch disks; 3.5 inches is normally the best choice, as you'll find a good range of disk capacities at affordable prices, but you may have to go to 5.25 inches if you want a monster disk.

Choose the Disk's Capacity

You may simply want to choose the highest-capacity disk you can afford, but typically you'll get the best value from buying a little way back from the cutting edge. For example, instead of buying a 200GB disk for a laptop, you might get a better deal on a 160GB disk. In some cases, you need to balance the disk's capacity against its rotational speed—if you want the highest capacity available, you may need to settle for a lower rotational speed.

Choose the Disk's Rotational Speed

The disk's rotational speed controls to a large extent how fast it can deliver data to the PC: the faster the rotational speed, the faster the data gets transferred. It also affects how much energy the disk uses, how hot it becomes, and how much noise it makes.

At this writing, 5400 rpm disks are the best choice for laptop PCs. 4200 rpm disks are less expensive but slower and are seldom worth buying; however, if your laptop uses a 1.8-inch disk, you may need to settle for a 4200 rpm disk. 7200 rpm laptop disks are also available, but they tend to have lower capacity than the 5400 rpm disks and produce more heat and noise.

For desktop PCs, 7200 rpm disks are normally the best choice, giving good performance with high capacity. Many 7200 rpm 3.25-inch disks are also impressively quiet, which can be welcome when you need to concentrate. Faster disks (for example, 10,000 rpm or 15,000 rpm) are typically designed for servers and tend to be too noisy for desktop use.

> **tip** *A factor that most people ignore when buying hard disks is the amount of noise they make. Given how close your laptop is to you while you are using it, a quiet or silent hard disk is usually a good idea. Even on a desktop PC that normally is several feet away from you, a quiet or silent hard disk can make the difference between peaceful work and struggling to concentrate through an irritating noise. Look for a disk that's specifically marketed as low-noise, quiet, or silent, and read users' reviews if possible to see if they support the manufacturer's claims. (Also, see Project 22 for more information about silencing your PC.)*

Step 4: Buy Any Software Needed

If you're adding a hard disk to your PC, you won't need to buy any extra software, as your current operating system remains in place. But if you're replacing your hard disk, you need to set up the new disk with your operating system.

There are two main ways of putting the operating system onto your new disk:

- **Reinstall Windows from scratch**   The basic way is to reinstall Windows from scratch on the new hard disk. You then need to apply any Windows updates and install all the programs you use. To reinstall Windows, you need your Windows DVD.

- **Clone your PC's hard disk**   Cloning your PC's existing operating system onto the new disk can save you plenty of time and effort, as you don't need to reinstall Windows and your programs. But to clone the disk, you need cloning software such as Norton Save & Restore.

Step 5: Install the New Hard Disk

At this point, you should be ready to install the new hard disk in your PC. The procedure is different depending on whether you're adding the hard disk to the PC or replacing the existing disk.

The first of the next two sections shows the steps for adding a hard disk. This section uses a desktop PC as the example. The second section shows the steps for replacing the hard disk. This section uses a laptop PC as the example.

Add a Hard Disk to Your PC

To add a hard disk to your PC, follow these steps:

1. Save any unsaved documents, close your programs, and shut down Windows.

2. Disconnect the cables from your PC, and put the PC on a suitable work surface.

3. Open the case. What this involves depends on how your PC is designed and built, but here are three examples:

   - **Tower-style PC**   Unscrew any retaining screws, and then remove the side panel on the side of the case away from the motherboard. If you're not sure which side this is, look at the back of the PC and see which side the parts and expansion cards are up against. That side is where the motherboard is, so you want the other side.

   - **Desktop-style PC**   Unscrew any retaining screws, and then remove the top panel or the entire cover. In a miniature case, you may need to remove other components before you can access the hard drive. In this case, consult the PC's manual to see which components you must remove, and how to remove them.

   - **Laptop PC**   Consult the documentation.

4. After opening the case, touch a metal part of the case to discharge any static electricity you may have built up.

5. Identify a suitable drive bay, insert the drive, and then screw it in place. Figure 7-3 shows the second disk in place.

Figure 7-3

If you have plenty of space, allow a gap between the disks rather than placing them right against each other.

6. Connect a drive cable and a power cable to the drive.

7. Close the case again.

8. Restore your PC to its usual location, and reconnect the cables.

9. Start the PC, and then log onto Windows.

Replace the Hard Disk in Your PC

To replace the hard disk in your PC, follow these steps (the example PC is a laptop):

1. Save any unsaved documents, close your programs, and shut down Windows.

2. Disconnect the cables from your PC, and put the PC on a suitable work surface. For a laptop, you may want to put down a cloth or a large mouse mat to prevent the PC getting scratched.

3. Turn the laptop so that you can access the cover or hatch that allows access to the inside or the hard disk. The example PC has hatches on the bottom for its field-replaceable units (see Figure 7-4), which makes the replacement procedure far easier.

Dealing with Masters, Slaves, and Jumpers

These days, you can often simply connect a disk to a drive cable without worrying about its configuration. This is because many PCs and disks use the Cable Select method of choosing the disk's role. With Cable Select, the cable connection used to connect the disk determines the drive's role.

If your PC doesn't use Cable Select, you need to check that the disk is set to the correct role, *master* (primary) or *slave* (secondary). To change the configuration, you use a *jumper* (a small connector) to connect two pins. This illustration shows the back of a disk drive with a jumper in place connecting two pins:

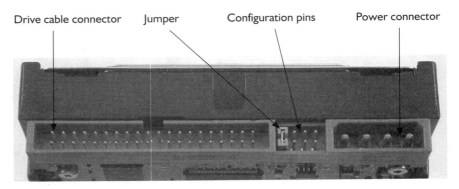

Drive cable connector   Jumper   Configuration pins   Power connector

Normally, you'll find on the disk's label a small and confusing diagram indicating which jumper configuration means what. Sometimes, you'll need to consult the disk's documentation or the manufacturer's website to find that small and confusing diagram.

When you're adding a disk, check the existing disk's configuration to determine how to configure the new disk. For example, if you're adding a second disk on the same cable, and you find the existing disk is configured as a master, configure the second disk as a slave.

When you're replacing a disk, the best approach is normally to set the same type of jumper configuration on the new disk as on the old disk, and to connect the new disk to the same connector on the same cable. For example, if the old disk is jumpered to the Cable Select position, jumper the new disk to Cable Select, and use the same connector on the same drive cable. That should give you the correct result.

4. Open the hard disk compartment, as in this example. Normally, the hard disk is obvious when you're in the right place.

5. Touch a metal part of the case to discharge any static electricity you may have built up.

Figure 7-4

This laptop is designed to allow you to replace the hard disk and memory easily.

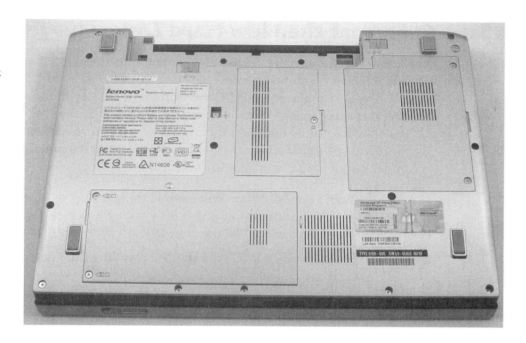

6. Detach the hard disk from its connector, and then remove it. The illustration shows an example of a drive that is held by its connector and by spring clips.

7. If the hard disk uses an enclosure, as in the example shown here, unscrew any retaining screws and then remove the disk from the enclosure. Insert the replacement disk, and then apply the retaining screws.

8. Insert the hard disk or enclosure in the bay or area that contains it, and then secure its connector.

9. Close the case again.

Step 6: Format the New Hard Disk

Before you can use the new hard disk, you must format it to apply a file system to it that enables Windows to access it.

If you've replaced your PC's existing hard disk with the new hard disk, formatting it is no problem: When you install Windows (or another operating system), the installation routine automatically prompts you to format the disk.

If you've added a hard disk, you need to format it manually. Follow these steps in either Windows Vista or Windows XP:

1. Start your PC. When Windows starts, you may see a notification-area pop-up message announcing that it is installing a device driver for your new hardware. This should be the new disk.

2. Press WINDOWS KEY-R. Windows displays the Run dialog box.

3. Type **diskmgmt.msc**, and then press ENTER or click the OK button. If you're using Windows Vista, go through User Account Control (unless you've turned User Account Control off) for the Microsoft Management Console feature. The Disk Management window opens. When Disk Management notices the new hard disk, it displays the Initialize Disk dialog box, as shown here.

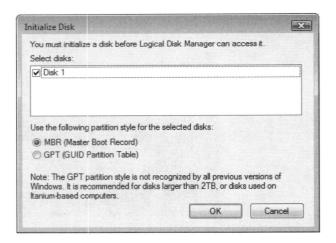

note *If Disk Management doesn't notice the new disk, choose Action | Scan Disks.*

4. Make sure the correct disk is selected in the Select Disks list box. (Disk Management should select the correct disk unless you've just added multiple new disks.)

5. Make sure the MBR (Master Boot Record) option button is selected rather than the GPT (GUID Partition Table) option button.

6. Click the OK button. Disk Management closes the Initialize Disk dialog box and initializes the disk, which then appears as Unallocated, as shown next for Disk 1 (the new disk).

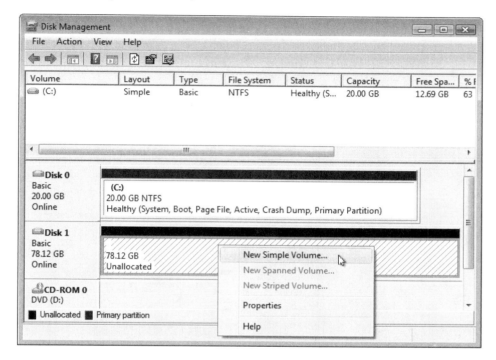

7. Right-click anywhere in the new disk's graphic and choose New Simple Volume. Disk Management launches the New Simple Volume Wizard, which displays its Welcome screen.

note A volume *is a defined section of a hard disk that enables Windows to access it. A volume is also called a* partition.

8. Click the Next button to display the Specify Volume Size screen. If you want to use less than the maximum space available on the disk for this volume, change the value in the Simple Volume Size In MB text box. This text box shows the full amount of space available by default, so if you want to create a single volume using all that space, you needn't make any change. This is often the easiest option.

9. Click the Next button to display the Assign Drive Letter Or Path screen. With the Assign The Following Drive Letter option button selected, choose the letter in the drop-down list that you want to assign to the drive. The wizard suggests the next available letter.

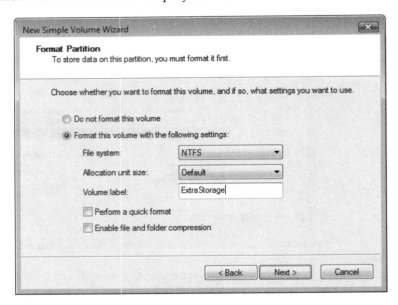

> **note** *If you prefer, you can mount the drive in an empty folder instead of assigning it a letter. This means that, for example, you can make the drive appear as a folder within your user folder, which can be handy if you're using the drive to store your documents or media files. To do this, select the Mount In The Following Empty NTFS Folder option button, click the Browse button, and use the resulting Browse For Drive Path dialog box to select the folder. As the option says, the folder must be empty, and it must be on a drive formatted with the NTFS file system (which both Windows Vista and Windows XP use as the default file system for hard disks).*

10. Click the Next button to display the Format Partition screen:

11. Make sure the Format This Volume With The Following Settings option button is selected, so that the File System drop-down list shows NTFS, and that the Allocation Unit Size drop-down list shows Default.

12. Type the name you want to use for the drive in the Volume Label text box. You can use up to 20 characters.

13. Clear the Perform A Quick Format check box. This option speeds up the formatting at the risk of missing bad sectors in the disk. This is a risk not worth taking with your data.

14. Select the Enable File And Folder Compression check box if you want to compress the contents of the drive. Compressing the contents slows down the drive's performance a little but enables you to store more data on the drive.

15. Click the Next button to reach the Completing The New Simple Volume Wizard screen, which summarizes the choices you have made.

16. Click the Finish button to close the wizard. The wizard creates the volume you specified. Disk Management formats the drive.

17. When the formatting is complete, Disk Management opens a Windows Explorer window showing the drive, so that you can begin using it.

Step 7: Turn Your Old Hard Disk into a Portable Disk

If you replaced your hard disk, and the reason you replaced it was because it was too small rather than because it had begun to lose data, you'll probably want to reuse it. If you have another PC with a smaller disk, one possibility is to use the disk you removed to replace that PC's disk. But what's usually a better bet is to turn your old hard disk into a portable disk. To do so, all you need do is buy an enclosure and install the hard disk in it.

Check the Disk's Dimensions

First, check the dimensions of the disk. The measurement given is the diameter of the disk's platter, so the dimensions of the disk case are somewhat bigger. Normally, the measurement is written on the disk.

Buy an Enclosure

Buy a suitable enclosure. You may find one at your local electronics paradise, but you'll find a better selection at online merchants such as CDW (www.cdw.com) or PC Connection (www.pcconnection.com).

There are three main criteria for choosing a disk enclosure:

- **Size**   Make sure the enclosure is the right size for the disk. You should also look for an enclosure that offers the degree of protection that you want.

2.5 inches	Most laptop hard disks are this size. (Some are 1.8 inches.)
3.5 inches	Most desktop hard disks are this size.
5.25 inches	Some desktop hard disks are this size.

- **Connection type**   The standard connection type is USB 2, which gives good performance as long as your PC has a USB 2 connector. (Most PCs built since 2004 have USB 2 connectors.) However, if your PC has FireWire rather than USB 2, or if you want to be able to use the drive with such a PC (or with a Mac), find an enclosure that offers both USB 2 and FireWire interfaces. They're a little more expensive, but the convenience is usually worth paying for.

- **Power supply**   Small enclosures, such as those used for low-powered laptop disks, are usually powered by the USB bus. Large enclosures that run hungrier disks normally have their own power adapters—so you'll probably need to plug in another "wall wart" when you use the disk.

Install the Drive in the Enclosure

Once you've bought an enclosure, installation should be straightforward. Follow these general steps:

1. Open the enclosure. You may need to unscrew it. The example enclosure came with its screws in a separate packet, so you can simply pop the top off without having to unscrew (and maybe lose) them.

2. Connect the drive's pins to the connector, making sure you get them aligned and keep them straight. (Push slowly and evenly.) If there's a power connector for the drive, connect it as well.

3. Slide the drive into the enclosure, and then close it using the screws or other means provided.

4. Connect the enclosure to the PC via USB or FireWire. If the enclosure has a power supply, connect that too.

5. Windows detects the disk and mounts it. You can then access the disk by choosing Start | Computer to open a Computer window showing your PC's drives.

Now you should have plenty of space to store all your files. But do you have enough space to view them satisfactorily? Maybe you need another monitor...or several more. Read on.

Project 8

Set Up a Multimonitor Monster

What You'll Need

- **Hardware: Extra monitor or monitors (required), extra graphics card or cards (optional), external video interface (optional)**
- **Software: None**
- **Cost: $100–$1500+ U.S.**

To use a PC at all, you need a monitor—but to use your PC to the max, you may need two monitors…or maybe many. Most people find that the more they can see onscreen, the faster they can get their computing done.

Even if you've got a laptop, you should be able to add two or three monitors to it—and that's even if it doesn't have an external display port.

This project starts at the sane end of the spectrum by assessing your options and discussing how to add one more monitor to your desktop or laptop. But then the project veers across to the enthusiast extreme—adding three monitors to a laptop and up to ten monitors to a desktop.

Step 1: Assess Your Options

First, figure out your options for adding monitors to your PC. If you're lucky, your PC is already equipped to drive another monitor, and all you need do is connect it.

Assess What Your PC's Graphics Card Can Manage

Your PC's graphics card should have at least one video connector, and may have two. PCs use two main types of video connector for their monitors:

- **Analog** Also called VGA or D-sub, this uses a D-shaped 15-hole socket into which a corresponding D-shaped 15-pin plug connects. (In "D-sub," the *D*

stands for the D shape, and "sub" is short for "subminiature," as other connectors were even larger.) The illustration here shows a D-sub connector.

● **Digital**   Usually called DVI (for Digital Visual Interface), this uses a 29-pin socket and plug. The pins are split into a bank of 24 (three rows of eight pins) and a group of five—four pins in a square around a cross-shaped pin, as shown here.

Some PCs use other kinds of connectors for monitors, but D-sub and DVI are by far the most widely used.

Desktop PC

Many recent desktop PCs have graphics cards with two video connectors—usually one DVI connector and one D-sub connector, but sometimes two DVI connectors. If your PC has two connectors, and one is currently free, you can easily add a second monitor.

If the spare connector is DVI, and you want to use it to drive a monitor that has a D-sub connection, get a DVI-to–D-sub converter cable such as the following:

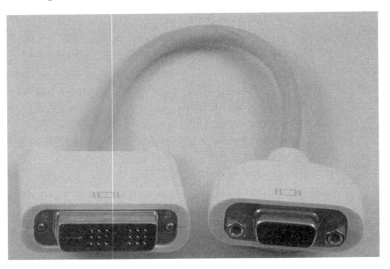

Laptop PC

Most laptop PCs have an external graphics connector that allows you to connect a monitor—for example, so that you can give a presentation. On high-end laptops, the external graphics connector is a DVI connector, but on most laptops, it's a D-sub.

Work Out How to Add Monitors

If you have a desktop PC with a graphics card that can drive a second monitor, or if you have a laptop PC with an external graphics connector, you're all set to buy that monitor (as discussed in the next step) and connect it.

If all your PC's graphics connectors are already in use, you need to add another graphics connector:

- **Desktop**   Install another graphics card or use special hardware. See "Step 6: Add Serious Numbers of Monitors to a Desktop," later in this project, and then return to Step 2.

- **Laptop**   Use an external-monitor PC card or other special hardware. See "Step 7: Add Two or More Monitors to a Laptop," later in this project, and then return to Step 2.

Step 2: Find a Suitable Monitor

Buy, beg, or borrow a suitable monitor. There are three main choices: monitor type, size, and resolution.

Choose Between LCD and CRT

You'll probably want to start by choosing a monitor type:

- **CRT (cathode ray tube)**   CRTs are the old-technology, TV-style monitors that have a large tube at the back. CRTs are inexpensive but bulky, almost all use an analog signal, and give a less sharp picture than LCDs. Apart from price, CRTs' only advantage is being able to show a good picture at various different resolutions. For example, you may need to set a lower resolution to run some software (such as children's educational programs).

- **LCD (liquid crystal display)**   LCDs are the newer, flatter monitors. LCDs are more expensive than CRTs, but prices have now fallen far enough for LCDs to be of better value than CRTs. LCDs come in three types: analog, digital, or capable of both. Digital LCDs give the best picture. Apart from price, LCDs' main disadvantage is that they normally can show only one resolution (the *native resolution*) crisply; you can use other resolutions, but the picture becomes "blocky" and jagged.

tip *Unless you're certain that you will use the monitor only with an analog input, it's usually worth paying the modest extra amount to get an LCD that can accept both analog and digital input.*

Choose a Monitor Size

Monitors come in sizes from modest to monster. Table 8-1 lists the most common sizes for external monitors and the maximum resolutions they typically support.

The bigger the monitor you get, the more you'll probably appreciate how much lighter LCDs are than CRTs. For example, a 21-inch CRT may well weigh 75lb, so you might need to reinforce your desk. By contrast, a 23-inch LCD typically weighs 20lb or less.

Monitor Type	Monitor Size (Diagonal)	Maximum Resolutions (Pixels, Horizontal × Vertical)
LCD or CRT	15 inches	1024×768
LCD or CRT	17 inches	1280×1024
LCD or CRT	19 inches	1280×1024
LCD	19 inches (widescreen)	1440×900
LCD or CRT	20 inches	1600×1200
LCD	20 inches (widescreen)	1680×1050
CRT	21 inches	1600×1200
LCD	22 inches (widescreen)	1680×1050
LCD	23 inches	1900×1200
LCD	24 inches	1900×1200
LCD	30 inches	2560×1600

Table 8-1   Common Monitor Sizes and Resolutions

 30-inch LCDs typically require a graphics card that supports dual-DVI output. These graphics cards are much more expensive than conventional cards.

Choose a Monitor Resolution

Along with monitor size, consider the resolution you need—the number of pixels ("picture elements" or dots) you want to have displayed at the same time. The greater the number of pixels, the more information you can see.

Different people prefer different resolutions and window sizes, but here are some illustrations of resolution:

- At 1024×768, you can have one good-size window open or two squashed windows.

- At 1280×1024 or (better) 1440×900, you can comfortably have two useful-size windows open.

- At 1600×1200 resolution, you can display two letter-size (8.5×11-inch) pages at an easy-to-read size.

Step 3: Add a Second Monitor to a Desktop

If your desktop PC has an unused video connector, you're all set to add a second monitor. Follow these steps:

1. Close all the applications you're running, and then shut down Windows.

note *On many modern PCs, you can hot-plug a monitor—that is, plug it in while the PC is running. However, some PCs are not capable of hot-plugging monitors, so unless you know that your PC is capable of hot-plugging, it is usually best to shut down the PC before connecting another monitor.*

2. Connect the second monitor to the unused connector on your video card. Use a DVI-to–D-sub cable if needed.

3. Turn the PC on. As Windows loads, it detects the new monitor.

4. Once you've logged in, Windows may open the Display Settings dialog box for you to arrange the monitors. Skip ahead to "Step 5, Tell Windows Where Your Monitors Are."

Step 4: Add a Second Monitor to a Laptop

This section describes how to add a second monitor to your laptop by using the external graphics connector. If your laptop doesn't have an external graphics connector, you'll need a more expensive solution. Go to the section "Step 7: Add Two or More Monitors to a Laptop," later in this project.

To add a second monitor to your laptop, follow these steps:

1. With the laptop running, connect the monitor to the laptop's graphics connector and to a power supply.

2. Turn the monitor on. If Windows notices the monitor, it displays the New Display Detected dialog box, shown here. When this happens, Windows may change the resolution of your laptop's screen to match the resolution it uses on the external monitor. As a result, your laptop's screen may go fuzzy. Don't worry; this is only temporary.

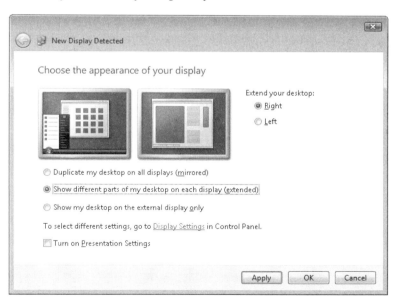

3. Select the appropriate option button:

   - **Duplicate My Desktop On All Displays (Mirrored)**   Select this option button if you want the external monitor to show the same picture as your laptop's screen. You'd choose this setting when giving a presentation on an external monitor, but it's no use for getting more screen real estate.

   - **Show Different Parts Of My Desktop On Each Display (Extended)**   Select this option button if you want to use both the laptop's screen and the external monitor. This is the choice you'll usually make. When you select this option button, Windows displays the Extend Your Desktop controls in the upper-right corner of the New Display Detected dialog box. Select the Right option button if the external monitor is positioned to the right of your laptop; select the Left option button if the external monitor is to your laptop's left.

   - **Show My Desktop On The External Display Only**   Select this option button if you want to use the external monitor but not your laptop's screen. This setting is useful if your laptop's screen is much smaller than the external display, or if you're connecting an external keyboard and mouse to your laptop and using it as if it were a desktop PC.

4. Click the Apply button. Windows applies the settings. If your laptop screen went fuzzy in step 2, the sharpness should return now if you selected the Show Different Parts Of My Desktop On Each Display (Extended) option button.

5. Click the OK button. Windows closes the New Display Detected dialog box.

Step 5: Tell Windows Where Your Monitors Are

Once you've installed your monitors, make sure that Windows knows how many monitors there are and where they are positioned relative to each other. Follow these steps:

1. Right-click the Desktop and choose Personalize. Windows displays the Personalization window.

2. Click the Display Settings link near the bottom of the window. Windows displays the Display Settings dialog box, which shows the monitors of which Windows is aware:

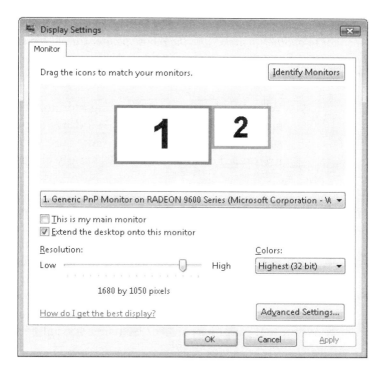

3. In the Drag The Icons To Match Your Monitors box, drag the monitor icons to show Windows where your monitors are positioned. For example, if you've positioned your second monitor to the left of the first monitor rather than to its right (as in the illustration), drag the monitor marked 2 so that it is positioned to the left of the monitor marked 1.

4. If you need to tell Windows which of the monitors is your primary monitor, click the monitor, and then select the This Is My Main Monitor check box. The main monitor is the monitor on which Windows displays the Start menu.

5. If Windows has disabled one of the monitors, and you want to enable that monitor, click the monitor, and then select the Extend The Desktop Onto This Monitor check box.

6. To change the resolution for a monitor, click the monitor, and then drag the Resolution slider along the Low–High axis.

7. When you're ready to apply the settings you've chosen, click the Apply button. Windows applies the settings and then opens the Display Settings message box to ask if you want to keep the settings.

8. Click the Yes button if you want to keep the settings. If you want to revert to the previous settings, either click the No button or wait for the timer at the bottom of the message box to count down to zero seconds, at which point Windows reapplies your previous display settings.

After positioning the monitors in the Display Settings dialog box, move the mouse pointer from one monitor to another to make sure the mouse pointer travels in a straight line rather than jinking up, down, or sideways as it moves to the other monitor. If your monitors are different sizes, you'll often need to adjust their horizontal or vertical placement to get a straight transition.

9. When you've finished choosing monitor settings, click the OK button. If there are any unapplied changes, Windows applies them and then opens the Display Settings dialog box to make sure the screen looks okay. If there are no unapplied changes, Windows simply closes the Display Settings dialog box.

Step 6: Add Serious Numbers of Monitors to a Desktop

Two monitors are enough for most mortals, but if you're one of the folks who has no wish to be mortal, there's no need to confine yourself to two monitors. Windows lets you add up to ten monitors to your PC—assuming you have enough connectors, monitors, and desk space.

You have two main choices for adding extra monitors to a desktop PC: by adding conventional graphics cards or by using special hardware.

Identify the Different Slots on Your Motherboard

Your PC's motherboard may contain any of three different types of slots that can accept a graphics card:

● **AGP**   Aperture Graphics Port is a widely used technology for graphics cards. Normally, a PC has only one AGP slot. If this slot is already in use, you need to add another type of graphics card—for example, PCI. AGP slots are normally colored brown. Most AGP cards have a locking tab at the end of the card that goes toward the middle of the PC, as shown in the lower-right corner here:

● **PCI**   Peripheral Component Interconnect is a widely used technology for connecting various PC components, including graphics cards, network cards, and sound cards. PCI graphics cards are not as fast as AGP graphics cards but can work alongside AGP graphics cards. PCI slots are often colored white. The following illustration shows a PCI card:

● **PCI Express**   PCI Express is a newer technology for connecting powerful graphics cards. PCI Express slots are different lengths, depending on the version of PCI Express, and are usually colored yellow.

Motherboard configurations vary widely, so it's a good idea to consult your PC's manual to determine which types of slots the motherboard contains. If one of them is an AGP or PCI Express slot, you should also check the version used—for example, AGP 4X or PCI Express x16—so that you can get a compatible graphics card.

Add Graphics Cards to Your PC

The conventional way to add extra monitors is to install extra graphics cards in your PC. Provided that the cards all work together with your motherboard and Windows to create an extended desktop, you can then connect a monitor to each graphics-card connector you want to use. You then have a multiple-monitor desktop.

To add extra graphics cards, follow these general steps:

1. Shut down Windows.

2. Disconnect the cables from your PC.

3. Open the case on the side opposite the motherboard.

4. Touch part of the case to discharge any static electricity that you have built up.

5. Locate an unused slot on the motherboard, insert a card of the appropriate type, and then fasten it with a screw. (See the sidebar "Identify the Different Slots on Your Motherboard" for information on identifying the different types of slots.)

6. Close the PC's case.

7. Reconnect the cables to your PC.

8. Restart the PC.

Use Special Hardware to Add Extra Monitors

If you've already installed as many graphics cards as your PC will take, or if for other reasons you need to take an alternative approach, you can install special hardware that enables you to use extra monitors without installing extra graphics cards in your PC.

If you need the extra monitors, evaluate products such as the following:

- **Zenview** Digital Tigers' Zenview series ranges from dual-monitor setups to eight-monitor arrangements. Prices start at $749 and go impressively high. See the Digital Tigers website (www.digitaltigers.com/multi-monitors.shtml) for details.

- **X-Top** 9X Media's X-Top series provides a huge variety of multimonitor configurations, ranging from two-monitor models (starting at about $1500) to complete video walls (which cost five figures). See the 9X Media website (www.9xmedia.com) for details.

Step 7: Add Two or More Monitors to a Laptop

To add two or more monitors to a laptop, you need to use special hardware. As you might expect, such hardware is expensive, so it's suitable only for those who must use a laptop rather than a desktop—for example, because they travel—but who also need to have more screen real estate than a laptop, plus one external monitor, can provide. Figure 8-1 shows a typical arrangement using an external video interface.

If you need to add two or more monitors to a laptop, evaluate products such as the following:

- **VTBook** VTBook from Village Tronic (www.villagetronic.com/vtbook/index.html) is an external video interface for laptops. VTBook lets you add one or two extra monitors to your laptop, so you can have up to four monitors total: your laptop's own screen, a monitor connected to the laptop's external graphics port, and either one or two monitors connected to the VTBook. VTBook costs around $249.

Figure 8-1

You can add extra monitors to a laptop by using an external video interface.

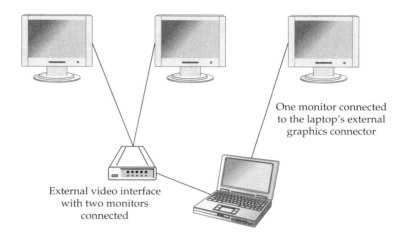

One monitor connected to the laptop's external graphics connector

External video interface with two monitors connected

- **DualHead2Go and TripleHead2Go** DualHead2Go and TripleHead2Go from Matrox (www.matrox.com/graphics/en/home.php) are external video interfaces that let you connect two or three monitors (respectively) to your laptop. DualHead2Go and TripleHead2Go connect to your laptop via the external graphics port; you then connect the monitors to the Matrox device. DualHead2Go and TripleHead2Go each come in an analog version and a digital version. Prices range from $169 for DualHead2Go Analog Edition to $299 for TripleHead2Go Digital Edition.

caution *Unlike VTBook and SideCar, DualHead2Go and TripleHead2Go are driven by your laptop's video card, so before you buy either product, make sure that your laptop's video card is powerful enough to drive the external monitors at the resolution you want. Go to www.matrox.com/ graphics/en/home.php, click the Support Center tab, click the GXM System Compatibility Wizard link under Support Options, and then follow the wizard steps.*

- **SideCar** SideCar from Digital Tigers (www.digitaltigers.com/sidecar .shtml) is an external video interface for laptops. You connect SideCar to your laptop via the PC Card slot, and then connect the monitors to SideCar. SideCar models start at $1299 for a model that adds two analog displays to your laptop's existing display or displays (giving three or four displays total) and go up to $1999 for a model that adds four digital displays (giving five or six displays total).

By now, you should at last be seeing enough of what's on your computer—or on the Internet. But what if you want to see what's on your other computers? Turn the page. It's time to network your home.

Build a Wired Network in Your Home

What You'll Need

- Hardware: Switch, cables, reel of cable (optional), cable crimper (optional), punch-down tool (optional), cable stripper (optional), cable tacker (optional)
- Software: Windows Vista or Windows XP
- Cost: $50–300 U.S.

This project shows you how to create a wired network in your house or other dwelling so that your PCs can communicate with each other and share your Internet connection. A wired network can transmit large amounts of data quickly and reliably and requires no maintenance once you have set it up. Installing the network takes some time and effort, but you will find that the usefulness and convenience of the network will repay these soon enough.

Time and effort…you may be wondering whether you should set up a wired network or take the easier route and set up a wireless network. I recommend that you choose a wired Ethernet network, because it is far faster and far more secure than a wireless network, and once you have installed the cables and other equipment, the network normally will run without trouble for several years. However, if you are still undecided, read through this project and then read Project 17, which explains how to set up a wireless network for home use, and then make your decision.

Step 1: Choose Hardware for a Wired Network

If you're lucky enough—or organized enough—to keep all your PCs in the same room, and you don't mind having cables in view, you can set up a wired network in minutes by connecting each PC and your Internet router to a switch. More likely, though, your network will be more extensive than this, either now or in the future. So this project shows you how to get cables discreetly from room to room and from floor to floor. Figure 9-1 shows an example of such a network, with dashed lines showing

Figure 9-1

If your PCs are in different rooms, you need to run cables from room to room.

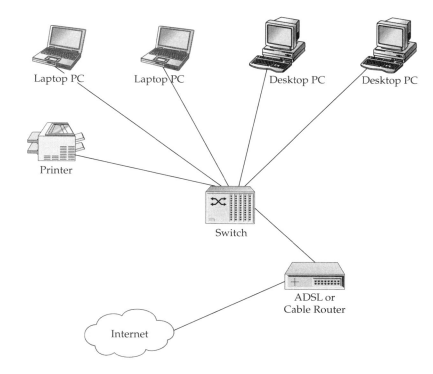

approximately where hidden cables run. You will use some or all of the equipment shown, as discussed in the following sections.

Network Switch

The switch forms the center point of your network. This is the device into which you plug the cables that connect the PCs and other devices to the network. Figure 9-2 shows an eight-port Gigabit Ethernet switch.

Normally, you should buy a switch that has enough ports to connect not only all of your current computers and network devices but also any others that you may buy in the foreseeable future.

Figure 9-2

The switch is the device at the center of the network into which you plug the Ethernet cables.

You can connect one switch to another easily enough, but each switch still requires its own power supply. So having, say, one 16-port switch is a neater solution than having two 8-port switches—at least, assuming that you want to have all the ports in the same place. If you need to have one set of ports in one room (or area of your home) and another set in a separate room, having two separate switches will be much easier, as you will be able to connect the PCs and other devices to each switch with short cables rather than needing to use longer cables.

note *You can also use a hub instead of a switch, but there's no point in doing so unless you already have an old hub that you want to reuse. Hubs are slower than switches, and whereas they used to be substantially less expensive, now they are only marginally less expensive at best. (FYI, "switch" is actually short for "switching hub"—in other words, a switch is a smarter kind of hub that switches data from one port to another.)*

Cables

Cables carry the Ethernet data from each PC to the switch, and vice versa. You also normally connect other devices, such as your cable or ADSL router or your printer, to the network with cables.

Computer stores offer precut cables in various lengths, including 30 meters (100 feet) or longer. These cables already have a network connector at each end, so you can plug one end into your PC's network adapter, plug the other into a port on the switch, and be in business.

Simply buying long cables lets you create a network throughout the house without much effort. The drawback is that the network connector on the end of the cable is substantially larger than the cable itself, so when you need to pass the connector through a baseboard, wall, or floor, you must drill a much larger hole than the cable itself would need.

caution *Depending on the laws where you live, you may need to follow building codes or fire regulations when running cables around your dwelling.*

If you're prepared to drill (and perhaps then fill) these holes, creating a network with precut cables is quite viable. But normally, your best option is to buy a reel of cable, and then cut from it the lengths that you need. If you're creating a network of any size, the reel of cable will work out to be less expensive than buying individual cables; and if you also buy RJ-45 plugs and a crimping tool, you can also create *patch cables*, shorter cables for connecting the computers to the wall plates (discussed next).

Buy Category 5E Cable or Category 6 Cable

The cable comes in different categories that set standards for the cable's performance. What you should normally buy is either Category 5 Enhanced ("Cat 5E") or Category 6 ("Cat 6") cable. Either of these cable types will handle both Fast Ethernet (100 Mbps) and Gigabit Ethernet (up to 1 Gbps) speeds—plenty even for streaming video. Cat 5E is fine for Gigabit Ethernet networks, but having Cat 6 cable may allow faster data rates with other technologies in the future.

Wall Plates

When you bring a cable into another room, you can simply crimp an Ethernet connector onto the end, and then plug that connector into your PC. But what's neater and more flexible is to use a *wall plate*, a plate or box that attaches to the wall and contains one or more Ethernet sockets. You then plug an Ethernet cable into the wall plate and into your PC. Because you can use different lengths of Ethernet cable, you can place the PC wherever you need it in the room.

You can buy wall plates with a single socket, two sockets, four sockets, and so on. Figure 9-3 shows a four-socket wall plate with cables plugged into two sockets. Each socket requires its own cable running to the wall plate and back to the switch—you can't share cables among the sockets. You can leave surplus sockets unconnected if you don't need them for the time being, but given the effort you're probably putting into cabling the network, connecting them all at the same time normally makes most sense.

Figure 9-3

A wall plate provides one or more Ethernet sockets, much like a telephone socket.

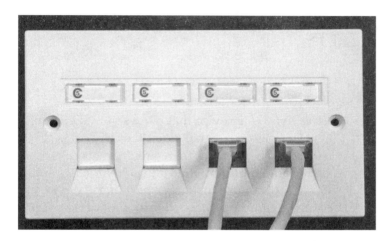

Raceways or Conduits

Where you need to run a cable along a baseboard or floorboard, you have two main choices: To simply tack it down using clips or staples, or to enclose it in a *raceway*, an enclosure that protects the cable and keeps it aligned. Raceways are good for keeping cables neat and hidden, especially when you're running several cables parallel to each other for a distance.

If you need to run a cable anywhere that it needs protection from the elements or wildlife, you can use a *conduit*. Conduits come in different types, but what you'll typically need is a kind of pipe or tube that shields the cable from where it enters the conduit at one end to where it emerges at the other end. For example, if you need to route a cable out through the wall of your house, around a corner, and then down into the basement, you can use a flexible plastic conduit that runs from one hole in the wall to the other.

Tools

For working with cable, you need some or all of the following tools, depending on exactly how much cabling you are doing.

You may also need an electric drill, sheet-rock saw, hammer, and other standard do-it-yourself tools. Wire cutters will cut cable easily, but so will strong scissors or a sharp pocket-knife. If you are looking to pull many cables inside walls or under carpets, also consider getting a wire snake, a flexible but protective guide that helps you steer the cables from their insertion point to where you want them to appear.

Punch-down Tool

If you are using wall plates, you need a punch-down tool to connect the wires of each Ethernet cable to the connectors in the wall plate. Figure 9-4 shows a punch-down tool.

Figure 9-4

A punch-down tool is vital for connecting the wires in a cable to the connectors in a wall plate.

Cable Tester

A *cable tester* is a device that allows you to ensure that a cable is connected correctly. The tester passes a signal along the cable to verify that all the wires are connected as they should be and that there aren't any breaks. The most useful cable testers include a detachable unit that you can use remotely, plugging it into one end of a cable run so that you can use the larger part of the device at the other end to test the cable in between. Figure 9-5 shows this kind of cable tester.

Figure 9-5

A cable tester with a detachable unit lets you test either a run of cable or a patch cable easily.

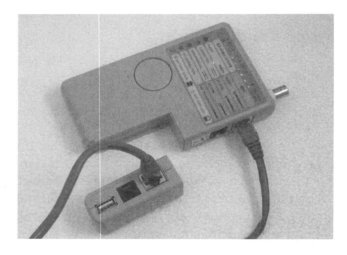

Cable Stripper

To remove the plastic sheath from an Ethernet cable easily and without damaging the insulation on the wires inside, buy a cable stripper. Figure 9-6 shows an example.

Figure 9-6

A cable stripper helps you remove the plastic sheath from an Ethernet cable. Make sure yours has an adjustable blade so that you can get the cut depth right.

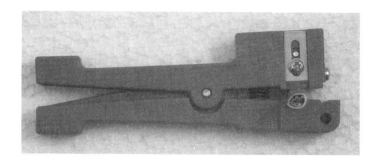

Crimping Tool

If you plan to create your own Ethernet cables, buy a crimping tool (see Figure 9-7), a drop-in die for RJ45 plugs, and a supply of RJ45 plugs for shielded twisted pair (STP) cable. You can then crimp a plug onto each end of a length of cable quickly and easily (after some fiddling to get the cables into order and alignment).

Figure 9-7

A crimping tool lets you create your own Ethernet cables, saving money over premade cables.

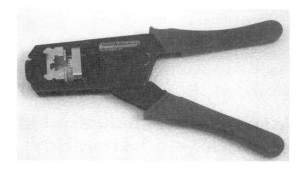

Cable Tacker

If you need to secure cables quickly to baseboards, floorboards, beams, or other wooden objects, consider buying a cable tacker (also called a *cable stapler*) such as the one shown in Figure 9-8. Alternatively, you can use plastic clips and a small hammer.

Figure 9-8

With a cable tacker, you can staple down cables quickly and securely.

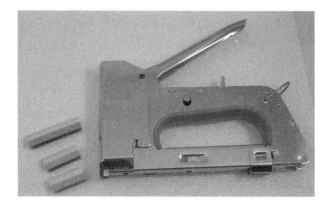

Step 2: Make Sure the PCs Have Network Adapters

First, make sure that each of the PCs that will connect to the network has a network adapter. In these days of widely available broadband Internet connections, it is now hard to buy a PC that *doesn't* have a network adapter. But if your network will include PCs that are several years old or more, you may find that you need to add a network adapter.

The best way to add a network adapter to a desktop PC is by opening the case and installing a PCI network card. If you have a spare Fast Ethernet PCI card lying around from an old PC, use that. Otherwise, buy a new Gigabit Ethernet PCI card.

If you're unwilling or unable to open your PC's case, or if it doesn't have a spare PCI slot to accommodate a network card, your main alternative is to connect a network adapter via USB. This is not such a good choice because USB is not fast enough for the fastest network connections even if the full bandwidth of the USB bus is available. (Normally the USB bus is carrying other signals as well—for example, from your keyboard or mouse to the PC.) However, a USB network connection is quite viable unless you simply must have the very fastest network speeds possible over a Gigabit Ethernet network.

For a laptop PC, the easiest solution is usually a PC Card or ExpressCard network adapter. Again, look for a Gigabit Ethernet card unless you already have a Fast Ethernet card you want to reuse. If neither of these options is available (for example, because you keep the PC Card slot occupied with another card), you can also use USB.

Step 3: Assess Your Hardware Needs for the Network—and Then Buy

Next, work out what you'll need for the network. Follow these general steps:

1. Draw a diagram of your home and mark where each of the PCs in the network will be.

2. Mark where you will place a wall plate with a connection for each PC or other network device. For example, if you will use a cable or ADSL router, that will need a connection to the network too. So will a network printer on which each PC can print.

3. Decide where you will place the switch (or switches).

4. Figure out where you will need to run the cables for the network and how many cables you will need to run to each point.

5. Establish which tools you need to buy.

With your needs established, you're now ready to buy the equipment for the network. A large computer store or a networking specialist will let you see the equipment before you buy, which will help you decide between competing products, especially if the staff is knowledgeable enough to provide useful advice. Alternatively, you will find plenty of online stores that sell networking equipment—often at good prices.

Step 4: Pull Cables Wherever They Need to Go

The next step is to pull cables from the location of your switch to each of the points at which you want to place a wall plate. Exactly what this step entails depends on your house or dwelling, the materials from which it is constructed, and where you're putting the cables. But chances are that you will need to route some cables from one room to another or between floors.

 Exercise extreme caution when drilling holes in the wall, floor, or ceiling. If you don't have a tool for detecting electric cables and pipes in walls or floors, now is a good time to invest in one.

Here are three tips that apply to almost all types of cabling:

- **Run the cable before cutting it**   If you can run the cable without having to cut it, do so, because being able to adjust the cable length easily to circumvent unforeseen obstacles can save you a great deal of time, effort, and wasted cable.

- **Pull plenty of cable**   If you need to cut the cable—for example, so that you can pass it through a hole in a wall or a floor—allow plenty of extra cable to get around unexpected snags and to give you enough cable to route and punch down at the far end. If you end up with a cable that is several feet too long, you can cut the surplus length off and turn it into a patch cable. But if you end up with a cable that's several feet too short, you will either need to adapt the network design on the fly or redo the whole run with a longer cable.

- **Treat the cable gently**   Try to avoid folding the cables or putting sharp bends in them, as doing so can reduce the speed at which they transmit data. When pulling cable through a wall or along a conduit, have someone feed the cable in at the other end to reduce the tension on the cable. Rather than pulling cable around two corners in a single action, pull it around the first corner, and then pull it around the second.

tip *Running a cable down through a floorboard (or out through a baseboard), through the basement, and then back up into another room can be an easy way to get from room to room.*

Step 5: Punch Down the Cables

Once you've pulled the cables to their destinations, punch them down into the wall plates. Follow these steps:

1. If the wall plate is the kind that attaches to a box (sometimes called a *wall wart*), punch a hole in the box, and then poke the cable through it. If the plate covers a hole in the wall, you don't need to take this step.

2. If the cable is much too long, cut it down to length.

3. Using a cable stripper, strip off the plastic cover from the last one-and-a-half inches of the cable to give yourself enough wire to work with.

4. Remove the connector block from the back of the wall plate, and then arrange the wires carefully in the slots on the block, as shown in Figure 9-9, following the guide in Table 9-1.

Figure 9-9

Arrange the wires in the connector block, and then punch them down.

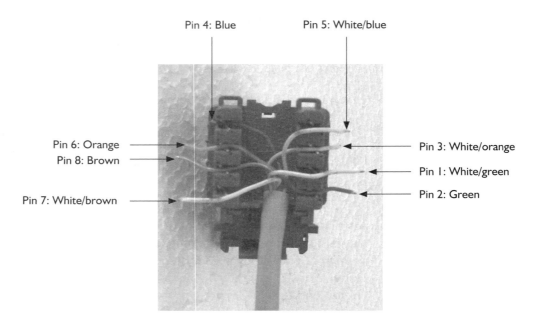

Pin 4: Blue   Pin 5: White/blue

Pin 6: Orange
Pin 8: Brown

Pin 7: White/brown

Pin 3: White/orange
Pin 1: White/green
Pin 2: Green

caution *Two wiring standards are widely used for Ethernet cables. The standard shown in this section is called T568A and is considered technically superior to the other standard, T568B, because it has better backward compatibility. The difference between the two standards is that the pin positions of the orange pair of wires and the green pair of wires are reversed. Both standards work fine as long as you make sure that each cable uses only one standard: each end of the cable must be connected in the same way, so the easiest approach is to choose one standard and stay with it.*

5. Starting with the first wire, align the punch-down tool with its trimming blades on the outside of the connector, and then press it down firmly. The punch-down tool pushes the wire into its slot, so that it makes contact with the blades on either side, and trims off any excess length of wire.

Pin #	Wire Color	Pin #	Wire Color
1	White/green	5	White/blue
2	Green	6	Orange
3	White/orange	7	White/brown
4	Blue	8	Brown

Table 9-1   Wiring Diagram for RJ45 in the T568A Standard

6. Once you've finished punching down a cable, install the connector block in the wall plate.

7. When you've punched down all the cables for a wall plate, screw the wall plate into place.

Step 6: Test the Cables

Once you've punched down a run of cable, test it with the cable tester to make sure that it is working:

1. Find (or create) two Ethernet patch cables, and then test them with the cable tester.

2. Connect the remote end of the cable tester to one end of a run of cable. If that end terminates in a wall plate, connect the tester's end using one of the patch cables.

3. Connect the main part of the cable tester to the other end of the run. Again, if that end terminates in a wall plate, use a patch cable to connect the tester.

4. Press the button on the tester, and verify that the tester shows a good connection.

If the cable tester shows a problem with the cable, follow these steps:

1. Check that the ends of the cable are correctly punched down or crimped.

2. Punch down or crimp each end again if necessary. Normally, the problem will be an incomplete connection. If you've crimped an RJ45 connector onto the cable, cut it off, strip a new section of cable, and then crimp on another RJ45 connector.

3. Test the cable again. If you still do not have a connection, and you're sure the cable is correctly punched down or crimped, you may need to replace the cable.

Step 7: Connect the Switch

When the cables are working, connect the cables to the switch at the center of your network. If you have two or more switches in the network, you need to connect them to each other. In some switches, you must use an *uplink port,* a port that's specially designed for connecting to another switch rather than to another network device. The uplink port may be a separate port or one of the regular ports with a switch to change it between regular mode and uplink mode. Read the switch's documentation to find out whether you need to use an uplink port. Some switches have auto-sensing ports that allow you to link to any port.

Step 8: Set Your Router to Assign IP Addresses via DHCP

When you connect each of your PCs and other network devices to the network, each must have an IP address that's unique on the network. The IP address allows the PCs and devices on the network to identify each other and transmit data to the right place.

The easiest way to assign IP addresses is to have your router assign them automatically by using Dynamic Host Configuration Protocol (DHCP). When a PC or device starts up, it looks for a *DHCP server*, a computer or device allocating IP addresses. The PC or device requests an IP address from the DHCP server and then uses that IP address until you shut it down. (And after you shut it down, the DHCP server marks the IP address as being available for use by another computer or device.)

Your router may already be set up to assign IP addresses via DHCP. To find out, connect a PC to your router following the instructions that come with the router. (For example, you may need to connect directly via a USB cable or via an Ethernet cable through a network switch.) Then access the configuration screens for the router and find the means for allocating IP addresses. If necessary, change this setting to use DHCP.

note *DHCP works well for most small networks, but in some circumstances, you may find that you need to assign IP addresses manually. For example, if you run your own web server or FTP server on your network, you may need to direct incoming requests for web pages or FTP files to a particular PC. In this case, assigning a fixed IP address to that PC makes directing the incoming requests much easier. Consult your router's documentation for instructions on which IP addresses you can assign.*

Step 9: Connect Your PCs and Other Devices

Now connect your PCs and other devices to the network:

- If you have used wall plates, connect one end of an Ethernet cable to a wall plate and the other end to the Ethernet connector on the PC or device.

- If you have used cables that end in Ethernet plugs, simply insert a plug in the Ethernet connector on the PC or device.

Step 10: Tell Windows to Get an IP Address via DHCP

When you connect your PCs to the network and power them on, you may find that Windows automatically requests an IP address from your router via DHCP. The easiest way to tell is by opening Internet Explorer and seeing if it's able to load a web page. If so, you're all set. If not, you may need to change the PC's network configuration to make Windows get an IP address via DHCP, as described next.

Set Windows Vista to Get an IP Address via DHCP

To set Windows Vista to get an IP address via DHCP, follow these steps:

1. Click the Start button, right-click the Network item, and choose Properties to open a Network And Sharing Center window.

2. Click the Manage Network Connections link in the Tasks list on the left of the window to display the Network Connections window.

3. Right-click the Local Area Connection item and choose Properties to display the Local Area Connection Properties dialog box. Unless you have turned off User Account Control, you need to go through User Account Control for the Network Connections program.

4. In the This Connection Uses The Following Items list box, double-click the Internet Protocol Version 4 (TCP/IPv4) item to display the Internet Protocol Version 4 (TCP/IPv4) Properties dialog box.

5. Select the Obtain An IP Address Automatically option button.

6. Select the Obtain DNS Server Address Automatically option button.

7. Click the OK button to close each dialog box, and then click the Close button (the × button) to close the Network Connections window.

Step 11: Share Files Using the Public Folder

Windows Vista comes equipped with folders for sharing files with other users of your PC or of your network. You may need to change settings on these folders to allow all users of the network to access them. When sharing files among the PCs on the network, you will probably want to share a folder on a PC that you keep running most of the time. (You can share one or more folders from any PC, but as soon as the PC goes to sleep, or you turn it off, those folders become unavailable.)

note *One way of making sure your shared files are available all the time is to have a server, a PC or device that you run all the time. See "Step 4: Set Up a Media Server for Your Household" in Project 13.*

To make Windows Vista's Public folder available to all network users, follow these steps:

1. Click the Start button, right-click the Network item, and choose Properties to open a Network And Sharing Center window (see Figure 9-10).

Figure 9-10

Use the Sharing And Discovery controls in the Network And Sharing Center window to share your PC's Public folder with other users of your network.

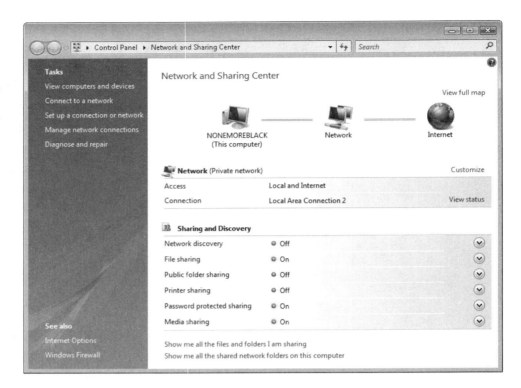

2. Click the down-arrow button on the Public Folder Sharing line to display the options.

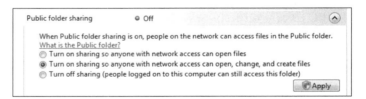

3. Select the Turn On Sharing So Anyone With Network Access Can Open, Change, And Create Files option button if you want other network users to be able to work with files in the shared folder. If you want to let them view the files but not change them, select the Turn On Sharing So Anyone With Network Access Can Open Files option button.

4. Click the Apply button, and then go through User Account Control for the Network And Sharing Center program (if you are using User Account Control). Windows applies the sharing.

5. Click the Close button to close the Network And Sharing Center window.

note *Windows Vista sometimes loses track of shared Public folders. If this happens, try restarting the PC that's sharing the Public folder that has vanished. If that doesn't help, try restarting the PC that's unable to see the shared folder.*

Step 12: Connect to a Shared Folder

Once you've shared a folder from one PC, you can connect another PC to it easily. To connect to a shared folder in Windows Vista, follow these steps:

1. Choose Start | Network to open a Network window showing all the PCs on the network.

2. Double-click the PC whose shared items you want to view. Windows Explorer displays those items, as in this example:

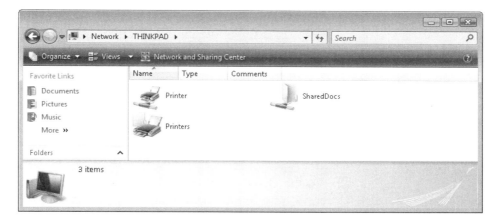

3. Double-click the folder you want to open. In the example shown, you would double-click the SharedDocs folder.

Map a Drive to a Network Folder

If you want to use the same network folder frequently, you can map a drive letter to it. Windows then establishes the drive mapping each time you log on, and you can access the folder via its drive letter directly from a Computer window. To map a drive to a network folder, follow these steps:

1. Using the instructions earlier in this section, open a Windows Explorer window, and then navigate so that the window shows the folder you want to map.

2. Right-click the folder in the main part of the window and choose Map Network Drive to display the Map Network Drive dialog box (shown here). Windows automatically enters the network path to the folder in the Folder text box.

3. In the Drive drop-down list, Windows automatically assigns the last unused letter of the alphabet—Z first, X if Z is used, and so on. You can choose another letter if you prefer.

4. Make sure the Reconnect At Logon check box is selected.

5. Click the Finish button. Windows maps the drive to the network folder.

Project 10

Recover from Windows Disasters with Knoppix

What You'll Need

- Hardware: USB key or USB drive (optional)
- Software: Knoppix
- Cost: Free to $10 U.S.

Sometimes Windows disagrees with itself—badly. Or with your PC's hardware. Or with its horoscope. Or maybe it gets a virus, Trojan horse, or other malware. Or your antivirus program decides it simply doesn't like you anymore. When one of these problems happens, you may find that you can no longer start Windows as usual. That means you can't access any of your files—your documents...your pictures...your videos...not even your e-mail messages.

To get Windows working again, you may need to repair it or reinstall it in a different folder. That can bring problems of its own, because you may not be able to access the files within your user account. So before you mess with your PC, you should make a copy of all the files you value so that they're safe even if the problems Windows is suffering turn out to be really bad.

This project shows you how to use Knoppix to copy those files to the safety of either a USB key or USB drive or a network drive. The project also shows you how to connect to the Internet so that you can download Windows updates, drivers, or other files you need to fix Windows.

note *Your copy of Windows may never suffer a disaster such as those described in this project—or it may suffer such a disaster tomorrow. To be prepared for such a disaster, read this project today and work through Steps 2 and 3, which show you how to get Knoppix, burn it to CD, and then run it. You can then store your Knoppix CD away safely with your other troubleshooting tools, ready for trouble—whether it strikes on your PC or that of a family member, friend, or colleague.*

Step 1: Understand What Knoppix Can Do

Knoppix is one of the many different distributions of the Linux operating system. Like many other Linux distributions, you can either download Knoppix for free or order a CD or DVD for little more than the cost of the media and shipping.

Knoppix is what's called a *live* distribution of Linux. That means that Knoppix boots directly from the CD or DVD in your PC's optical drive without you having to install it to your PC's hard disk. Booting from the optical drive has several advantages, including not changing the contents of the hard disk and being able to work when the hard disk (or its boot sector) is out of service. (There are also disadvantages, such as needing to access the optical drive whenever the operating system needs more instructions—but when you're recovering from a disaster, this price is easy enough to pay.)

Knoppix is modest in its hardware requirements, needing only 128MB of RAM to run all its features. But as usual with operating systems, the more RAM, the merrier: Knoppix will run better, and you can even load the operating system into RAM to make it run faster and to free up your PC's optical drive.

Knoppix is a full operating system and even includes the OpenOffice.org program suite (which includes a word processor, a spreadsheet program, and a presentations program), so it can take care of most of your computing needs. However, in this project we look only at how to use Knoppix to recover files from a Windows computer that's having problems.

Step 2: Download Knoppix and Burn Your Recovery CD

First, download the latest version of Knoppix and burn it to CD.

 If you have a slow Internet connection, you may prefer to order a Knoppix CD or DVD from a vendor such as On-Disk.com (http://on-disk.com). You'll find a full list of these vendors on the Knoppix web site. The cost is typically around $10 U.S. including delivery.

Download the Latest Knoppix CD

Steer your web browser to the Knoppix web site (www.knoppix.com), and then click the Download link. This link takes you to a page where you can choose to download Knoppix via BitTorrent or Emule or via HTTP or FTP from a mirror site. (A *mirror site* is a site that hosts files on behalf of other web sites to make them more widely available.)

There are two main distributions of Knoppix: a CD distribution (which is the one you most likely want) and a DVD distribution, which is far larger and contains many more programs and tools. Unless you have an extremely fast Internet connection, downloading the DVD distribution will take all night, whereas you should be able to download the CD distribution via a DSL or cable connection in less than two hours.

The Knoppix distribution file you want probably has a name that looks like this: KNOPPIX_V5.1.1CD-2007-01-04-EN.iso. Here, 5.1 is the version number; the file is for one CD and is an ISO image for creating a CD; and the language is English (EN).

The file size of the ISO file will be 700MB or a bit less, because 700MB is the amount of data that fits on a standard recordable CD. (If the web site's directory is crammed with files, the file size can be a useful identifier.)

When you click the link to download the disk image, Internet Explorer may display a dialog box asking if you want to save the file or find a program online to open it. Click the Save button, and then choose where to save the file—preferably in a folder on your PC's hard drive so that you can easily burn it to CD.

When Internet Explorer displays the Download Complete dialog box, click the Open Folder button to open the folder containing the Knoppix disk image.

Burn the Knoppix Disk Image to CD

Next, burn the Knoppix disk image to CD. How you do this depends on the burning software installed on your computer. For example, if you have the widely distributed Roxio DigitalMedia LE, click the Copy button, click the Burn Image item below it, choose the disk image on the screen, and then click the Burn Image button.

tip   *If your PC doesn't have a program for burning disk images to CD or DVD, have a look at ISO Recorder (http://isorecorder.alexfeinman.com/isorecorder.htm), donationware (if you like it, you can make a donation to the author's development fund) that can burn CDs on Windows XP and both CDs and DVDs on Windows Vista.*

Step 3: Take Knoppix for a Spin to Make Sure It's Working

This step shows you how to launch Knoppix, view some files, attach a USB drive, access the Internet via a broadband connection, and then close down Knoppix.

Launch Knoppix

To launch Knoppix, follow these steps:

1. With Windows running, insert the Knoppix disc. If Windows opens an Internet Explorer window showing information about the Knoppix distribution, browse it if you wish to.

2. Close your Windows programs, and then restart your PC. The PC boots from the Knoppix disc, and the Knoppix screen appears.

note   *If your PC doesn't boot from the Knoppix disc, you may need to change the PC's BIOS settings to make the PC boot from the optical drive. See Project 6 for instructions on doing this.*

3. Press ENTER to start loading Knoppix. You'll see several screens full of text in various colors as Knoppix loads, displaying messages that track its progress.

The Knoppix graphical user interface (GUI) then appears for the rest of the loading process.

4. When Knoppix is fully loaded, it opens a Konqueror window (see Figure 10-1). Konqueror is the file browser and web browser that Knoppix uses.

Figure 10-1

Knoppix is now up and running, having booted from your PC's optical drive rather than the hard disk.

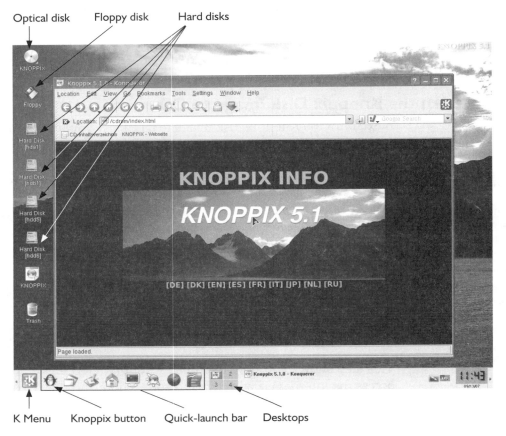

Have a quick look at the files on your PC:

1. Click the Close button (the × button) to close the Konqueror window.

2. Click the Hard Disk (hda1) icon to open a Konqueror window showing the contents of the first hard disk in your PC (see Figure 10-2). The PC shown here has three hard disk partitions, but your PC may well have only one partition.

> **tip** *Konqueror opens a file with a single-click rather than a double-click, as Windows Explorer requires. Until you become accustomed to Konqueror, you may find it easier to right-click a file (and then cancel the context menu if you don't need to issue one of its commands) than to click a file and open it inadvertently.*

3. Click the Maximize button in the upper-right corner of the Konqueror window to maximize the window.

Figure 10-2

Here are the contents of hda1, the first hard disk partition on the computer.

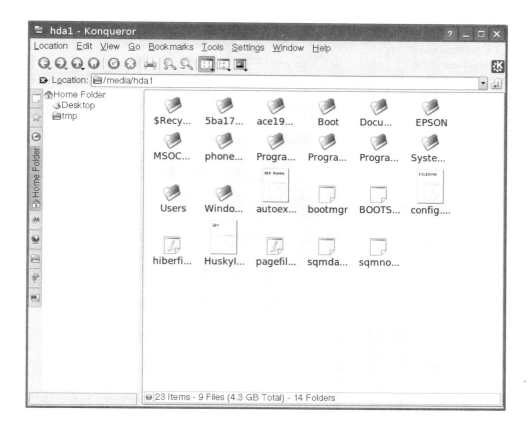

4. Choose View | View Mode | Detailed List View to display the details of the files and folders (see Figure 10-3). Here, you can see all the files and folders, including the hibernation file (hiberfil.sys), the page file (pagefile.sys), and the boot manager (bootmgr), which are normally hidden.

5. Click the Users folder to display its contents, which include a folder for each user's user account, an Administrator account, and the All Users account.

6. Click the account name for a user whose account you normally cannot access. (Or, if you prefer, click your own account.) Konqueror displays its contents, which you can then access as needed.

7. Click the Close button or press ALT-F4 to close the Konqueror window.

Explore the K Menu to get an idea of its contents. It contains a wide range of programs and utilities—and even some games.

Attach a USB Drive

When you're using Knoppix to repair Windows or to recover files from your PC, it's often handy to have a drive to which you can copy files or that you can use to supply files to the PC. The easiest solution is to use a USB key (sometimes also called a *flash drive* or a *thumb drive*) or another USB-connected drive that enables you to copy files easily to or from the PC.

Figure 10-3

Detailed List View gives you a better view of the files and folders on the drive.

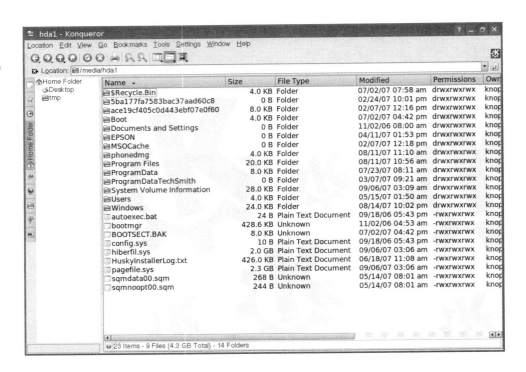

note   *In Linux terminology, you* mount *a drive to add it to the PC's file system. To remove a drive from the file system, you* unmount *it.*

To use a USB key or USB drive with Knoppix, follow these steps:

1. Connect the USB key or drive to your PC. Knoppix recognizes the key or drive, mounts it automatically in the file system, and then displays a dialog box saying that a new medium has been detected.

2. Select the Open In New Window item in the list box.

3. Click the OK button. Knoppix displays a window showing the contents of the key or drive, as in the example shown here:

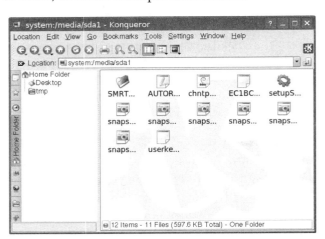

You can then work with the files and folders on the key or drive much as you would in a Windows Explorer window on Windows. For example, to copy a file or folder, right-click it and choose Copy. You can then right-click the folder in which you want to paste the file or folder, and choose Paste to paste it.

When you have finished using the USB drive, unmount it from the file system before you detach it from the PC. Right-click the drive's icon on the desktop and choose Unmount. You can then safely remove the drive from your PC.

Connect to Your Network and the Internet

If you have a broadband Internet connection, you should be able to get Knoppix to connect to the Internet easily by choosing suitable settings for your PC's network adapter. This is handy for when you need to download patches or update files to fix Windows or run a virus check on Windows.

note   *If you have a network with a typical setup, when you connect to the Internet, you can also connect to any shared drives on your network. For example, you may need to copy files from another computer on the network to the PC on which you have booted Knoppix.*

Set Up a Network Connection or Broadband Connection

To connect to your network, and thus to connect to the Internet via a broadband connection shared via the network, follow these steps:

1. Click the Knoppix icon (the penguin) on the quick-launch bar and choose Network/Internet | Network Card Configuration. Knoppix launches the netcardconfig program in a console window.

2. If your computer has two or more network interfaces (for example, an Ethernet connection and a wireless connection, or an Ethernet connection and a FireWire card), Knoppix displays an Xdialog box like the one shown here, prompting you to choose the network device. (If your computer has only one network interface, skip to step 3.) Select the eth0 item, as this is usually the Ethernet connection, and then click the OK button.

3. Knoppix displays a dialog box asking whether you want to obtain an IP address automatically via DHCP. If your network uses Dynamic Host Configuration Protocol (DHCP) to allocate available IP addresses automatically, as many networks do by default, click the Yes button, and then go to step 5.

Otherwise, click the No button, and then specify the following information in the dialog boxes that appear in the sidebar "Find Out Your Network's Gateway and DNS Settings" if you don't have this information:

● **IP address**   For example, 192.168.0.14 or 10.0.0.5

● **Network mask**   The subnet mask, usually 255.255.255.0.

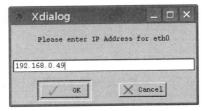

● **Broadcast address**   Usually the last address in the subnet you're using—for example, 192.168.0.255 or 10.0.0.255.

● **Default gateway**   The IP address of the Internet connection device. This is usually a low value in the subnet—for example, 192.168.0.1 or 10.0.0.2.

● **Name server**   The IP address of the Domain Name Service (DNS) server your Internet connection uses. Your ISP normally provides this IP address.

4.   When you click the OK button in the last dialog box, the netcardconfig program applies the settings, displays several lines of text as it does so, and then closes.

Find Out Your Network's Gateway and DNS Settings

If you don't have your network's gateway and DNS settings written down, but you have another functional PC running Windows Vista, you can find them out easily:

1.   Click the Start button, right-click the Network item, and choose Properties to open a Network And Sharing Center window.

2.   Click the View Status link for the network connection to display the connection's Status dialog box.

3.   Click the Details button to display the Network Connection Details dialog box, which contains readouts of the IP address, subnet mask, default gateway, and DNS servers.

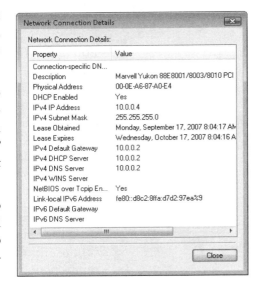

4.   Click the Close button to close each dialog box, and then click the Close button to close the Network And Sharing Center window.

Verify That Your PC's Internet Connection Is Working

To verify that your PC's Internet connection is working, access a web site:

1. Click the Konqueror button on the quick-launch bar to launch Konqueror.

2. Click in the address bar to place the focus there.

3. Type the address of a web site (for example, **www.mhprofessional.com**) and then press ENTER.

Verify That You Can Connect to Your Network

If your PC can connect to the Internet, it's definitely connected to your network. You can then view shared folders on the network as well. Follow these steps:

1. Click the Knoppix button on the quick-launch bar and choose Utilities | Samba Network Neighborhood. Knoppix opens a Konqueror window that shows the workgroups of computers sharing files via the Server Message Block (SMB) protocol. (*Samba* is a geek's way of saying SMB.) The following illustration shows an example:

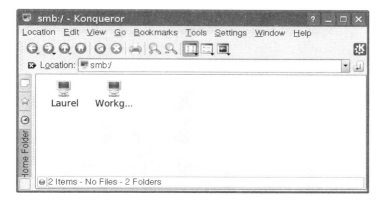

2. Click the workgroup that contains the computer that shares the drive (you may well see only one workgroup). The Konqueror window shows the computers that are sharing drives:

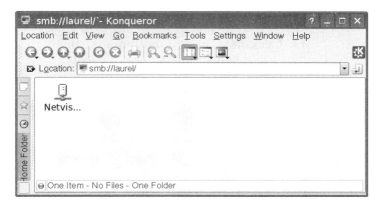

3. Click the computer that shares the drive. The Konqueror window shows the shared drives:

note *Any drive whose name is a drive letter followed by $ is one of Windows' hidden shares that are used for administrative purposes. You will not normally be able to connect to these drives from Knoppix.*

4. Click the drive you want to connect to. The Konqueror window shows its contents:

When you've finished browsing the network, click the Close button to close the Konqueror window.

Log Out from Knoppix and Return to Windows

To log out from Knoppix and return to Windows, follow these steps:

1. Click the Knoppix button, and then choose Log Out. Knoppix displays the End Session dialog box.

2. Click the Restart Computer button. Knoppix closes down with several screens full of multicolored text, and then prompts you to remove the CD.

3. Remove the CD, close the optical drive if it's the kind that opens, and then press ENTER. Windows starts as usual, and you can log on.

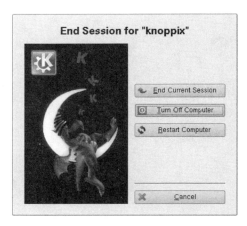

If you want to turn the PC off rather than restart it with Windows, click the Turn Off Computer button instead of the Restart Computer button in the End Session dialog box. After you remove the CD and press ENTER, your PC shuts down.

Step 4: Back Up Your Files Using Knoppix

If Windows starts giving problems and refuses to boot, follow these general steps to back up your files, referring back to Step 3 for specific techniques:

1. Insert the Knoppix CD in your PC's optical drive, and then boot Knoppix.

2. Choose the drive or folder to which you will back up the files: either connect a USB key or USB drive to your PC or establish a connection to another computer on your network that has a shared folder.

3. Use Konqueror to copy the appropriate files to the drive or folder.

Step 5: Download Windows Updates or Drivers to Fix Problems

If Windows has suffered problems that allow you to log on but not connect to a network, you can use Knoppix to download Windows updates, tools such as the Windows Malicious Software Removal Tool, or hardware drivers to fix the problem. Follow these general steps, referring back to Step 3 for specific techniques:

1. Insert the Knoppix CD in your PC's optical drive, and then boot Knoppix.

2. Establish an Internet connection.

3. Open Konqueror, and then download the files you need:

    ● **Windows updates and tools** Go to the Microsoft Download Center (www.microsoft.com/downloads/).

    ● **Hardware drivers** Start at the hardware manufacturer's web site. If it no longer exists, try searching using a search engine, such as Google.

4. Shut down Knoppix.

5. Boot Windows, and install the updates or drivers.

Making Knoppix Run Much Faster

If you find Knoppix useful and run it frequently, you may grow impatient at Knoppix's need to access the optical drive every other time you issue a command. If your computer has 1.5GB RAM or more, you can make Knoppix run much faster by copying Knoppix to RAM. (RAM responds far faster than the optical drive, and in silence.) To do so, when your PC starts booting Knoppix and displays the introductory screen, instead of simply pressing ENTER, type the following command, and then press ENTER:

```
knoppix toram
```

Copying the CD to RAM takes a few minutes, but once that's done, Knoppix runs much faster, and much more quietly.

Modify Your PC's Case

What You'll Need

- **Hardware:** Rotary tool, file saw, tapered reamer, metal cutter
- **Software:** None
- **Cost:** $100–200 U.S.

This project shows you how to get started on modifying the case of your desktop PC—preferably after its warranty has expired. The project shows you the tools you typically need, gives you examples of a couple of simple projects, and then leaves you to exercise your imagination and do-it-yourself skills.

There are two main reasons to modify your PC's case:

- **Practical** To make a component fit that wouldn't otherwise fit. This project explains how to create the space for and mount a larger fan to keep a PC cool.

- **Aesthetic** To make your PC's case look better (or worse, or simply more interesting) than the manufacturer made it. For example, enthusiastic "modders" have created cases made of wood, of see-through acrylic (with lights inside), and of other materials. Others have created a PC that looks like a weapon of mass destruction, a PC that looks like a gingerbread house, and even a PC that looks like a toilet. (If you want to see some of these, look at http://gadgets .fosfor.se/the-top-10-weirdest-case-mods/.) This project shows you how to cut a hole in the side panel of the case, and then put a transparent panel over the hole, so that you can see the inside the computer while the side is on.

note *This project doesn't cover modifying laptop PCs. You can of course attack them with the tools described in this project—but unless the laptop is unusually roomy inside, you will be able to achieve little change without inflicting damage. If you feel an insatiable urge to modify a laptop PC, try scrounging some broken ones to practice on before you attack your pride and joy.*

Step 1: Get the Tools for the Job

You can severely modify a PC—or wreck it completely—by using conventional household tools. But for good (or even acceptable) results, you'll probably want to use specialized or semi-specialized tools. Exactly which tools you need depends on what you're planning to do to your PC. This section discusses the main tools you're likely to need.

 Normally, you'll want to modify only your PC's case, not any of the PC's components. This should go without saying, but if you've seen the tech-support horror-story forum stories that describe users finding that a new video card "had too many pins" to fit in the slot on the motherboard, and "fixing" the problem by cutting off the extra pins, you'll know it doesn't go without saying. (The video card is the wrong kind for the slot on the motherboard, and the extra pins are vital to the card.)

Rotary Tool

For minor drilling, precision cutting, grinding, sanding, or buffing, you'll probably want a rotary tool such as a Dremel. Figure 11-1 shows a cordless Dremel with a starter kit of attachments, which include attachments for cutting and sanding.

Figure 11-1

A rotary tool can perform a wide variety of case-modification tasks with the right attachments.

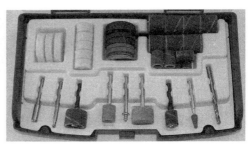

 Always wear goggles or other full-eye protection when using a Dremel or other rotary tool.

File Saw

If you need to put a hole through a plastic part of your PC's case, one possible tool is a file saw (see Figure 11-2). This is an inexpensive tool with a drill-like tip and serrated shaft that you can use to cut holes. The results are rough, but you can tidy them up afterward with other tools as needed.

Figure 11-2

You can use a file saw to cut holes in a plastic case.

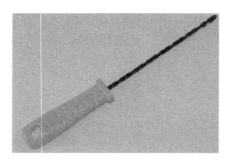

Tapered Reamer

If you need to put things through your PC's case in ways the case's maker didn't intend, you probably need to create some holes and enlarge others. Where there's an existing hole, you can drill with a larger bit to make it bigger, but what's usually easier and neater is to use a *tapered reamer*, a spike that tapers from a narrow point to a thicker haft, and which has cutting blades along the taper. You push the reamer through an existing hole, and then turn it while pushing it in to enlarge the hole to exactly the right size. Figure 11-3 shows a tapered reamer.

Figure 11-3

A tapered reamer is a great tool for enlarging existing holes to exactly the size you need.

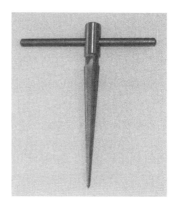

 Most reamers are designed to work in one direction only—for example, clockwise. Even though this may appear to be a tool where you don't need to read the two lines of instructions on the packaging, do just that.

Metal Cutters

Metal cutters, also called *tin snips*, tend to look like a particularly macho pair of kitchen shears (see Figure 11-4). They're useful for cutting through sheets of metal—for example, for enlarging an existing hole you've made in a side panel—or for trimming off extra bits of metal left over from your work with other tools.

 Apart from these specialized and semi-specialized tools, you'll probably also need household tools such as a metal file and a pair of pliers. Work gloves are also a good idea.

Figure 11-4

Metal cutters let you trim metal to fit or cut through sheets of metal.

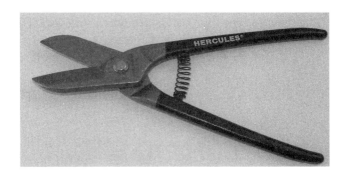

Step 2: Mount a Larger Fan

This step explains how to mount a larger fan to keep your PC cool.

 A larger fan is especially handy if you're looking to reduce the amount of noise your PC makes. See Project 22 for a detailed look at how you can silence your PC.

To mount a larger fan than your PC's case is designed for, follow these steps:

1. Shut down Windows, turn off the PC, and disconnect all its cables. Put the PC on a work surface.

2. Open the case. For example, undo the thumbscrews or screws that secure the case.

3. Touch a part of the metal chassis to discharge any static electricity you have built up.

4. Choose the fan you will use, and then measure the amount of space it takes up. The fan may come with a template for marking the ventilation hole and screw holes it needs. If it doesn't, you may find it helpful to make your own template by using a piece of cardboard or stiff paper.

5. Find a suitable location for the fan:

    ● To keep the noise down, you should mount the fan on the frame of the PC's case. You *can* mount a fan on a panel (for example, the top panel) in a pinch, but it's a recipe for producing vibration as well as airflow.

    ● If possible, site the fan so that it will be removing heat from, or providing cool air to, the PC's hotter components, such as the processor, processor fan, or graphics card.

6. Make sure the fan is oriented the right way:

    ● A fan at the front of the case should normally be drawing air into the case.

    ● A fan at the back of the case should normally be blowing air out of the case.

7. Measure where the screw holes will need to go.

    ● If possible, use one or more existing holes intended for mounting fans. For example, if your case is designed to take an 80mm fan and you're trying to shoehorn in a 120mm fan, you may be able to use one of the corner holes.

    ● You may be able to simply stick your template to the case and drill through it.

8. Drill small holes for the screws, and then use a tapered reamer to enlarge them carefully to the right size for the screws.

9. If necessary, enlarge the ventilation hole for the fan.

10. Mount the fan and screw it in place, using any vibration-damping mounts provided.

11. Connect the fan to a power connector. If you're using a variable-speed fan controller, mount it too. (For example, some variable-speed fans have a controller that mounts in a spare expansion slot, with a control knob outside the PC.)

12. Put your PC back together, connect its cables, and restart it.

Step 3: Create a Viewing Window in the Case

To make a viewing window in your PC's case (see Figure 11-5), follow these general steps:

1. Shut down Windows, turn off the PC, and disconnect all its cables. Put the PC on a work surface.

2. Open the case. For example, undo the thumbscrews or screws that secure the case.

3. Remove the panel in which you will create the hole.

4. Measure and mark the hole on the inside of the panel. CD pens and permanent markers work well on light-colored case panels. If the panel is dark-colored, use a grease pencil or paper tape to mark the hole.

Figure 11-5

A viewing window in your PC's case lets you see what's going on inside while it's running.

5. Drill through the case at one corner of the shape. Position the drill hole a little way within the shape so that the hole will not pass the extreme of the shape even when you expand the hole.

6. Using a tapered reamer or similar tool, ream the hole until it is large enough for your cutting tool to pass inside.

If you're using metal cutters as your cutting tool, you may need to drill several holes and then ream them together into a slot. Keep each of the holes inside the shape rather than placing them on the line.

7. Cut the hole. This is easier said than done:

   ● In an ideal world, you'll be able simply to cut smoothly and evenly all the way along the outside of the hole.

   ● In practice, you'll often need to hack out the center of the hole, and then work your way around the edges, cutting off small pieces at a time.

   ● Stay within your shape. You can always extend the hole later, but you'll have a tough time making it smaller once you've cut outside it.

8. Tidy up the hole:

   ● File off any large rough edges.

   ● Use a rotary tool to sand down smaller rough bits.

   ● Use pliers to straighten any parts of the metal that you've bent out of shape.

9. Cover the hole with your window material on the inside of the panel, and then secure the window in place. For example, you might use adhesive to bond a sheet of clear or colored acrylic over the hole.

10. Clean up the case panel and your workspace, and then put the case back together. If the result lacks polish, consider painting parts of the case, or decorating it with stickers or decals, to disguise any flaws.

If you put a viewing window in your PC's case, you may also want to add an internal light to make the PC's innards easier to see—or to make them glow in the dark. An online or offline computer store will offer various options.

Use Your PC as Your Home Theater

What You'll Need

- Hardware: Your existing TV or projector, cables
- Software: Windows Vista Home Premium Edition or Windows Vista Ultimate Edition
- Cost: Free, as long as you have a TV or projector

If your PC started life as a Media Center, or if you've turned it into one (as described in Project 5), you've probably gotten used to watching TV on it, and maybe recording one show while you're watching another. Watching is great on your large-screen LCD—but doesn't it spoil your enjoyment when the other members of your family park themselves around your desk, peering over your shoulder as you bite your nails through the final few minutes of the ballgame? Or maybe they decide that the DVD you're watching beats any available TV channel hands down.

Either way, if you want your family or household members to be able to enjoy the TV as much as you do, you probably need to display the picture on a larger screen. This project shows you how to use your PC as your home theater by connecting the PC to either your TV or to a projector.

Step 1: Choose a Connection Type

The first step—and in some ways the most complex—is choosing the right type of connection to use between your PC and the TV or projector. Depending on your PC and the TV or projector, you may have only one choice of connection, but in many cases, you'll need to decide among two, three, or more types of connection. Let's examine the connections first so that you know which connectors to look for on the PC and the TV or projector.

Understand Which Connection Types Are Preferable

Here are the types of connections, in descending order of quality:

- HDMI (High-Definition Multimedia Interface)
- DVI (Digital Visual Interface)
- VGA (Video Graphics Array)
- Component video
- S-Video
- Composite video

The following subsections explain the different connections and show pictures of what their ports and connectors look like.

tip *Ideally, you should avoid converting the signal from digital to analog if the TV can handle digital input. Even if you must convert the signal to analog, try to avoid converting the signal from one connection type to another, as doing so will always degrade the signal. That said, the results may be quite acceptable, especially as most TVs are far less sharp than PC monitors.*

HDMI

An HDMI cable transmits uncompressed digital audio and video signals, conveying the audio and video information from your PC to the TV without loss, so it should be your first choice if both your PC and output device have it. Figure 12-1 shows an HDMI port and an HDMI connector.

Figure 12-1

If your PC and TV both have HDMI ports, an HDMI cable should be your first choice for connecting them at full quality.

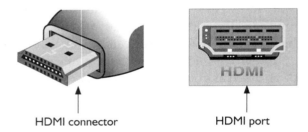

HDMI connector   HDMI port

Many new and recent LCD TVs include one or more HDMI ports, as do higher-end projectors. Older TVs are less likely to have HDMI ports.

DVI

DVI is widely used for connecting desktop PCs to LCD monitors and to projectors, but few laptops have DVI ports (usually only high-end laptops), and even fewer TVs have them. Look for the connection anyway—if your TV has DVI, you'll get a high-quality picture. Figure 12-2 shows a DVI port and a DVI connector.

Figure 12-2

DVI gives a high-quality signal, but you are more likely to find a DVI port on a projector than on a TV.

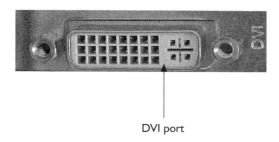
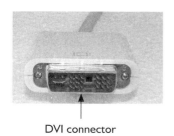

DVI port   DVI connector

VGA

VGA cables carry an analog signal rather than the digital signal that HDMI and DVI carry, so the PC has to convert the video signal from digital to analog before sending it along the VGA cable. VGA is widely used for connecting both desktop PCs and laptop PCs to monitors and to projectors. Few TVs have VGA ports. Figure 12-3 shows a VGA port and connector. You will also see VGA ports and connectors referred to as D-sub, which is short for D (indicating the shape) and *subminiature* (indicating that the connector was smaller than other connectors used at the time—but not anymore).

Figure 12-3

VGA uses a D-sub connection that has 15 pins.

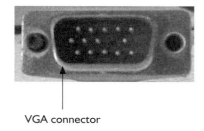
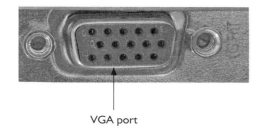

VGA connector   VGA port

 VGA D-sub connectors and ports are the same size as some other types of D-sub connectors and ports that have different numbers of pins and are used for different purposes. For example, a nine-pin D-sub connector is used for serial ports. Before inserting a D-sub connector in a D-sub port, check visually that the number and arrangement of pins on the connector matches the number and arrangement of holes on the port.

Component Video

Component video uses a three-stranded cable to carry an analog signal, with each strand terminating in a separate RCA connector. Each strand carries a different component of the video signal—hence the name. Figure 12-4 shows a component video cable.

Figure 12-4

Component video uses three RCA connectors at the ends.

S-Video

An S-Video cable uses a two-stranded cable to carry an analog video signal. The cable terminates in a single connector, making for an easy connection. Figure 12-5 shows an S-Video port and connector.

Figure 12-5

An S-Video cable uses a single connector, so it's easy to connect.

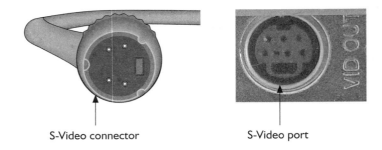

S-Video connector   S-Video port

RCA/Composite Video

A composite cable carries the entire video signal on a single cable. Image quality suffers, so make a composite cable your last choice—the one you use only if none of the other connection types is available. The composite cable carries only the video, so you'll also need to use an RCA cable to carry the audio from the PC to the TV or projector. Figure 12-6 shows a composite cable and an RCA cable.

Figure 12-6

When you use a composite cable (left) to carry a video signal, you also need to use another cable (such as the RCA cable shown on the right) to carry the audio signal.

Check the Ports on Your PC's Graphics Card and TV or Projector

Now that you know what the ports and connectors for the various connection options look like, check which ports are on your PC's graphics card and on your TV or projector.

Normally, a desktop PC gives you far more choices than a laptop PC does—and if necessary, you can change the graphics card in most desktops without much difficulty, whereas only a few laptops let you change their graphics cards, and then only with considerable expense and minimal choice of replacement cards.

Most TVs offer one or more of HDMI, component video, S-Video, and composite video. Choose the highest-quality connection type available for both your TV and the PC. Many projectors offer both DVI and VGA ports. Some also offer HDMI ports. Again, choose the highest-quality connection type available.

Step 2: Find or Buy a Cable

Now that you've established what kind of cable you need, see whether you already own one. For example, your shiny new TV may have included an HDMI cable that you've left sleeping in its Styrofoam nest, or your camcorder box may have packed an S-Video cable along with its tangle of other cables. Or maybe a dusty old box contains an unused component video cable that came with your DVD player…even if the cable is several years old, it should work.

If your search comes up dry, you'll need to beg, borrow, or buy a cable. Any electronics retailer worth patronizing—online or bricks-and-mortar—should be able to help you here.

note *Another means of connecting your PC to your TV is to use a media extender, a TV set-top box to which your PC transmits the video signal wirelessly. At this writing, Microsoft and hardware partners including Linksys, D-Link, and Niveus Media have just announced media extenders that work with Windows Media Center in Windows Vista, so these devices should be available by the time you read this.*

Step 3: Connect Your PC to Your TV or Projector

With the cable in hand, you're ready to connect your PC to the TV or projector. How exactly you proceed depends on what kind of PC and what kind of TV or projector you have, but in general, you need to follow these steps:

1. If the PC is running, shut down Windows, and then turn the PC off.

2. Make sure the TV or projector is powered off as well.

3. Connect a cable of the appropriate type to the port you're using on the PC and to the input on the TV or projector.

4. Turn on the TV or projector. If necessary, switch the TV's or projector's input to receive the signal from the cable you're using. For example:

   ● On a TV, you may need to choose a different AV input instead of the usual one.

   ● On a projector, you may need to press a button to cycle among the possible input sources until it finds the signal from the PC.

5. Turn on the PC. Depending on the connection you're using, you may see the PC's bootup sequence on the PC's monitor, on the TV screen, or on both.

6. If Windows Vista detects the TV or projector as a new display and opens the New Display Detected dialog box to let you configure the new display, choose the appropriate option button, each of which is described next, and then click the Apply button:

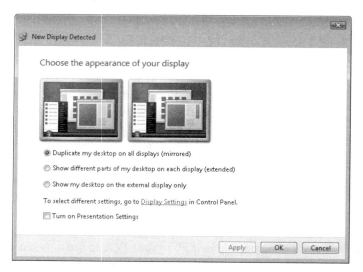

- **Duplicate My Desktop On All Displays (Mirrored)** Select this option button if you want to display the same picture on your PC's screen and on the TV or projector. This setting is useful when you're setting up the TV or projector, but usually either the PC's screen or the external image will be at an unsuitable resolution for long-term viewing.

- **Show Different Parts Of My Desktop On Each Display (Extended)** Select this option button if you want to make the external image an extension of your desktop. You can then drag a window from the PC's screen to the external image.

- **Show My Desktop On The External Display Only** Select this option button if you want to shut off your PC's screen and see only the external image.

note *On a laptop PC, you may need to press a function key combination (for example, FN-F7) to send the video output to the external graphics port. Consult your laptop's documentation or look for a key bearing a graphic of multiple monitors (usually in the color used for the lettering on the FN key).*

7. If at this point you're not seeing any image on the TV or projector, use the Display Settings dialog box to set up the display:

- Right-click the Desktop and choose Personalize to open the Personalize window.

● Click the Display Settings link at the bottom to open the Display Settings dialog box:

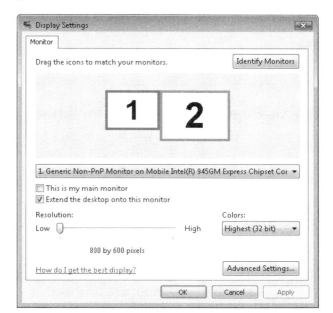

● Click the monitor icon that represents the TV or projector. If you're not sure which it is, click the Identify Monitors button to make Windows flash up a large number on each monitor.

● Select the Extend The Desktop Onto This Monitor check box.

● Click the Apply button.

● If necessary, change the resolution on the monitor by dragging the Resolution slider, and then click the Apply button. For a TV, start with the lowest resolution available, and then work upward. For a projector, start with the lowest recommended resolution in the projector's specs, and then experiment with higher resolutions that the projector supports.

● When you've got the external display to your satisfaction, click the OK button to close the Display Settings dialog box.

Step 4: Run Windows Media Center and Play Content

Now you're all set to run Windows Media Center and enjoy content on it:

1. Choose Start | All Programs | Windows Media Center.

2. If you extended your desktop, drag the Windows Media Center window to the TV or projector's part of the desktop, and then maximize the window.

3. Start the program or DVD playing. Enjoy!

If you're using a projector, when you switch the projector off, the fan may continue to run even after the lamp has gone off. Allow the fan to finish cooling the projector before you unplug the projector's power supply. Disconnecting the power supply to stop the fan running may damage the lamp in the projector.

Is It Worth Buying a Projector for Enjoying TV or Media?

Since you ask: Only if you have money to burn. Projector prices have dropped from the levels of causing severe financial pain to being borderline affordable, but unless you plan to enjoy movies frequently, the expense probably doesn't justify the enjoyment. Besides, with a projector, you usually need to darken the room somewhat before you can see the picture well. The gloom or darkness can be atmospheric—romantic or scary, take your pick—especially for movies, but it's less than ideal for regular viewing.

What you may be able to do, though, is rent or borrow a projector. Your local video store may rent them out. Many organizations and social clubs have projectors that are seldom used but available to the members. Or you could tell your boss that it's essential you practice your presentation at home…

If you do buy or borrow a projector, you'll also need a surface onto which you can project the image. Ideally, you'll have a screen (maybe borrowed from the same source), but a white wall, a white board (such as a sheet of 8×4-foot chipboard sanded down a bit and painted with matt paint), or even a sheet stretched taut can all serve the purpose.

Share Your Household's Music and Movies Easily and Effectively

What You'll Need

- Hardware: Extra PC (optional), network-attached storage device (optional), or external USB hard disk (optional)
- Software: Windows Media Player or iTunes
- Cost: Free or up to $500 U.S., depending on the method you choose

If your household has more than one computer, you'll probably want to share your music and movies between the computers so that each computer can play all the songs and video files. This project shows you how to share your household's music and movies easily and effectively. You have a choice of several ways to share your music and movie files with other people whose computers connect to the same network as yours. Before you start sharing, it's a good idea to understand your options, because this will let you choose and implement the way of sharing that's best for you. We'll look at this first.

Step 1: Assess Your Options and Decide Your Plan of Attack

Your first step is to assess your options for sharing music and movies, figure out exactly what you need, and then decide how to proceed. The easiest way to start is by using a network-aware media player, such as Windows Media Player or iTunes. You build your media library in the player, and then choose to share either the whole library or just parts of it.

Sharing is simple and effective. Here's how it works:

- The shared library remains on the computer that's sharing it, and when a participating computer goes to play a song or other item, the sharing computer streams that item across the network to the playing computer. This means that the item isn't copied from the sharing computer to the playing computer in a way that leaves a usable file on the playing computer.

note Streaming *is a way of sending a file across a network connection in order so that the computer receiving the file can start playing it before receiving the whole file. If you view a video on YouTube, that's streaming.*

- Participating computers can play the shared items but can't do anything else with them; for example, they can't burn shared songs to CD or DVD, download them to a player such as an iPod or Zune, or copy them to their own libraries.

- When a computer goes offline or is shut down, library items it has been sharing stop being available to other users.

As you no doubt spotted, that last bullet point holds a major drawback. Unless you keep all the sharing computers running all the time (and prevent any laptops from leaving the building or your wireless network), you will lose access to some of the shared items. Not being able to burn shared items or download them can also be a problem, depending on how much freedom you expect to have with your shared files.

note *The sharing described here is limited to computers on the same TCP/IP subnet as your computer is on. (A subnet is a logical division of a network.) Any home network uses a single subnet, so this won't be a problem. But if your computer connects to a medium-sized network (such as one in a dorm), and you're unable to find a computer that you know is connected to the same network somewhere, it may be on a different subnet.*

If you want to make sure that all your media files are available all the time, and that you can do with them whatever you want (subject to the law), you may need to step up to the next level—for example, by repurposing an old PC as a server, by using Windows Home Server, or by using a purpose-built network storage device. Step 2 shows you how to share music and video using Windows Media Player. Step 3 shows you how to share music and video using iTunes. Step 4 discusses your options for running a server or a network storage device.

note *Windows Media Player makes sharing media files with other PCs easier than iTunes does—and it gives you finer control over which media files you share with whom. (For example, you can share all your files with one computer but share only a select few files with another computer.) However, iTunes also lets you share media files with Macs running iTunes and play the media files those Macs are sharing.*

Step 2: Share Music and Video Files via Windows Media Player

Unless you've installed an operating system other than Windows on your PC (see Project 23 for suggestions), the chances are high that you've got Windows Media Player installed on your computer. Windows Media Player is a friendly program that wants to help you share your computer's music and video files with other computers on the same network—and enjoy the files that they're sharing. Let's look at how you set up Windows Media Player for sharing.

Understand How Windows Media Player Shares Files

Before you set up sharing on Windows Media Player, you need to know a little about how it shares files.

First, you probably have your own user account, as every user should. The user account lets you maintain your settings—everything from your Desktop background to where you position the Taskbar, from your screensaver to the items on the Start menu—independently from those of each of the other users.

Your user account contains a whole suite of folders in which Windows intends you to store your files: Documents, Music, Pictures, Videos, and so on. Any files you keep in the folders in your user account are private from other users—unless they're media files and you tell Windows Media Player to share them.

Set Up Sharing on Windows Media Player

To set up sharing on Windows Media Player, follow these steps:

1. Start Windows Media Player if it's not already running. For example, choose Start | All Programs | Windows Media Player.

2. Move the mouse pointer over the Library button on the toolbar, click the down-arrow button that appears on the bottom part of the button, and then choose Media Sharing from the menu. Windows Media Player displays the Media Sharing dialog box.

3. If you want Windows Media Player to automatically locate media libraries that other computers running Windows Media Player are sharing, select the Find Media That Others Are Sharing check box. Normally, you'll want to do this.

4. If you want Windows Media Player to share your own media, select the Share My Media check box.

5. Click the OK button, and then go through User Account Control for the Windows Media Player Configuration feature. Windows Media Player displays an expanded version of the Media Sharing dialog box, as shown next.

Any computer or item marked with a yellow triangle and an exclamation mark doesn't yet have a sharing setting applied to it.

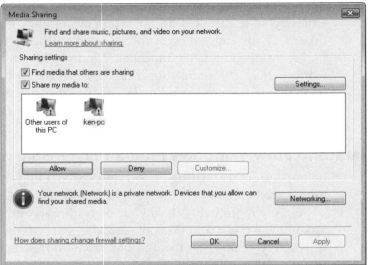

6. To allow other users of your computer to access your media library, click the Other Users Of This PC icon in the Share My Media To list box, and then click the Allow button. Windows Media Player changes the exclamation-mark icon for a checkmark icon and makes the Customize button available.

7. To allow users of a particular other computer to access your media library, click the computer's icon in the Share My Media To list box, and then click the Allow button. Windows Media Player replaces the exclamation-mark icon with a checkmark icon and makes the Customize button available.

8. To block users of a particular other computer from accessing your media library, follow these steps:

   ● Click the computer's icon in the Share My Media To list box, and then click the Deny button. Windows Media Player displays the Deny dialog box for the computer.

   ● If you want to prevent any other user of your computer from sharing media with the computer you're blocking, click the Yes button, and then go through User Account Control for the Windows Media Player Configuration feature. If you want to leave other users of your computer free to share their media with the computer you're blocking, click the No button. Either way, you can select the Don't Show This Message Again check box before clicking a button if you don't want Windows Media Player to ask you this question again.

9. If you don't want to share your entire media library with the other users of your PC or the specified computer, follow these steps:

   ● Click the computer's icon or the Other Users Of This PC icon (as appropriate) in the Share My Media To list box.

● Click the Customize button. Windows Media Player display the Media Sharing – Customize dialog box:

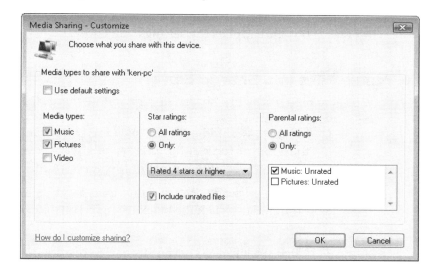

● Clear the Use Default Settings check box. (Using the default settings means sharing all media types—music files, picture files, and video files—with minimal-quality screening and without parental ratings.) Windows Media Player makes all the Media Types, Star Ratings, and Parental Ratings controls available.

● In the Media Types column, select only the check boxes for the media types you want to share. For example, if you want to share only music, select the Music check box, and clear both the Pictures check box and the Video check box.

● In the Star Ratings column, choose what you want to share. Select the All Ratings option button only if you're determined to share your dross as well as your diamonds. Normally, you're better advised to select the Only option button, and then choose either Rated 5 Stars or Rated 4 Stars Or Higher in the drop-down list. Clear the Include Unrated Files check box unless you really want to share everything.

tip *To get the most out of your media library, rate all the files it contains—eventually, not all at once. You can then be confident of sharing only quality media. Better yet, you can keep the library's size down by removing the low-rated files.*

● In the Parental Ratings column, select the All Ratings option button if you want to share all items no matter how low they're rated. Otherwise, select the Only option button, and then select the check boxes for the unrated items you want to share: Music, Pictures, or Video.

note *The check boxes that appear in the Parental Ratings list box correspond to the check boxes you've selected in the Media Types column. For example, if you clear the Video check box in the Media Types column, the Parental Ratings list box doesn't have a Video: Unrated check box.*

● Click the OK button. Windows Media Player closes the Media Sharing – Customize dialog box, returning you to the Media Sharing dialog box.

10. Click the OK button. Windows Media Player closes the Media Sharing dialog box and applies the settings you chose.

Play Media Files in a Shared Library

To play media files in a shared library, follow these steps:

1. In Windows Media Player, click the Library button on the toolbar to display the Library (unless the Library is already displayed). The shared libraries appear toward the bottom of the left column.

2. Double-click the library name to expand its listing, displaying its contents. (You can also click the black triangle, but double-clicking the name is usually easier.)

3. Click the view you want to use to display the library's contents, as in the example in Figure 13-1, which shows Artist view. You can then play items as usual—for example, double-click a song to start it playing.

Figure 13-1

Once you've set Windows Media Player to look for shared media libraries, you can easily play shared music and video files.

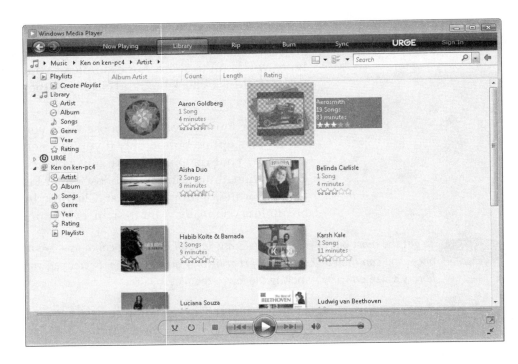

Start Sharing Your Media Library the Easy Way

This section shows you how to set up sharing of your media library manually, but there's an even easier way to get started. When Windows Media Player notices a shared media library that you haven't used before, it displays a pop-up message above the notification area:

Click the pop-up message to open the Windows Media Player Library Sharing dialog box. If you want to share your media library with this computer, click the Allow button. If you're feeling surly, click the Deny button. And if you're feeling really surly, select the Disable Future Notifications check box, and then click the Deny button.

That's enough possibilities to satisfy most people, but if you want to customize your sharing settings, click the Sharing Settings button. Windows Media Player displays the Media Sharing dialog box, in which you can set up custom sharing as discussed in step 9 of the preceding list.

Step 3: Share Music and Video Files via iTunes

If you have an iPod or an iPhone rather than a player that's compatible with Windows Media Player, you'll probably want to manage the iPod or iPhone using iTunes, the program that Apple provides—for free—for managing iPods and iPhones. (There are several alternative programs that you can use to manage iPods from Windows, but most of them involve paying money.)

Like Windows Media Player (discussed in Step 2), iTunes makes it easy to share your music and video files with other iTunes users on your network and to play the files they're sharing. You may also want to share files with other users of your computer—which, interestingly, requires a little more effort.

Get and Install iTunes

If you're already using an iPod or an iPhone, chances are that you've already downloaded and installed iTunes. If not, open your web browser, go to the Apple web site (www.apple.com/itunes/download/), and download the latest version of iTunes for Windows.

iTunes has a straightforward installation procedure except for one minor issue on Windows Vista: the User Account Control dialog boxes that make sure you're intending to install the software (rather than having accidentally triggered some malware that's trying to run it) tend to get stuck behind the main installation window. If installation seems to have gotten stuck, look at the Taskbar to see if there's a flashing button for User Account Control. If so, click it, and then go through User Account Control as usual. Because the installer installs not only iTunes but also QuickTime and other components, you may have to go through User Account Control twice or more.

Once you've installed iTunes, start it, and then follow through its prompts for adding media files to your media library (iTunes offers to search your folders for files). You can add other files to the media library easily:

- Drag the files from a Windows Explorer window to the Library area of the Source pane (the pane on the left of the iTunes window).

- Choose File | Add Folder To Library to add a whole folder of files.

- Choose File | Add File To Library to add an individual file.

Share Your Library with Other Local iTunes Users

You can share either your entire library or selected playlists with other users on your network. You can share most items, including MP3 files, AAC files, Apple Lossless Encoding files, AIFF files, WAV files, and links to radio stations. You can't share Audible files or QuickTime sound files.

note   *At this writing, you can share your library with up to five other computers per day, and your computer can be one of up to five computers accessing the shared library on another computer on any given day. However, Apple can change the details of library sharing, so you may see different restrictions from these.*

To share some or all of your library, follow these steps:

1. In iTunes, choose Edit | Preferences or press CTRL-COMMA or CTRL-Y to display the iTunes dialog box.

2. Click the Sharing tab, shown in Figure 13-2 with settings chosen.

3. Select the Share My Library On My Local Network check box (which is cleared by default). By default, iTunes then selects the Share Entire Library option button. If you want to share only some playlists, select the Share Selected Playlists option button, and then select the check boxes for the playlists you want to share.

4. By default, the items in your shared library are available to any other user on the network. To restrict access to only those people with whom you share a password, select the Require Password check box, and then enter a strong (unguessable) password in the text box.

tip   *If there are many computers on your network, use a sharing password to help avoid running up against the five-users-per-day limit. If your network has only a few computers, you may not need a password to avoid reaching this limit.*

Figure 13-2

On the Sharing tab, choose whether to look for shared libraries and whether to share part or all of your library.

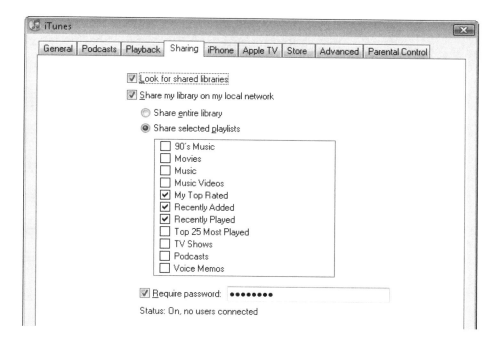

5. Click the General tab to display its contents. In the Shared Name text box , set the name that other users trying to access your library will see. The default name is *username*'s Library—for example, Mimi's Library. You might choose to enter a more descriptive name, especially if your computer is part of a well-populated network (for example, in a dorm).

6. Click the OK button to apply your choices and close the dialog box.

note *When you set iTunes to share your library, iTunes displays a message reminding you that "Sharing music is for personal use only"—in other words, remember not to violate copyright law. Select the Do Not Show This Message Again check box if you want to prevent this message from appearing again.*

Once you've shared your library, other iTunes users on the same network can access it as described in the upcoming section "Access and Play Another Local iTunes User's Shared Library."

Disconnect Other Users from Your Shared Library

To disconnect other users from your shared library, follow these steps:

1. In iTunes, choose Edit | Preferences or press CTRL-COMMA or CTRL-Y to display the iTunes dialog box.

2. Click the Sharing tab to display it.

3. To see how many users are connected to your shared library, look at the Status readout toward the bottom of the Sharing tab.

4. Clear the Share My Library On My Local Network check box.

5. Click the OK button. If any other user is connected to your shared library, iTunes displays a message box that indicates so and asks whether you are sure you want to turn off sharing.

6. Click the Yes button or the No button, as appropriate. If you click the Yes button, anyone playing an item from the library will be cut off abruptly without notice.

Access and Play Another Local iTunes User's Shared Library

To access another person's shared library, you must first set your computer to look for shared libraries. You may already have done so when you turned on sharing on your own computer. If not, do so first.

Set Your Computer to Look for Shared Libraries

First, set your computer to look for shared libraries:

1. In iTunes, choose Edit | Preferences or press CTRL-COMMA or CTRL-Y to display the iTunes dialog box.

2. Click the Sharing tab to display its contents.

3. Select the Look For Shared Libraries check box.

4. Click the OK button to close the iTunes dialog box.

Access Shared Libraries on Your Local Network

Once you've selected the Look For Shared Libraries check box on the Sharing tab, iTunes automatically detects shared libraries when you launch the program while your computer is connected to a network. If a shared library comes online after that, iTunes detects it almost immediately.

If iTunes finds shared libraries or playlists, it displays them in the Source pane on the left. Figure 13-3 shows an example of browsing the music shared by another computer.

If a shared library has a password, iTunes displays the Shared Library Password dialog box. Type the password, and then click the OK button to access the library. Select the Remember Password check box before clicking the OK button if you want iTunes to save the password to speed up future access to the library.

tip   *Double-click the entry for a shared library in the Source pane to open a separate window that shows the library's contents.*

Figure 13-3

Computers sharing libraries appear in the Source pane in iTunes, allowing you to quickly browse the songs and other items that are being shared.

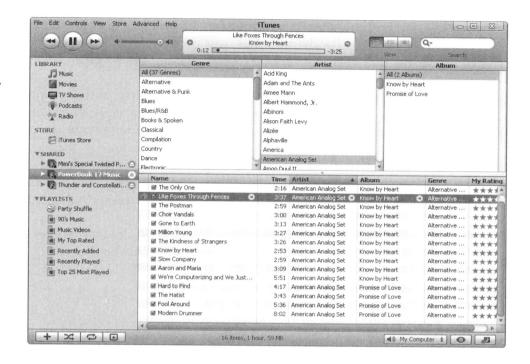

Disconnect a Shared Library

To disconnect a shared library you've connected to, take one of these actions:

- Click the Eject icon next to the library in the Source pane.

- Click the library in the Source pane and then either press CTRL-E, click the Eject icon in the lower-right corner of the iTunes window, or choose Controls | Disconnect *Library* (where *Library* is the name of the shared library).

- Right-click the library in the Source pane and choose Disconnect.

Share Your Music More Effectively with Other Local Users

As you saw earlier in this step, iTunes makes it easy for you to share either your library or specific playlists with other iTunes users on your local area network (LAN). You can share with up to five different computers per day, and your computer must be attached to the network and powered on for other computers to be able to access your shared files.

You may also want to share your music and videos with other users of your computer. As you saw in Step 2, Windows Media Player knows the ins and outs of Windows Firewall and can share your media files even if you've put them in the folders within your user account that are normally barred to anyone but you. iTunes doesn't have this inside knowledge, and as a result, you have to work around the security features built into Windows before you can share your music and video files.

Your iTunes library, which is stored by default in your Music\iTunes\iTunes Music folder, is securely protected from other users of your computer. That's great if you want to keep your music to yourself, but not so great if you want to share it with your friends, family, or coworkers.

The easiest way to give other users access to your library is to move it to the Public folder. Windows creates this folder automatically when you install it, and shares it automatically with other users of your computer but not with other computers on the network. The Public folder appears at the top level of the file system from the user's point of view. Choose Start | Computer to open a Computer window, click the drop-down arrow at the left end of the Address bar, and choose Public. In the Public folder, you'll find a full set of folders for sharing, including Public Music, Public Pictures, and Public Videos.

Moving your library to the Public Music folder involves two steps: Moving the files, and then telling iTunes where you've moved them to.

Move Your Library Files to the Shared Folder

To move your library files to the Public Music folder or the Shared Music folder, follow these steps:

1. Close iTunes if it's running. (For example, press ALT-F4 or choose File | Exit.)

2. Open your library folder. Choose Start | Music to open a Windows Explorer window showing your Music folder.

3. Double-click the iTunes folder to open it. You'll see an iTunes Music Library. xml file, an iTunes Music Library.itl file, and an iTunes Music folder. The first two files must stay in your library folder. If you remove them, iTunes won't be able to find your library, and it will create these files again from scratch.

4. Right-click the iTunes Music folder and choose Cut to cut it to the Clipboard.

5. In the Music folder, double-click the shortcut to the Sample Music folder. (The Sample Music folder is in the Public Music folder, so double-clicking the Sample Music folder's shortcut is a handy way to jump to inside the Public Music folder.) In the Address bar, click the Public Music item to display the folder's contents.

6. Right-click an open space in the Public Music folder, and then choose Paste to paste the iTunes Music folder into the folder.

7. Close the Windows Explorer window. (For example, press ALT-F4 or choose File | Close.)

Tell iTunes Where the Media Files Are Located

Next, you need to tell iTunes where the song files and other media files are:

1. Start iTunes. (For example, double-click the iTunes icon on your Desktop.)

2. Press CTRL-COMMA or choose Edit | Preferences to display the iTunes dialog box.

3. Click the Advanced tab to display its contents.

4. Click the Change button to display the Browse For Folder dialog box.

5. Navigate to the Public Music folder, and then click the OK button to close the Browse For Folder dialog box.

6. Click the OK button to close the iTunes dialog box.

After you've done this, iTunes knows where the files are, and you can play them back as usual. When you rip further song files from CD or import files, iTunes stores them in the Public Music folder.

You're all set. The other users of your PC can do either of two things:

- Move their library to the Public Music folder, using the techniques described here, so that all files are stored centrally. Instead of moving the library folder itself, they should move the folders it contains. Users can then add songs they import to the shared library, and all users can access them.

- Keep their library separate, but add the contents of the shared library folder to it:

  1. Choose File | Add Folder To Library to display the Browse For Folder dialog box.

  2. Navigate to the Public Music folder.

  3. Select the iTunes Music folder.

  4. Click the Open button. iTunes adds all the latest songs to the library.

Whichever approach the other users of your PC choose, the songs that they add to the shared library don't appear automatically in your library. To add all the latest songs, use the Add To Library dialog box, as described in the previous list—but be careful not to add the same songs twice.

note *If you do add the same songs to your library twice (or more), click the Music item in the Library area of the Source pane, and then choose View | Show Duplicates to reveal duplicate songs. You can then delete any unwanted duplicates once you've made sure they're actually duplicates rather than other versions of the same songs.*

Step 4: Set Up a Media Server for Your Household

If you find that trying to play songs stored in libraries that keep disappearing off the network is too tedious, another option is to set up a media server for your household. In the old days, a server would be a dedicated computer that you kept running the whole time, but there's also a modern alternative that you may find preferable—a network-aware drive or an external hard drive connected to a network router.

If you have an old computer that you can turn into a server, and you're prepared to leave it running the whole time, cranking up your electricity bill, the server is a good option. But if getting a server would mean buying a new computer, a network drive may be a better choice. Let's look at the network drive option first.

note *This section assumes that you're using the server primarily to share media files—but you can also use it to share other files (such as documents or spreadsheets) or to back up files.*

Choose a Network Drive

A network drive tends to be a neater solution than running a full-bore server—and it is usually much lighter on the electricity than is a server. And if you're really lucky, you may already have a network router that can share a drive. So start by making sure you know the capabilities of your network router. An increasing number of these include one or more USB ports to which you can attach an external drive, and then share it on the network. The configuration process varies depending on the router manufacturer, but it is usually easy. If your router has this capability, all you need do is buy an external drive, connect it via USB, and configure it for sharing.

If your network router doesn't have the capability to share an attached USB drive, look at independent network-attached storage (NAS) devices designed for consumers rather than corporations. You can find these at any computer store worth patronizing, but you may find a wider variety at online stores such as Amazon (www.amazon .com) and CDW (www.cdw.com).

Examples of NAS devices include those in the following list. On most of these sites, you'll want to follow a Network Storage link to find the devices if they don't have links on the home page.

- **LinkStation series**   Buffalo Technology Inc. (www.buffalotech.com)
- **StorCenter series**   Iomega Corporation (www.iomega.com)
- **Ethernet Big Disk NAS Server series**   LaCie (www.lacie.com)
- **Shared Storage NAS Server**   Seagate Technology LLC (www.seagate.com)

Once you've bought the NAS device, connect it to your network via an Ethernet cable, and then configure it following the instructions that come with it.

Set Up a "Real" Server

You can either build a server from scratch on a new computer or change the role of one of your existing computers—even a pensioned-off computer that's too old to run Windows Vista or XP at a decent speed. Whether you buy (or build) a new computer or repurpose an existing computer will color your choices for your server. Here are notes on the key components for the server:

- **Operating system** The server can run Windows Vista or Windows XP if you have a copy that you can spare; if not, you might consider using a less expensive (or even free) operating system, such as one of the many distributions of Linux.

> **note** *Another possibility is to use Windows Home Server. After installing Windows Home Server, you can manage the server remotely through a management console, so the computer running Windows Home Server doesn't even need a monitor or a keyboard.*

- **Processor** The server can run on a modest processor—even an antiquated one by today's standards, such as a 500-MHz or faster processor for a Windows or Linux server.

- **RAM** The server needs only enough RAM to run the operating system unless you'll need to run applications on it. For example, 256MB of RAM is adequate for a server running Windows XP. Windows Vista requires 512MB or (preferably) 1GB.

- **Disk space** The server must have enough disk space to store all the songs and other files you want to have available. A desktop computer is likely to be a better bet than a notebook computer, because you can add internal drives to it. Alternatively, you might use one or more external USB or FireWire drives to provide plenty of space.

- **Network connection** The server must be connected to your network, either via network cable or via wireless. A wireless connection is adequate for serving a few computers, but in most cases, a wired connection (Fast Ethernet or Gigabit Ethernet) is a much better choice.

- **Monitor** If the server will simply be running somewhere convenient (rather than being used for other computing tasks, such as running applications), all you need is an old monitor capable of displaying the bootup and login screens for the operating system. After that, you can turn the monitor off until you need to restart or configure the server.

- **Keyboard and mouse** Like the monitor, the keyboard and mouse can be basic devices, because you'll need to use them only for booting and configuring the server.

- **CD-ROM drive**   Your server needs a CD-ROM drive only if you'll use the server for ripping. If you'll rip on the clients, the server can get by without one.

- **Sound card**   Your server needs a sound card only if you'll use it for playing music or other media files.

- **Reliability**   Your server may be modest, but it must be reliable—otherwise the files won't be available when you want to play them. Make sure also that the server has plenty of cooling, and configure its power settings so that it doesn't go to sleep.

- **Location**   If you choose to leave your server running all the time, locate it somewhere safe. To keep down the noise, you may be tempted to hide the server away in a closet. If you do, make sure there's enough ventilation so that the server doesn't overheat.

Place the Files and Media Libraries on the Server

Once you've gotten your NAS device or server up and running, perform these general steps:

1. Create a folder that will contain the songs.

2. Share that folder on the network so that all the users you want to be able to play music are allowed to access it.

3. On each of the client computers, move the library into the shared folder.

Turn Your PC into a Recording Studio

What You'll Need

- Hardware: Audio interface, microphones, your existing instruments, a room
- Software: Audacity
- Cost: $100 U.S. and up to wherever you choose to stop

Back in the old days before PCs became ubiquitous and multipotent, recording high-quality audio was a complex process involving expensive equipment, reel-to-reel recorders, and usually a studio. Recording a track worth other people's listening time usually meant a serious investment of time, money, and effort.

Now that PCs powerful enough to handle audio and video are easily affordable, recording is far easier, though it can still be as complex as you choose to make it. For example, if you want to record an entire rock band (or other musical group) all together, you'll need a load of microphones, pickups, and mixing gear. But if you're happy to proceed by recording one or two instruments at a time, and then mixing the tracks together on your PC, you can get impressive results using only a minimum of equipment.

This project shows you how to turn your PC into a recording studio by getting the hardware and installing the software you need for recording. The next project demonstrates how to use the software to record and mix tracks together.

Step 1: Prepare a Room for Recording

If you will use a studio for recording, you can skip this section. But if you're not in a position to afford burning handfuls of dollars every hour, you'll do better to work at home. The basic rule of home recording is to make the most of what you've got. Chances are that you won't have a spare room that you can devote to recording, so you will probably need to repurpose an existing room—for example, your bedroom or the living room.

tip *A bedroom can actually be a great choice for home recording, because it contains curtains and soft objects that help absorb sound.*

Whatever type of room you have available, you'll need to prepare the room acoustically as far as possible and set up the PC in a suitable and (preferably) quiet way. The next sections offer suggestions for how to go about these tasks.

Work on the Room's Acoustics

Have you ever walked into a big, empty room with bare walls—a community hall, perhaps, or a school gym—and heard your footsteps echoing back at you? Or your voice booming when you spoke? In such rooms, *standing waves* tend to occur when something makes a noise. Your heel cracks down on the floor, and the noise bounces off one wall, reflecting across the room to the other wall, where it bounces off again. The waves meet up again in the middle of the room, producing the standing waves.

Unless you're deliberately aiming for a recording that sounds as though it was made in a garbage can, you'll want to minimize standing waves by taming the sound reflections. To tame the reflections, you need to break up any bare walls or similar surfaces (such as fitted closet doors) in the room. For example:

- *Draw the curtains.* The curtains will damp down the window.

- *Hang a blanket over and around the door.* This will damp down the door and also reduce the amount of sound leaking out of the room.

- *Remove any sliding closet doors.* These loose, flat objects can vibrate beautifully. After removing such doors, hang a blanket over the open space to deaden it.

- *Put a rug on a bare floor.* Polished hardwood floors are beautiful, but the sound bounces off them big-time. Use a rug or some off-cuts of carpet to absorb the sound.

- *Add furniture.* Your first reaction is probably to shift all the furniture out of the room so that you have space for your instruments (and for you and your bandmates to express yourselves). But a bed, sofa, armchairs, and so on are great for reducing standing waves.

- *Put a cushion or bean-bag in each open corner.* If the room has open corners, you need to damp them down. One easy way is to put a pillow, cushion, bean-bag, or folded blanket in each open corner. Alternatively, move furniture into the corners. For example, put an armchair in a corner.

note *If you have pets, remove them from not only your studio but the surrounding area when you're playing. This is not just to avoid the potential cruelty of forcing them to listen to your music but also to prevent them from adding vocal contributions—for example, your dog might decide to howl when a stringed instrument hits the animal's resonant frequency.*

You also need to, within reason, remove any objects that may resonate or vibrate. When you and your bandmates start playing your instruments, any loose objects in the room will start getting a sonic workout. When an object, or part of it, hits its resonant frequency, it starts to vibrate or rattle. This is awkward enough when a single object starts vibrating noisily when you're playing, but if your band goes in for a wall-of-sound sonic assault, you'll probably get multiple objects vibrating or rattling at the same time. Musical instruments tend to be prime culprits here, though they're not the only ones (your mom's collection of china plates, tastefully arranged on display racks, might collect an interesting range of vibrations). For example, if you have a piano in your recording room, other instruments from drums to guitars will make its strings vibrate, so you'll probably want to remove it from the room if you're not using it. Bass guitar often sets the snare wires on a snare drum vibrating. And other instruments can trigger vibrations in guitars.

Set Up Your PC in the Recording Room

Next, set up your PC in the recording room so that you can connect your sound sources to it. Normally, you'll have two main considerations when setting up the PC:

- Position the PC where it is as easy to use as possible.

- Avoid recording any noise that the PC itself makes.

Make the PC Easy to Use When Recording

Set up your PC in the room so that you'll be able to access it easily while you're recording. For example, if you're wearing a guitar or bass, you will probably find it easier to use the PC while standing than while sitting, so putting the monitor, keyboard, and mouse on a higher surface than usual may be helpful. On the other hand, if you'll be hammering away at musical keyboards most of the time, having the computer keyboard somewhere you can reach from a seated position will usually be preferable.

Avoid Recording Noise from Your PC

To make sure that their recordings contain no noise from the computers used for recordings, professional sound studios use computers that are almost totally silenced. You too can have a totally silent PC, but they tend to be expensive.

note *See Project 22 for instructions on reducing the amount of noise your PC makes—and to learn sources for buying totally silent PCs.*

More likely, though, you'll want to get started with your existing PC. If the PC is noisy enough to create problems with the recording, try these workarounds:

- Place the PC's CPU in a corner of the room as far as possible from your microphones and pickups. Screen the CPU off with furniture, cushions, or other sonic baffles. If you're tempted to cover it with blankets, make sure it doesn't overheat.

> **note**   *If your PC is a noisy laptop, treat the whole of the laptop as the CPU, positioning it away from your microphones and pickups. Attach an external monitor, keyboard, and mouse to the laptop.*

- Position the monitor, keyboard, and mouse where you need to control the recording, and connect them to the CPU via extension cables.

- If you can run cables under a door, through a vent, or through a serving hatch, you may even be able to position the CPU in a different room from the monitor, keyboard, and mouse.

- If you're using an external audio interface, as recommended in this project, position it with the monitor, keyboard, and mouse. Again, you'll probably need an extension cable.

Step 2: Get the Audio Hardware You Need

Since around the turn of the millennium, it has been hard to buy a PC that doesn't have multimedia capabilities, so there's every chance that your PC includes at least basic sound hardware. But if you're planning on serious amounts of recording, you may want to beef up your PC's audio capabilities.

Choose an Audio Interface

For most people starting out with recording audio, the easiest choice usually is an *external audio interface*, which is basically a sound box into which you can connect your instruments. The sound box sits outside your PC and transfers the sound to the PC via USB or FireWire. Figure 14-1 shows the MobilePre USB audio interface from M-Audio (www.m-audio.com), which this project uses as its example.

Figure 14-1

An external audio interface such as the MobilePre USB makes it easy to get a high-quality audio signal into your PC.

Having a single cable going to your PC tends to be much easier than simply plugging instruments or microphones into the sound card—especially on a laptop PC, which normally has only a single audio input. However, if you do want to be able to plug multiple instruments and microphones directly into a desktop PC, and you're prepared to install a PCI sound card, you can use an audio interface such as the Delta 1010LT (see Figure 14-2), also available from M-Audio.

Figure 14-2

An internal audio interface such as the Delta 1010LT lets you plug a wide array of instruments directly into a desktop PC.

Connect Your Audio Interface to Your PC

If you're using an external audio interface, you need to connect it to your PC and install any drivers that Windows needs in order to recognize and use the interface. This section shows you the general steps you need to follow. The example uses an M-Audio MobilePre USB interface; the precise steps needed to connect any other audio interface will almost certainly be somewhat different.

To connect your audio interface, follow these general steps:

1. Install the driver software for the interface:

   - Even if the interface included a disc containing drivers, it's a good idea to visit the manufacturer's web site to see if an updated version is available.

   - Even though an interface may appear to be a single object to the human eye (for example, a box with knobs, switches, and connectors), to Windows it may appear as several different components. For example, the M-Audio MobilePre USB appears as both a USB controller (as shown on the left here) and a sound, video, or game controller (as shown on the right).

2. When the software installation is complete, or when the installation routine prompts you to do so, plug in the audio interface.

3. When Windows tells you that your device or devices are ready to use, click the Close button. If Windows prompts you to restart your PC, do so.

Step 3: Connect or Mike Your Instruments

The next step is to connect your instruments to the audio interface. How you will do this depends on what types of instruments you have and what types of audio interface, but here are brief examples.

Vocals

Use a good-quality dynamic microphone designed to pick up a full range of vocals, *not* that extra webcam mike that has been sitting unused for three years because you bought a Bluetooth headset. Normally, you'll plug the microphone directly into the audio interface unless you need to run it through any effects boxes first—for example, to multitrack your voice.

> **tip** *Use a pop shield to protect the microphone from any excesses in your voice stream. If you don't have a pop shield, you can create a workable substitute quickly by stretching an old pair of nylons over a coat hanger.*

If you'll be playing an instrument while singing, you'll need a microphone stand. If you can devote your full energy to singing, holding the microphone will give you more freedom.

Acoustic Guitar

To record an acoustic guitar, use a dynamic microphone positioned about a hand's breadth away from the sound hole in the guitar. Normally, you'll want to use a microphone stand to hold the microphone in place, but if you're short of a stand, you may be able to tape the microphone to the back of a chair. (If so, tape it securely, and make sure the chair is stable enough to avoid vibration.)

Electric Guitar or Bass

When recording electric guitar, you have two main options:

● Run the guitar through your effects pedals or processors (reverb, wah-wah, or whatever), and then run a cord from the last pedal or processor to your audio interface so that you can record the processed sound. This approach lets you create your preferred sound in your regular way, and then simply record it.

- Connect the guitar directly to the audio interface and record it "clean," and then apply audio effects in Audacity as needed (Audacity is introduced in Step 4). This approach gives you more flexibility in Audacity, but you will need to learn a different way of creating your preferred sound.

If you're in a hurry to get results, go with the first option. Given more time, you will probably want to experiment with both approaches and find out which suits you the best.

note *When recording electric bass, proceed as for electric guitar.*

Drums

Most drummers swear by acoustic drums and swear at electronic drums, but electronic drums are far easier to record than acoustic drums, as you can run the signal directly into your audio interface. This section assumes you've got acoustic drums.

In the olden days, big-band recording engineers would devote a single microphone to the drums, positioning it with great care but often not a great deal of success. As you'll know, if you've listened to such recordings, unless the engineer was very good (or got lucky), some of the drums would be dominant and others barely audible. These days, many professional recording studios mike each drum or percussion item (for example, a hi-hat or a cymbal) separately. Some of the key drums or percussion items may even enjoy two or more microphones to give the engineer more flexibility in processing the sound.

In a pinch, you can create acceptable drum tracks by positioning one microphone on either side of the drum kit. You'll need to experiment to find the best placement, and you may need to vary your normal drumming style—for example, by striking some drums less hard than usual so that they don't swamp the other drums. If you're looking for optimum results, grit your teeth, buy the microphones and microphone stands, and then position them as follows:

- **Bass drum** Take off the front skin (the one away from the drum pedal and beater), and place a folded blanket against the back skin (the one the drum beater strikes) to dampen the sound. Position a dynamic microphone inside the bass drum. If you need to deepen the bass drum's sound, place a thick blanket over the drum (but not over the back skin).

- **Snare drum** Position a dynamic microphone a few inches away from the drum head on the side opposite the drummer. If the snare rings too loud, use damping gels (widely available in music stores) or cloth and tape to damp the sound.

note *When positioning microphones on drums, your challenge is to get them close enough to the drum head to pick up the sound clearly without the sound of other percussion but far enough away from the drummer's flailing sticks. A well-struck microphone makes a fine, dramatic sound on a recording—but usually only once.*

- **Toms** For each tom, position a dynamic microphone a few inches away from the drum head on the side opposite the drummer.

- **Hi-hat** Position a condenser microphone a few inches away from the top plate of the hi-hat at the upper extent of its travel.

- **Cymbals** Position a condenser microphone six inches to a foot from each of the most important cymbals (for example, your primary ride cymbal). Cymbals that you use less—for example, ancillary crash or splash cymbals—may be able to share a microphone effectively.

If you're short of microphones, cut down your drum kit to a minimum. For example, by ditching the second tom, the floor tom, and a couple of crash or splash cymbals, you can save yourself a handful of microphones.

Step 4: Download and Install Audacity

Many different recording programs are available, but if you're feeling the knock-on effects of the subprime pinch, the best place to start is with a free program. Luckily, there's a great one, Audacity, which runs not only on Windows but also on Linux and the Mac. Go to the Audacity page on the SourceForge.net web site (http://sourceforge .net/projects/audacity/) and download Audacity by following the link that leads to the latest stable version for Windows. (There's also an unstable version that's suitable only for the adventurous.) You want the version described as ".exe (32-bit Windows)," not the zip file.

Internet Explorer may try to block you from downloading Audacity. If nothing happens when you click the download link, click the Information Bar (the yellow bar that appears between the lowest toolbar and the top of the window) to display a menu that allows you to circumvent the blocking.

To install Audacity, follow these steps:

1. Run the file you've downloaded. For example, if you're using Internet Explorer, click the Run button in the Download Complete dialog box.

2. If Internet Explorer displays a Security Warning dialog box to let you know that "The publisher could not be verified," click the Run button. As long as you've downloaded Audacity via SourceForge, the file should be fine, even though it has not been signed with a digital certificate. You also need to go through User Account Control for the audacity-win program (unless you have turned off User Account Control).

3. Accept the license agreement.

4. Specify where to install Audacity. The default location, in an Audacity folder inside your Program Files folder, is fine unless you particularly want to put it somewhere else.

5. On the Select Additional Tasks screen, choose whether to create a Desktop icon (you may find it useful) and create Windows file associations with the Audacity project file extension (.aup; usually a good idea).

6. On the Completing The Audacity Setup Wizard screen, leave the Launch Audacity check box selected so that the wizard launches Audacity for you.

The first time you run Audacity, choose the language you want to use. You then see an Audacity window. Project 15 shows you how to use the Audacity interface, so for now, your next step is to configure Audacity for sound recording.

Step 5: Configure Audacity for Sound Recording

Part of Audacity's power comes from the wide variety of configurable settings it offers. By choosing suitable settings, you can greatly increase your chances of making a high-quality recording that others will listen to with pleasure rather than with horror or embarrassment. To access the settings, choose Edit | Preferences. Audacity opens the Audacity Preferences dialog box.

Configure Input/Output Settings

With the Audacity Preferences dialog box open, start by configuring the audio input/output settings:

1. Click the Audio I/O tab to display its contents (see Figure 14-3).

Figure 14-3

Choose your playback and recording devices, and the number of channels, on the Audio I/O tab.

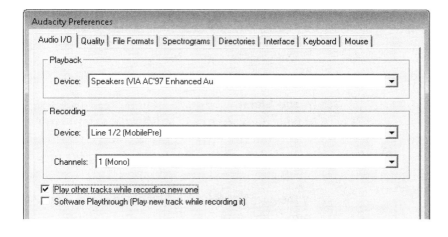

2. In the Playback drop-down list, select the audio device you want to use for playing back audio. For example, you may want to output audio through your audio interface so that you can play it through an amplifier rather than merely listen to it on speakers.

3. In the Device drop-down list in the Recording group box, select the item for your audio interface.

4. In the Channels drop-down list, select 1 (Mono) if you're getting mono input or 2 (Stereo) for stereo input. Audacity supports up to 16 channels if your input device can supply them.

5. If you want to play back the existing tracks in the audio project while recording a new track, select the Play Other Tracks While Recording New One check box. This setting lets you play along with what you've recorded so far.

6. If you want Audacity to play back each new track as you record it, select the Software Playthrough check box.

Leave the Audacity Preferences dialog box open for the moment so that you can choose recording quality settings.

Choose Recording Quality Settings

To choose recording quality settings, follow these steps:

1. Click the Quality tab to display its contents (see Figure 14-4).

Figure 14-4

Choose the default sample rate and default sample format on the Quality tab.

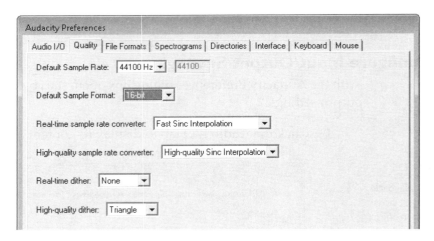

2. In the Default Sample Rate drop-down list, select 44100 Hz unless you know you want to use a different sample rate. 44100 Hz (often described as 44.1 kilohertz, or kHz) is the sample rate used for CDs, and provides very high audio quality. Audacity does offer much higher sample rates—up to 96000 Hz—if you need them.

3. In the Default Sample Format drop-down list, choose 32-bit Float if your sound card supports 32-bit sound. This gives you the best audio quality—but if your sound card maxes out at 16-bit sound, there's no point in using 32-bit sound, so choose 16-bit instead, and you will reduce the file sizes by half. If your sound card supports 24-bit sound, choose 24-bit, which is the stage in

between 16-bit and 32-bit sound. (Check your sound card's documentation if you're not sure of its capabilities.)

4. In the Real-Time Sample Rate Converter drop-down list, choose Fast Sinc Interpolation.

5. In the High-Quality Sample Rate Converter drop-down list, choose High-Quality Sinc Interpolation.

6. In the Real-Time Dither drop-down list, choose None.

7. In the High-Quality Dither drop-down list, choose Triangle.

Again, leave the Audacity Preferences dialog box open so that you can continue choosing settings.

Choose File Formats Settings

To choose file formats settings, follow these steps:

1. Click the File Formats tab to display its contents (see Figure 14-5).

Figure 14-5

The most important setting on the File Formats tab is the Uncompressed Export Format drop-down list. You can also use the controls on this tab to add an MP3 encoder to Audacity.

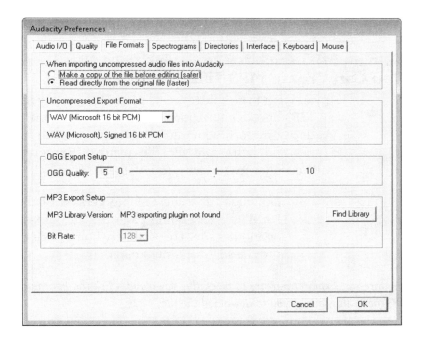

2. In the When Importing Uncompressed Audio Files Into Audacity group box, select the Make A Copy Of The File Before Editing option button if you want to avoid even the possibility of damage to your existing uncompressed audio files (for example, WAV files) when importing them into Audacity for your projects. Select the Read Directly From The Original File option button if you're prepared to tolerate the faint possibility of damage occurring while Audacity reads the files.

3. In the Uncompressed Export Format drop-down list, choose the format in which you want to export uncompressed audio:

    ● This is the format in which you will export your project files unless you compress them using the OGG encoder or an MP3 encoder that you add (as described in the sidebar, "Add an MP3 Encoder to Audacity so that You Can Create MP3 Files").

    ● Normally, the best choice here is WAV (Microsoft 16 Bit PCM) if you're working with a 16-bit sample size, or WAV (Microsoft 32 Bit Float) if you're working with a 32-bit sample size.

4. If you will export audio files to the Ogg Vorbis file format, choose a quality on the OGG Quality slider.

 Ogg Vorbis is a free, open-source encoder for compressed audio. Ogg Vorbis competes with the MP3 encoder (which is proprietary), but at this writing, MP3 is much more widely used.

5. If you will export audio files to the MP3 file format, add an MP3 encoder to Audacity, and then choose settings. See the following sidebar, "Add an MP3 Encoder to Audacity so that You Can Create MP3 Files," for details.

Add an MP3 Encoder to Audacity so that You Can Create MP3 Files

If you want to be able to create MP3 files directly from Audacity, you must add an MP3 encoder to Audacity. Alternatively, you can export WAV files from Audacity, import them into a media player such as Windows Media Player or iTunes, and then create MP3 files using that program's MP3 encoder. To add an MP3 encoder to Audacity, follow these steps:

1. Download the latest stable version of the LAME encoder from the LAME Project home page (http://lame.sourceforge.net/index.php) or another site. The Audacity home page maintains a link to a site that provides LAME downloads.

 Internet Explorer may try to block this download. Click the Information Bar to display a menu that allows you to download the file.

2. Extract the lame_enc.dll file from the download package and put it in the System32 folder in your Windows folder:

    ● The easiest way to open a Windows Explorer window to this folder is to choose Start | Run, type **%windir%\system32**, and then press ENTER.

    ● Windows may try to hide the contents of the System32 folder from you. If so, click the Show The Contents Of This Folder link.

3. Display the Audacity Preferences dialog box by pressing CTRL-P or choosing Edit | Preferences.

4. Click the File Formats tab to display its contents.

5. Check the MP3 Export Setup area. If the MP3 Library Version readout says "MP3 exporting plugin not found," you need to add an MP3 encoder.

6. Click the Find Library button. Audacity displays the Export MP3 dialog box, which explains that you need to supply the LAME MP3 encoder and asks if you want to provide it.

7. Click the Yes button and use the resulting dialog box to find lame_enc.dll in the folder to which you extracted it in step 2.

8. Click the Open button. Audacity adds the LAME version to the MP3 Library Version readout.

9. In the Bit Rate drop-down list, select the bitrate at which you want to export MP3 files. For example, choose 128 Kbps if you want acceptable-quality audio at small file sizes (for instance, so that you can cram more songs onto a low-capacity iPod) or choose 320 Kbps for maximum quality at the expense of file size.

10. Click the OK button to close the Audacity Preferences dialog box.

---

note *The Spectrograms tab of the Audacity Preferences dialog box lets you change the way in which Audacity displays spectrograms of audio tracks. (To display a spectrogram, click the track's drop-down menu and choose Spectrum.) You probably won't need to change the default Fast Fourier Transform (FFT) setting from 256 until you're experienced with Audacity, but you may want to select the Grayscale check box to view the spectrograms in grayscale rather than in color. You can also change the maximum frequency on this tab, but try using the default setting at first.*

Choose Interface Settings

Audacity is highly customizable, and the Interface tab and Keyboard tab of the Audacity Preferences dialog box let you configure how Audacity's interface appears and how you can use the keyboard to control the program. The Mouse tab is informational only. When you're getting started with Audacity, the settings you're most likely to want to change are those on the Interface tab (see Figure 14-6).

Here are the key settings, with suggested choices:

● **Autoscroll While Playing** Controls whether Audacity automatically scrolls the display of the tracks while recording or playing back. Turn this setting on unless you find that you get breaks in the audio because your PC is struggling to keep up. (This should be a problem only on an underpowered PC.)

Figure 14-6

The Interface tab lets you control which toolbars are available and the minimum decibel display range that Audacity uses.

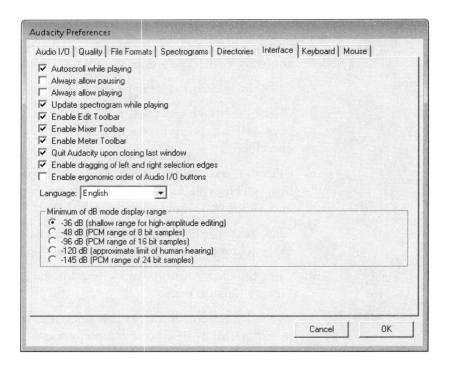

- **Always Allow Pausing**   Controls whether Audacity enables the Pause button even when you're not playing or recording. Selecting this check box lets you click the Pause button to put Audacity on Pause, and then click the Record button to get Audacity ready to record; you can then click the Pause button to set the recording going. This action may seem familiar if you've recorded on cassette recorders. On cassette recorders, starting recording this way made sense because applying the recording heads made a noise. In Audacity, most people find it easier simply to click the Record button when they're ready to start recording.

- **Always Allow Playing**   Controls whether Audacity enables the Play button even when you don't need it for controlling playback. Normally, it is best to leave this check box cleared.

- **Update Spectrogram While Playing**   Controls whether Audacity updates the display of the spectrogram while playing audio. As long as your PC can manage the updating without the audio breaking up, you'll probably find this setting helpful.

- **Enable Edit Toolbar**   Controls whether Audacity lets you use the Edit toolbar. Normally, you'll want to keep this check box selected.

- **Enable Mixer Toolbar**   Controls whether Audacity lets you use the Mixer toolbar. This toolbar also is usually helpful to have, so keep this check box selected.

- **Enable Meter Toolbar**   Controls whether Audacity lets you use the Meter toolbar. Most people find this toolbar vital to making good recordings, so keep this check box selected too.

- **Enable Dragging Of Left And Right Selection Edges**   Controls whether Audacity lets you drag the left and right edges of a selection to change the length of the selection. If you clear this check box, clicking the left or right edge of a selection will create a new selection.

- **Minimum Of dB Mode Display Range**   Controls the scale that Audacity uses for displaying logarithmic waveforms. Briefly, you have a range of choices. At a low setting (such as –36 decibels), quiet sounds appear to be silent, but you get a clear view of the sounds at the louder end of the scale. At a high setting (such as –145 decibels), you get a clear view of the quieter sounds, but the sounds at the louder end of the scale have less differentiation. Try starting with –48 decibels, but change the setting depending on whether you're working with primarily loud sounds (choose a low setting) or primarily quieter sounds (choose a high setting).

Choose a Temporary Folder

Audacity automatically sets itself up to use a temporary folder for recording data that you haven't yet explicitly assigned to a specific file. This folder has a name such as audacity_1_2_temp and is located within the Temp folder in your user profile. For example, if your username is Dave, you'll find the Audacity temp folder somewhere like this on Windows Vista: C:\Users\Dave\AppData\Local\Temp\audacity_1_2_temp. You can change where the temporary folder is located by clicking the Directories tab in the Audacity Preferences dialog box and using the controls in the Temp. Directory group box:

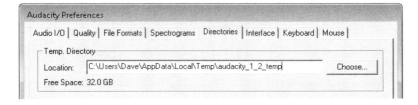

You can place the temporary folder anywhere in your PC's file system, but for best performance, follow these simple guidelines:

- **Use a local hard drive**   To ensure that the temporary folder is always present, use a local hard drive rather than an external hard drive or a removable drive. A local hard drive will normally also give better performance.

tip   *The Keyboard tab of the Audacity Preferences dialog box lets you set up custom keyboard shortcuts for Audacity so that you can work faster.*

- **If you have two hard drives, avoid the system drive**   In a desktop system (or one of the rare laptops) that has two or more physical hard drives, put your temporary folder and your project folders on a drive other than the system drive. The system drive is the drive on which Windows is installed. Windows puts the paging file (which Windows uses for extra memory space) on the system drive, keeping the system drive busy. If your PC has only one hard drive, don't worry about this.

- **Make sure there's plenty of space**   The Free Space readout at the bottom of the Temp. Directory shows you how much space is available on the disk on which the temporary folder is currently located. To ensure worry-free recording, allow yourself at least 5–10GB of free space on the disk.

> **note**   *Recording 32-bit audio at 44.1 kHz and in stereo takes up about 20MB of space per minute. Each gigabyte buys you around 50 minutes of jamming. If you find yourself running short of disk space, you may want to archive your old recordings to recordable CDs or DVDs—or simply delete them.*

When you've finished choosing settings, click the OK button to close the Audacity Preferences dialog box.

At this point, your home recording studio is set up, and all systems are ready to go. It's time to start recording.

Record Music on Your PC

What You'll Need

- **Hardware: Recording gear (as discussed in Project 14)**
- **Software: Audacity**
- **Cost: Free**

In the previous project, you learned to set your PC up for recording audio, such as that from your band or your solo performances, by setting up a room to act as a studio, adding an audio interface to your PC, and installing and configuring the freeware program Audacity. This project shows you how to perform the recording itself. You'll start by meeting the Audacity user interface, which the previous project skipped over.

Step 1: Meet the Audacity User Interface

If you've continued straight from Project 14, you probably have an Audacity window open on your screen. If not, choose Start | All Programs | Audacity to open an Audacity window so that you can meet the main components. When you launch Audacity, the program displays an empty project window, as shown in Figure 15-1.

Audacity's four toolbars provide controls for the actions you'll take most frequently:

- **Control toolbar** Contains selection tools and playback and recording controls.

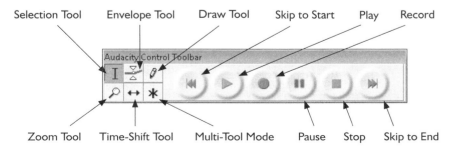

Figure 15-1

Audacity opens a blank project and displays its toolbars docked at the top of the window.

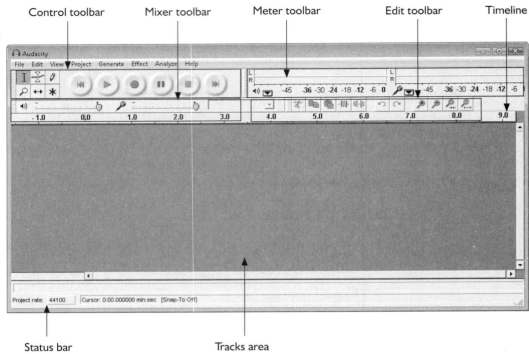

- **Edit toolbar**   Contains tools for performing common editing actions (such as cut, copy, and paste), trimming and silencing, undo and redo, and zooming.

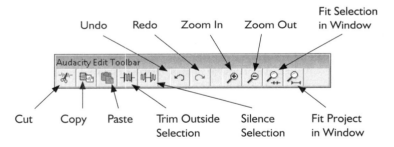

- **Mixer toolbar**   Contains an input volume slider, an output volume slider, and a source-selection drop-down list.

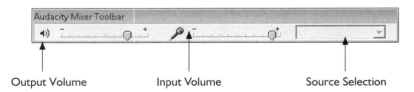

● **Meter toolbar**   Contains an input level meter and an output level meter. Also provides access to related commands.

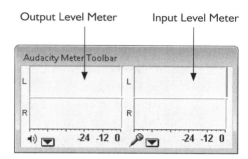

Apart from the four toolbars, you see four other main elements in the Audacity window shown in Figure 15-1:

● **Menu bar**   Like most programs, Audacity provides a set of menus that divide commands into manageable categories. For example, the File menu includes commands that let you create, save, open, and close project files.

● **Timeline**   Below the toolbars, at the top of the main area of the window, is the timeline, which shows a readout in seconds.

● **Tracks area**   In the middle of the window, this large open area is where you create and manipulate tracks, as you'll learn to do shortly.

● **Status bar**   At the bottom of the window, the status bar shows information such as the sample rate of the active project and details about the current selection (when there is one).

tip   *Having the four toolbars together at the top of the Audacity window can be handy for keeping your most-used controls in one place, but it squashes the toolbars together, particularly in a small window (for example, on a small screen). However, you can float any of the toolbars, either by dragging the dotted handle at its left end or by opening the View menu and choosing its corresponding Float command. Once you've floated a toolbar, the View menu displays a Dock command that you can use to dock the toolbar again—for example, Dock Control Toolbar. You'll see an example of floating a toolbar shortly.*

Step 2: Create a Recording Project

Normally, your first step in making a recording should be to create a new recording project for it.

To create a recording project, follow these steps:

1. Start Audacity if it's not currently running. For example, choose Start | All Programs | Audacity. Audacity automatically creates a new, blank project file when you open it.

Understand How Audacity's Project Files Work

A *recording project* is the set of files in which Audacity saves the audio files and configuration files that make up an audio project. For example, to create a project, you typically either import existing audio files, record new audio files from scratch, or both. You then decide which files are worth using, and tell Audacity how to mix them.

An Audacity project file uses the .aup file extension, which is associated with Audacity. Most other audio programs can't open Audacity project files, so when you want to use another program to listen to or work with audio you've recorded or created with Audacity, you export the appropriate mix of a project to a common file format (such as WAV or MP3).

---

note   *If you've got another project file open, choose File | New or press CTRL-N to open a new project file.*

2. Choose File | Save Project As. Until you tell Audacity not to warn you anymore, Audacity displays a Warning dialog box. Read the warning (which briefly explains Audacity's file formats), select the Don't Show This Warning Again check box, and then click the OK button to close the dialog box.

3. Audacity displays the Save Project As dialog box, which is a standard Save dialog box. Choose the folder in which to save the project. As mentioned in Project 14, you should allow plenty of disk space for your Audacity recordings. Type the name for the project file, and then click the Save button.

Start Recording Without Saving a Project...When You Must

If you don't explicitly save a project, you can simply click the Record button to start recording audio to Audacity's temporary folder. (See the section "Choose a Temporary Folder" in Project 14 for an explanation of what the temporary folder is and where it's located.) Such ad hoc recording usually works fine, which is handy for those times when a jam that's going nowhere shows signs of turning into a scorcher, or when you're noodling out the chords to a song and suddenly find yourself inspired to sing something you might want to keep. Other times, start by creating and saving a project first to keep your files in order.

Step 3: Set the Recording Level

Before you record any music, make sure you've got the recording level set at the right level to capture even the loudest sounds you will generate, as loud as possible, without distorting those sounds. To set the recording level, follow these steps:

1. In Audacity, choose View | Float Meter Toolbar to display the Meter toolbar as a separate floating window rather than docked at the top of the Audacity window.

2. If the Audacity Meter Toolbar window isn't a suitable size or shape, resize or reshape it by dragging its lower-right corner down and to the right. Once you drag to a certain size, Audacity automatically changes the configuration of the meters:

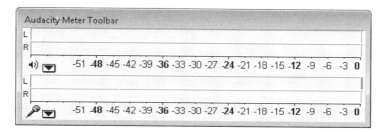

3. Start an input source and crank it up to full volume. For example, tell your guitarist to start playing—and to turn his amp up to 11.

4. Click the drop-down button next to the microphone icon and choose Monitor Input.

5. The Audacity Meter Toolbar window displays the strength of the input signal, as shown here. Adjust the signal's strength so that the loudest sound you will record registers close to, but below, 0 at the right end of the scale. For example, turn down the volume on the audio interface.

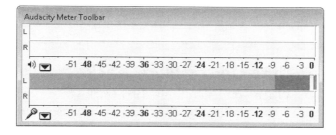

6. For precise work, you may find it easier to have the Audacity Meter Toolbar window displayed vertically. To switch dimension, click the drop-down button next to the microphone icon and choose Vertical Stereo. Again, drag the window to the shape and size you want.

If you have plenty of screen space, you may prefer to keep the Audacity Meter Toolbar window floating. If you're pushed for screen space, you can dock the toolbar again once you've set the recording level. To dock the toolbar, choose View | Dock Meter Toolbar.

 If you have time, test the recording level further by making a test recording that you can play back to make sure there's no distortion. Most people find it hard to predict in advance exactly how loud they will play—especially when there is competition from other band members.

Step 4: Record the First Track

caution *Be sure not to record anybody else's copyrighted work without permission.*

At this point, you should be all set to add the first track to your recording project. Follow these general steps:

1. Get the input ready. For example, wake your drummer, feed him a cup of coffee, and point him toward the drum kit.

2. In Audacity, click the Record button. Audacity adds a new track to the project and starts recording input.

3. Start the input. For example, gesture vigorously and explicitly at your drummer until he starts playing.

4. When you're ready to stop recording, click the Stop button.

5. Play back the track by clicking the Play button. Decide whether it's worth keeping. If not, click the Close button (the × button) at the upper-left corner of the track to delete the track, and then go back to step 1 of this list.

6. Rename the track with a descriptive name. Click the drop-down menu button and choose Name to display the Track Name dialog box. Type the new name in the Change Track Name To text box, and then click the OK button.

7. Press CTRL-S or choose File | Save Project to save the project file (and its components).

Solo or Mute One or More Tracks

When you listen to the first track you've recorded, you'll hear only that track when you hit the Play button, because there isn't any other. But once you've recorded two or more tracks, Audacity plays them all together unless you tell it to do otherwise.

To listen to a track on its own, without hearing any other tracks you've recorded, click the Solo button for the track, and then click the Play button. You can solo multiple tracks at once, so you can use this feature to listen to different mixes of tracks. Click the Solo button again to remove soloing from a track.

Alternatively, you can mute any track by clicking its Mute button. Click the Mute button again to remove muting.

Step 5: Apply Effects to a Track

As mentioned in the previous project, you can either record effects into an audio stream that you then record in Audacity, or record a clean audio stream and then apply effects in Audacity. You can also combine both approaches and apply effects in Audacity to a stream that already includes effects.

The advantage of applying effects in Audacity is that you can remove them. By contrast, any effects that you've recorded into an audio stream normally remain there. You may be able to use Audacity's effects to reduce or remove effects you've deliberately recorded in an audio stream, but you'd be unwise to rely on doing so.

Audacity offers a good range of effects, from echo and compression to pitch-changing and wah-wah. You'll find all the effects on the Effects menu. To apply an effect, follow these general steps:

1. Click the track you want to affect.

2. Open the Effects menu and choose the effect you want to apply. For example, choose Effect | Compressor if you want to apply dynamic compression to a track.

note *Dynamic compression is useful for punching up a track by reducing its overall dynamic range: Quiet sounds become somewhat louder, and the range of difference between the quieter sounds and the louder sounds is reduced.*

3. If Audacity displays a dialog box, such as the Dynamic Range Compressor dialog box shown here, choose settings to achieve the sound you want. Most of these dialog boxes include a Preview button that lets you audition an effect before you actually apply it. When you've produced the sound you want, click the OK button to apply the effect to the track.

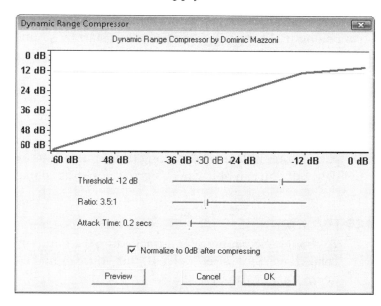

Step 6: Add Further Tracks to Your Recording

To add the next track to your recording, you can follow much the same steps as for recording the first track: Cue the sound source, click the Record button to add a new track and start recording in it, and then set the sound source going. Stop the recording, listen to the resulting track, and apply any effects that are needed.

If you want to hear the existing tracks while you are playing the next track, choose Edit | Preferences, make sure the Play Other Tracks While Recording New One check box on the Audio I/O tab of the Audacity Preferences dialog box is selected, and then click the OK button.

Step 7: Set the Gain and Panning for Each Track

When you've recorded all the tracks for your project, you'll be ready to set the relative volume of each track (by adjusting the gain) and its left-right positioning (by adjusting the panning).

note *You may choose to set gain and panning earlier in the process of adding tracks. For example, after recording the first track for a project, you may decide that it belongs on the left of the mix and deserves a moderate volume; and you may then pan the next track to the right. However, you will probably need to tweak the gain and panning of the tracks further as you add subsequent tracks to your project, because adding tracks normally makes the dynamics of the overall sound change.*

Different people find that different balancing techniques work best for them, but in general, it's usually best to start with the underpinning tracks—those that form the basis of the music you are producing. For example, if you're recording rock music, you will probably use the drum tracks and the bass tracks as the underpinning for the other tracks. Once you've set up these tracks, you can decide where the other tracks belong in the mix. By contrast, if you start by setting up an intricate arrangement of guitar tracks, you may have trouble working in the drum and bass tracks because of their relative lack of subtlety.

Change the Gain for a Track

To change the gain for a track, (controlling the volume at which the track is played back), drag the Gain slider along its minus-to-plus axis. Each movement is three decibels, but you can hold down SHIFT as you drag to make one-decibel adjustments.

Change the Panning for a Track

To change the panning for a track, drag the Panning slider along the Left–Right axis. Each movement is ten percent, but you can make smaller adjustments by holding down SHIFT as you drag.

Step 8: Align Tracks with the Time-Shift Tool

When your PC is both recording audio and playing back audio at the same time, as when you use the Play Other Tracks While Recording New One feature to play back your existing tracks, the audio can easily get out of sync. This usually happens because your PC introduces *latency*—a delay, in lay terms—into the recording process. You'll notice this problem immediately when you play it back; depending on the track type, you may also be able to see the problem on the track display, as in the example shown in Figure 15-2. Here, you can see that the main beats in the Drums 1 track and the Tambourine track are severely out of time.

Figure 15-2

When your tracks are out of sync, like the tracks shown here, you can use the Time-Shift Tool to align them.

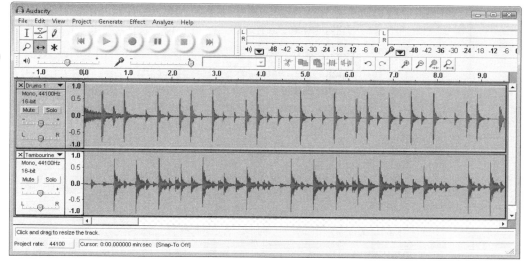

To fix the synchronization problem, use the Time-Shift Tool. Follow these steps:

1. Choose View | Zoom In one or more times to zoom the view in so that you can see the tracks more spaced out:

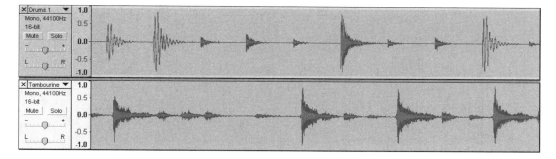

2. Click the Time-Shift Tool button on the Control toolbar.

3. Click the track you want to shift, and then drag it left or right to align its waveforms with those in the other track.

4. Play back the tracks, and verify that the alignment is accurate.

5. Choose View | Zoom Normal to restore normality to the view.

Step 9: Turn Two Tracks into a Stereo Track

When you're recording on a shoestring, you will often need to record a single track at a time, and in mono. You can then use Audacity to turn two mono tracks into one stereo track, giving your project a more interesting sound:

1. Make sure the tracks are aligned. If not, align them as described in Step 8.

2. Position the two tracks together in the Audacity window, so that one of the tracks is directly above the other track, as shown in the following example. If the tracks are currently separated, click one of them, open the track's drop-down menu, and then use the Move Track Up command or the Move Track Down command to move the track so that it is next to the other track.

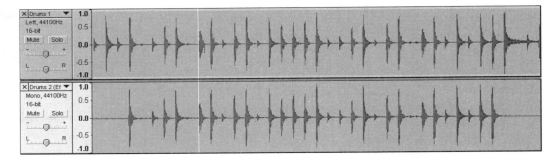

3. Open the drop-down menu for the upper of the two tracks and choose Make Stereo Track. Audacity turns the two tracks into a single track, as shown here:

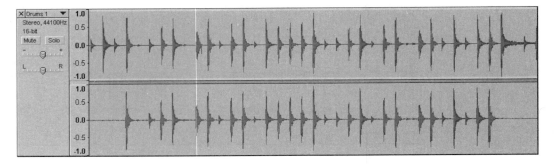

4. Play back the stereo track, and verify that it sounds correct. If you need to adjust it (for example, to align the tracks better), choose Edit | Undo Make Stereo to separate the two tracks again.

Step 10: Export Your Project to an Audio File

When you've finished mixing your project in Audacity, listen to it several times to make sure you're satisfied with the sound. Adjust the mix or effects as necessary.

note *If you have bandmates, make them listen to it too, and get their approval. Otherwise, marshal some friends or family, but be prepared to take their views with several pinches of salt, because they probably don't have a firm grasp on your artistic vision.*

To export your project, take the following steps. These assume that you are exporting your project to a WAV file, but the process for creating an MP3 file is similar.

1. If your project contains unsaved changes, press CTRL-S or choose File | Save Project.

2. Choose File | Export As WAV. Audacity displays the Save WAV (Microsoft) File As dialog box.

3. Click the Browse Folders button to display the remainder of the dialog box if you need to be able to access other folders.

4. Select the folder in which you want to save the file.

5. In the File Name text box, type the name you want to assign to the exported file.

6. If necessary, in the Save As Type drop-down list, choose the format in which you want to save the exported file. This should seldom be necessary, because the Save As Type drop-down list displays the format corresponding to your choice in step 2. For example, if you choose Save As WAV, the Save As Type drop-down list automatically displays WAV (Microsoft) Files.

7. Click the Save button or press ENTER. Audacity saves the audio file in the format you chose.

If you've exported the audio file in an uncompressed format (such as WAV), you will probably want to create a compressed version that you can distribute comfortably across the Internet. For example, import the audio file into Windows Media Player or iTunes, and then use that program's features to create an MP3 file or an AAC file containing a compressed version of the file.

Step 11: Tag Your Song File

After creating a compressed audio file, be sure to tag the file with suitable information so that those who receive the file are in a position to appreciate it fully. The basic components of a tag are the artist's name, the CD or album name, the song name, and the song number, but it's good to add any further data you have available. For example, if you have artwork for the song, include it in the audio file. Likewise, also include any lyrics the song has, no matter how clearly you suppose them to be audible—some listeners will find them helpful.

To tag a file, you can use a media-player program such as Windows Media Player or iTunes; many other audio-editing programs also provide tagging capabilities. Figure 15-3 shows the Song Information dialog box from iTunes, whose title bar displays the song's title (rather than the words "Song Information").

Figure 15-3

Use a tagging tool such as the Song Information dialog box in iTunes to make sure that your song is tagged with a full complement of information.

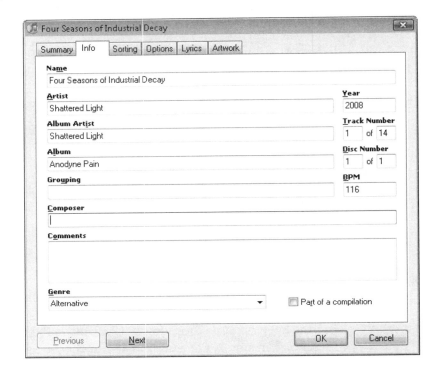

Step 12: Distribute Your Song

When you've finished tagging your song, it's time to unleash it on the waiting world. Once upon a time, you needed to enlist the services of a record company to get your song distributed, but now the Internet offers you a wide variety of ways to distribute the song yourself. Here are four ways to consider:

● **Post your song on music sites**   Sites such as Amie Street (www.amiestreet .com) let artists post their own songs—and earn money when other people buy them. On this particular site, song prices rise as the songs become more popular (or at least as they are downloaded more), so thrifty listeners can get a song for free or for only a few cents. While the price of your song is low, enlist a few friends to help you drive the price up to a level at which it starts receiving attention.

● **Create a video for YouTube**   Creating a full-scale video may be beyond your budget, but there's nothing to stop you from getting creative with whatever you have. For example, you can use photos and animations in a PowerPoint presentation to create a visually attractive or arresting accompaniment to your song. Windows Movie Maker (or iMovie, if you have access to a Mac) also lets you create effective movies out of still photos or video clips.

● **Send your song to local radio stations or podcast stations** Both local radio stations and podcast stations have an insatiable hunger for content, especially if you can supply it to them with an angle, such as your being a local citizen or a long-standing listener.

● **Post your song to your web site** As soon as you have a band, you should set up a web site for it—either on your own site, or on a social networking site. Make the file available at a moderate quality (for example, 128 Kbps MP3) so that people can download it easily but enjoy the audio.

note *If the file size of your song is less than a few megabytes, you can even send it to people via e-mail—but usually, sending a message that tells people how to download a full-quality version of the song from your web site (or from another site) is a better idea.*

Once you've gotten the hang of recording, you'll probably want to work at it and become more expert with the many features that Audacity offers. This project has barely scraped the surface, but if it has whetted your appetite, then it has done its job. The next project explains how to avoid losing your precious compositions.

Back Up and Restore Your Computer

What You'll Need

- Hardware: External USB hard drive (optional)
- Software: Your existing copy of Windows Vista Business Edition or Windows Vista Ultimate Edition, or another version of Windows Vista plus a third-party program
- Cost: Free to $250 U.S.

Backups are the dental floss of computing. Everyone knows they should floss their teeth...all of them...regularly. Some do. Similarly, everyone knows that they should back up their data...all of it...regularly. Few do.

Windows Vista Business Edition and Windows Vista Ultimate Edition include a feature called Complete PC Backup and Restore. Provided you have enough space on a hard disk or other storage medium (such as recordable DVDs), you can back up all of the data on your PC. You can also choose to back up some drives but not others, which is useful when you want to use one hard drive as the backup location for another hard drive. With other versions of Windows Vista, you need to use a third-party program if you want to back up your entire PC.

Step 1: Back Up Your Entire PC on Windows Vista Business Edition or Ultimate Edition

Backing up every file on your PC requires far more space than just backing up essential files, but it has the great advantage of preventing you from missing any files that you've stored in folders other than your regular ones.

note *If you're looking for a backup solution for one or more PCs that don't have Complete PC Backup and Restore, consider Windows Home Server, which can run automatic backups on all computers connected to the server.*

Programs to Back Up and Restore Other Versions of Windows

Neither Windows Vista Home Basic Edition nor Windows Vista Home Premium Edition includes a program that lets you back up your whole PC or your entire system drive, so if you want to perform this task, you need to use third-party software.

At this writing, perhaps the best program for doing this is Norton Ghost from Symantec (www.symantec.com). Ghost lets you back up your full system to a wide variety of media, including external drives (connected via either USB or FireWire) and recordable DVDs. You can also control backups from other computers, which is useful if you have more than one PC.

Symantec also offers a more limited program called Norton Save & Restore that offers much of Ghost's backup functionality but does not provide remote management.

Another program you may want to evaluate is True Image Home from Acronis (www.acronis.com), which offers similar features to Save & Restore.

To back up your entire PC, follow these steps:

1. If you plan to use an external hard disk for the backup, make sure that it's connected to your PC and that it's working.

2. Choose Start | All Programs | Maintenance | Backup And Restore Center to open a Backup And Restore Center window (see Figure 16-1).

Figure 16-1

The Backup And Restore Center window provides quick access to the commands for backing up and restoring your entire PC.

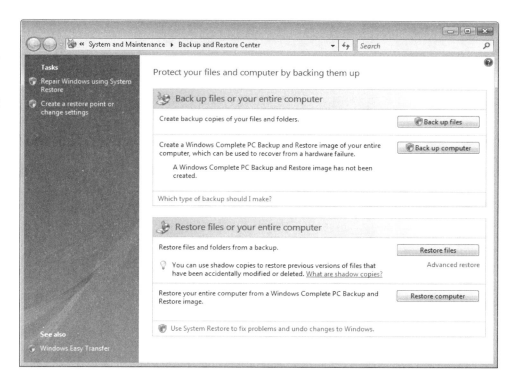

3. Click the Back Up Computer button, and then go through User Account Control for the Microsoft Windows Backup feature (unless you've turned off User Account Control). Windows launches the Windows Complete PC Backup Wizard, which displays the Where Do You Want To Save The Backup? screen.

4. Choose where to save the backup:

- **Hard disk**   If you want to save the backup on a hard disk, select the On A Hard Disk option button, and then choose the correct hard disk in the drop-down list.

- **DVDs**   If you want to save the backup on as many DVDs as it takes, select the On One Or More DVDs option button, and then make sure that the correct drive is selected in the drop-down list.

5. Click the Next button to display the Which Disks Do You Want To Include In The Backup? screen (see Figure 16-2).

Figure 16-2

Choose which disks you want to include in the backup.

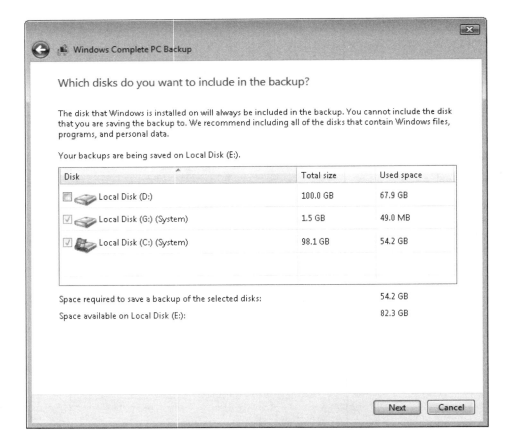

6. Select the check box for each disk you want to include. The wizard automatically selects your system disks for you and doesn't let you deselect them. The readouts show how much space is needed to back up the selected disks and how much space is available.

7. Click the Next button to display the Confirm Your Backup Settings screen (see Figure 16-3).

Figure 16-3

Verify your backup settings before you start the backup running.

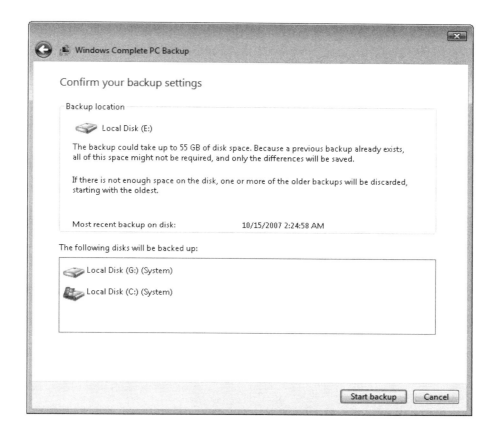

8. Make sure you've chosen the right disks to back up and the right backup location.

9. Click the Start Backup button to start the backup running. The wizard keeps you informed of its progress.

10. When the Windows Complete PC Backup window shows the message "The backup completed successfully," click the Close button to close the wizard, and then click the Close button (the × button) to close the Backup And Restore Center window.

11. If you're using a removable medium for the backup, label it and store it safely.

Step 2: Restore Your Entire PC

If things go wrong with your PC, you can restore it from the latest backup you made using Complete PC Backup and Restore. To restore your entire PC, follow these steps:

1. To start the restore process, your PC must be switched on and your Windows Vista installation DVD must be in the optical drive:

   ● If Windows is running, insert the Windows Vista installation DVD, close the AutoPlay dialog box if it opens, and then restart Windows.

   ● If Windows is not running (for example, because it won't run), start your PC, and then insert the Windows Vista installation DVD. If Windows has already reached the point at which it hangs by the time you insert the DVD, restart the PC by pressing the Reset button or the Power button.

2. When your PC prompts you to "press any key to boot from CD or DVD," press a key to launch the boot process. Windows displays the Install Windows screen.

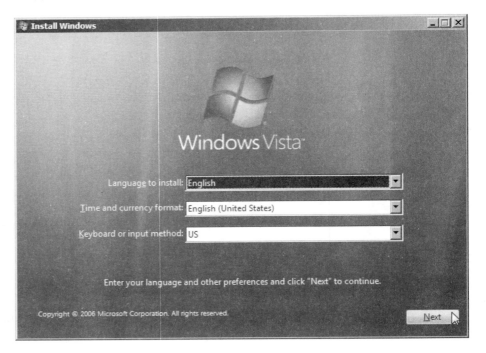

If your PC doesn't offer to boot from the Windows DVD, you may need to change BIOS settings. See Project 6 for instructions.

3. Choose the language in the Language To Install drop-down list and the keyboard layout in the Keyboard Or Input Method drop-down list.

4. Click the Next button to display the Install Now screen.

5. Click the Repair Your Computer link in the lower-left corner of the Install Now screen to display the first System Recovery Options dialog box.

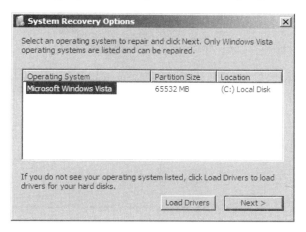

6. Click the operating system you want to restore, and then click the Next button to display the second System Recovery Options dialog box.

7. Click the Windows Complete PC Restore link to display the Restore Your Entire Computer From A Backup screen:

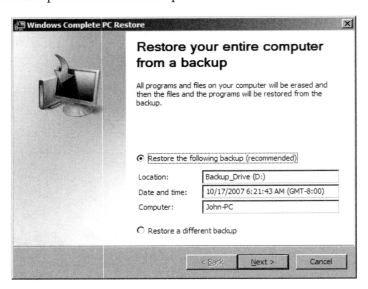

8. In the Restore The Following Backup area, make sure that Windows has chosen the backup you want to use, and then click the Next button. If Windows has not chosen the backup you want to use, select the Restore A Different Backup option, and then click the Next button. On the Select The Location Of The Backup screen, select the backup you want to use, and then click the Next button.

9. Windows displays a confirmation screen to confirm the restoration:

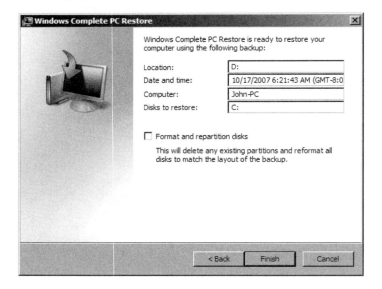

10. Make sure the settings are correct. Select the Format And Repartition Disks check box only if you want to reformat your PC's hard disk and return its partitions to the way they were when you made the backup. (This is not usually necessary.)

11. Click the Finish button to display Windows' double-check confirmation dialog box:

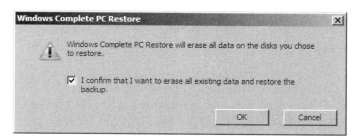

12. Take a deep breath, and then select the I Confirm That I Want To Erase All Existing Data And Restore The Backup check box.

13. Click the OK button. Windows restores the PC, keeping you informed of its progress.

14. At the end of the restoration, Windows restarts your PC.

15. When the logon screen appears, you can log on, and then start using the PC.

You May Need to Reactivate Windows Vista After Restoring Your PC

If you've just restored your PC successfully, you'll probably be relieved enough to put up with a little inconvenience…and some may be coming your way. After restoring your PC, you may need to reactivate Windows Vista. This normally happens only if Windows Vista has cause to believe it's running on different hardware than it was before. For example, if you've replaced your PC's hard drive because it failed, Windows Vista may detect the new hard drive as a different PC. But this problem also seems to occur even without hardware replacements.

If Windows Vista prompts you to activate it, follow through the online activation process. If the process fails (as it may, because the activation mechanism might think you are trying to install the same copy of Windows on a second PC), call the telephone number the activation mechanism provides, have yourself transferred from the automated system to a human, and persuade them to give you a new activation code to enter.

Now that you've backed up your PC, should you think about flossing your teeth?

Create a Wireless Network

What You'll Need

- Hardware: Wireless access point, wireless network adapter, USB flash drive
- Software: Your existing copy of Windows Vista
- Cost: $150 U.S.

In Project 9, you learned how to run a wired network through your home to connect all your PCs, share your Internet connection, and share files. Setting up a fully wired network gives great results, but it takes a serious commitment of time and effort (not to mention money).

If you don't want to take the time and effort to set up a wired network, or if you live in a dwelling whose landlord won't let you run cables and make holes in the walls and floors, a wireless network may be a better choice. This project shows you how to set up a wireless network, making sure you know about the limitations and dangers of wireless networks as well as their advantages.

Step 1: Decide Whether a Wireless Network Is Right for You

Wireless networks have several highly appealing benefits over wired networks. For example, you don't need to drill holes or run cables, and if your PCs already have wireless network adapters, you may not need to buy any hardware except a wireless access point. So if you need to set up a new network, the choice between wired and wireless may seem a no-brainer: Creating a wireless network is easier and much faster, and it may even be cheaper than creating a wired network.

Plus, your computers won't be tethered to Ethernet wall plates in the various rooms that the network serves. You'll be able to move your computers freely throughout the entire area covered by the network. That may include the whole house, your yard, or even several neighboring buildings. You may even be able to connect to your network from the coffee shop down the street. This means that anyone else within range of your network can also connect as well, so you need to secure the network using encryption to prevent unauthorized people connecting to it.

Despite rapid advances in wireless technology, wireless networks are still far slower than up-to-date wired networks—even though they have now become faster than wired networks were a few years ago. See the sidebar "Have Realistic Expectations of Wireless Network Speeds" for details on this. However, unless you need to transfer large files among the PCs on your network frequently, current wireless network speeds may be more than adequate. For example, streaming video via a Slingbox (see Project 21) typically works fine over an 802.11g wireless network. And even an 11 Mbps–max 802.11b wireless network is usually adequate for sharing a DSL or cable Internet connection.

Have Realistic Expectations of Wireless Network Speeds

Wireless network equipment is based on various standards set by the Institute of Electrical and Electronics Engineers (IEEE). At this writing (February 2008), the latest standard to have been approved (in 2003) is 802.11g, also called Wireless-G, which provides for transmission speeds of up to 54 Mbps. Wireless-G equipment generally works well and is the best choice for creating a wireless network.

The 802.11b standard, approved by IEEE in 1999, provides for transmission speeds of only up to 11 Mbps but is very widely used. The 802.11a standard, also approved in 1999, provides for speeds of up to 54 Mbps but is not used nearly as widely. 802.11b equipment and 802.11a equipment are not compatible, but most 802.11g equipment is backward compatible with both 802.11b and 802.11a equipment. 802.11a equipment was not successful in the consumer market, largely because it was not only incompatible with 802.11b equipment but also more expensive.

However, 54 Mbps is not very fast, so manufacturers have been releasing equipment based on the draft of the forthcoming 802.11n standard, which provides for transmission speeds of 270 Mbps or faster. Some manufacturers claim speeds of 300 Mbps or more for their Draft-N equipment. 802.11n equipment is typically backward compatible with 802.11g, 802.11b, and 802.11a equipment.

There are three problems with the manufacturers' claimed speeds:

● The fastest speeds are only available under *greenfield* conditions—that is, when only 802.11n equipment is involved. Having a mix of 802.11n equipment and equipment based on earlier standards (such as 802.11g or 802.11b) typically requires even the 802.11n equipment to use lower speeds. In the real world, greenfield conditions seldom occur.

(Continued)

- Because the equipment is based on the Draft-N standard rather than on a final standard, equipment from different manufacturers may not interoperate at the higher speeds.

- In the real world, data transmission is almost always much slower than the maximum theoretical speeds, especially when multiple devices are accessing the same network. If other wireless networks overlap with yours, your equipment may need to lower its speeds in order to communicate. Other nonnetworking equipment (such as cordless phones and microwave ovens) can also contribute to lowering transmission speeds.

For these reasons, don't expect the wireless network equipment you buy to achieve anything like its claimed speeds. Because of the Draft-N issue, if you buy 802.11n equipment, buy it all from the same manufacturer to ensure the devices work together successfully at acceptable speeds.

Step 2: Understand the Types of Wireless Network and Assess Your Needs

There are three main types of wireless network:

- **Infrastructure wireless network**   A network that is built around one or more wireless access points. This is the type of network covered in this project. For a home network, you'll normally need only one access point, unless you need the network to cover a large area (for example, all the way down the back yard). Figure 17-1 shows an infrastructure wireless network.

Figure 17-1

In an infrastructure wireless network, a wireless access point provides wireless connectivity to the PCs and other devices.

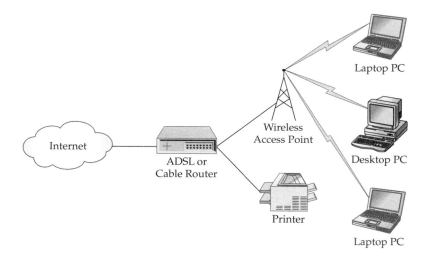

● **Ad hoc wireless network** A network created among computers without the use of an access point. For example, if your main PC has an Internet connection, you can create an ad hoc wireless network to share that Internet connection by using your PC to share the Internet connection, as shown in Figure 17-2.

Figure 17-2

An ad hoc wireless network lets you quickly share your files and Internet connection with another wireless-enabled PC.

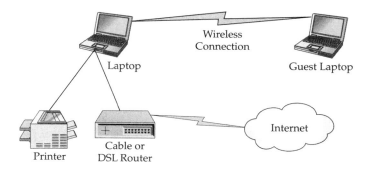

● **Hotspot wireless network** This is actually an infrastructure wireless network, but behaves in a different way from an infrastructure wireless network that you may create in your home. When you connect to a hotspot wireless network, such as the network in a coffee shop or an airport, your browser is typically redirected to a *captive portal*, a web page at which you log in (and usually agree to terms of service) and that lets the wireless network authenticate your computer and prevent it from taking nonapproved actions (such as sending spam or accessing web sites that are on a blocked list).

note *A fourth type of wireless network is a citywide or metropolitan wireless network, which provides either free or paid wireless Internet access throughout a city or the major part of it. If your city provides a wireless network, its authorities will make sure that the taxpayers know how to access the network.*

Step 3: Buy the Wireless Network Equipment

For your wireless network, you'll almost certainly need a wireless access point. Many different models are available, depending on the features you need. These are the features that you will typically need:

● **IEEE standard** 802.11g is the safest choice. If you choose to buy draft-standard 802.11n equipment, buy both the access point and any network adapters from the same manufacturer.

● **Wired Ethernet ports** Look for a wireless access point with enough switches to connect any wired Ethernet devices you want to use. For example, you may need to connect your printer or your cable or DSL router—or both—to the wireless access point to share them through the network.

tip *If you don't already have a cable or DSL router, look for an access point that incorporates the type of router you need. That way, you have one less device to configure.*

- **USB ports** Having one or more USB ports on the access point is useful for two reasons. First, some wireless access points let you configure them by using a USB flash drive. Second, some access points let you share a hard drive on the network by attaching it to the access point. Given that the access point keeps running all the time to maintain the network, this is an easy way to share files on the network.

If your PCs already have wireless network adapters (as many recent PCs do, especially laptops), you will not need to buy adapters. Otherwise, these are your choices for adding wireless network adapters:

- **Desktop PC** Either connect a USB wireless adapter or open the case and install a PCI network adapter. USB is the easier choice, especially if you buy a cabled adapter that you can reposition to get good reception.

- **Laptop PC** Either insert a PC Card or ExpressCard wireless adapter, or connect a USB wireless adapter. A PC Card or ExpressCard is usually a neater solution than a USB adapter, as the USB adapter projects farther from the laptop and is easy to damage. As with a desktop PC, however, a cabled USB adapter that you can reposition to improve reception is a good alternative if the wireless signal is weak.

Step 4: Position the Wireless Access Point and Power It On

Once you've got the wireless gear you need, position the wireless access point where you can connect it to your Internet router and to any devices that it will share—for example, a printer or a USB hard drive. You also need a power socket for the wireless access point's power supply. When you've connected the power supply, power on the access point.

Step 5: Create the Settings for the Wireless Network

The next step is to create the settings for the wireless network and save them to a USB flash disk so that you can then apply them to the access point and to each PC that will be part of the network.

To create the settings file for the wireless network on Windows Vista, follow these steps:

1. Click the Start button, right-click the Network item (in the list of folders on the right), and then click Properties to open a Network And Sharing Center window.

2. In the left panel, click the Set Up A Connection Or Network link to launch the Set Up A Connection Or Network Wizard. The wizard displays the Choose A Connection Option screen.

3. In the Choose A Connection Option list box, select the Set Up A Wireless Router Or Access Point item, and then click the Next button. The wizard displays the Set Up A Home Or Small Business Network screen.

4. Click the Next button. The wizard tries to detect your wireless access point. If it fails to do so, it displays the Windows Did Not Detect Any Wireless Network Hardware screen. If the wizard detects your access point but cannot configure it directly, it displays the Windows Detected Network Hardware But Cannot Configure It Automatically screen.

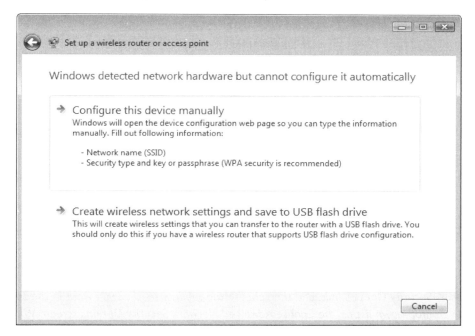

5. If your wireless access point supports USB configuration, click the Create Wireless Network Settings And Save To USB Flash Drive option. The wizard displays the Give Your Network A Name screen.

note *If your wireless access point does not support USB configuration, and the wizard has displayed the Windows Detected Network Hardware But Cannot Configure It Automatically screen, you can click the Configure This Device Manually option. The wizard opens your browser (for example, Internet Explorer) to the login screen for the wireless access point. Type the username and password (these will be in the manual unless you have changed them), and you will then reach a screen for entering the network name (or SSID), the security type (for example, WPA), and the passphrase to use for security.*

6. In the Network Name (SSID) text box type the name you want to give the network, using up to 32 letters and numbers.

7. Click the Next button to reach the Help Make Your Network More Secure With A Passphrase screen.

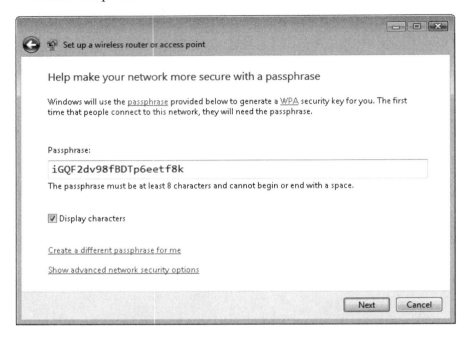

8. The Passphrase text box contains an automatically generated passphrase that is very hard to break. For the best security, accept this passphrase. If you prefer, you can type another passphrase manually (for example, one that's easier to remember) or click the Create A Different Passphrase For Me link to create another passphrase automatically.

 If you want to change the wireless security method used, click the Show Advanced Network Security Options link, and then choose the security method you want in the Security Method drop-down list on the Choose Advanced Network Security Options screen. Windows Vista's default security method is good enough for securing most wireless networks.

9. When you've finished choosing the passphrase, click the Next button to display the Choose File And Printer Sharing Options screen.

10. Choose the appropriate option button:

   ● **Keep The Custom Settings I Currently Have**   This option button appears only if you have chosen custom sharing settings. In this case, you will normally want to leave this option button selected (as it is by default) to preserve those custom settings.

   ● **Do Not Allow File And Printer Sharing**   Select this option button if you want to turn off sharing. The PCs can still connect to the Internet.

   ● **Allow Sharing With Anyone With A User Account And Password For This Computer**   Select this option button if you want users with accounts on this PC to be able to reach this PC's Public folder and shared printer from any other PC on the network.

- **Allow Sharing With Anyone On The Same Network As This Computer**   Select this option button if you want anybody using another PC on this network to be able to reach this PC's Public folder and shared printer (even if they don't have a user account on this PC).

11. Click the Next button, and then go through User Account Control (unless you've turned User Account Control off) for any option except keeping your current network settings. The wizard displays the Insert The USB Flash Drive Into This Computer screen.

12. Insert the flash drive (if it's not already connected), and then choose the drive letter in the Save Settings To drop-down list.

13. Click the Next button to make the wizard copy the wireless network settings to the flash drive. The wizard then displays the To Add A Device Or Computer, Follow These Instructions screen.

14. Unplug the flash drive from your PC, and then click the Close button to close the wizard.

Step 6: Apply the Wireless Network Settings to the Wireless Access Point

To apply the settings to the wireless access point, follow these steps:

1. Plug the flash drive into the wireless access point's USB port.

2. Wait for 30 seconds while the wireless access point reads the settings and applies them.

3. Unplug the flash drive.

Step 7: Apply the Wireless Network Settings to Each PC

To apply the network settings to a PC, follow these steps on Windows Vista:

1. Plug the USB flash drive containing the network settings into a USB port. Windows Vista automatically opens the AutoPlay dialog box, as shown here.

2. Click the Wireless Network Setup Wizard button to launch the wizard, which prompts you to add the PC to the network.

3. Click the OK button to add the PC to the network. When the wizard has done so, it displays a message box confirming the action.

4. Click the OK button. You can then unplug the USB flash drive and use it to connect other PCs to the network.

Step 8: Connect a PC to the Wireless Network

Once you've applied the wireless network settings, Windows automatically connects to the wireless network if it is within range. Windows displays a connection icon in the notification area. You can hover the mouse pointer over the icon to display its current status, as shown here.

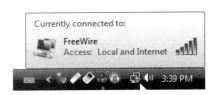

You can then start using the network. For example, choose Start | Internet to open an Internet Explorer window and connect to the Internet through the wireless network.

Step 9: Disconnect from and Reconnect to the Wireless Network

Normally, you'll want to keep using your wireless network until you put your PC to sleep or shut it down. But sometimes you may need to disconnect from your wireless network—and then reconnect to it.

To disconnect from the wireless network on Windows Vista, right-click the wireless network icon in the notification area, click or highlight the Disconnect From item, and then click the network name:

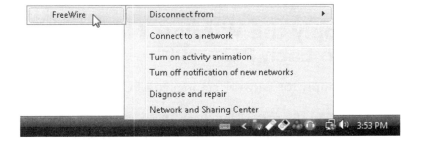

To reconnect to the wireless network on Windows Vista, follow these steps:

1. Right-click the wireless network icon in the notification area, and then choose Connect To A Network to launch the Connect To A Network Wizard, which displays the Select A Network To Connect To screen:

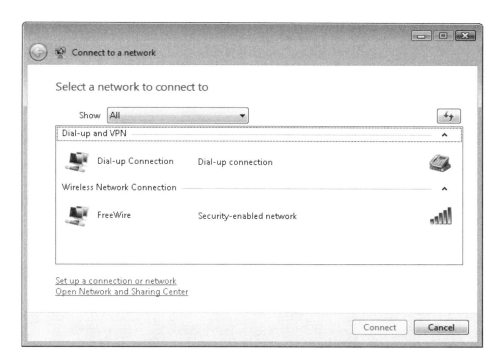

2. In the Select A Network To Connect To list box, click the wireless network, and then click the Connect button.

3. When the wizard displays the Successfully Connected To screen, click the Close button.

Step 10: Manage Multiple Wireless Networks

If you connect your PC to two or more wireless networks, you need to tell Windows the order in which you want it to use the networks, so that Windows doesn't automatically connect to the wrong network.

To manage wireless networks on Windows Vista, follow these steps:

1. Click the wireless network icon in the notification area, and then click the Network And Sharing Center link to open a Network And Sharing Center window.

2. In the left pane, click the Manage Network Connections link to display the Manage Wireless Networks window (see Figure 17-3).

3. In the Networks You Can View And Modify list box, drag the networks into the order in which you want Windows to attempt to connect automatically.

4. When you've finished rearranging the networks, click the Close button (the × button).

Figure 17-3

Use the Manage
Wireless Networks
window on Windows
Vista to arrange the
wireless networks into
your preferred
connection order.

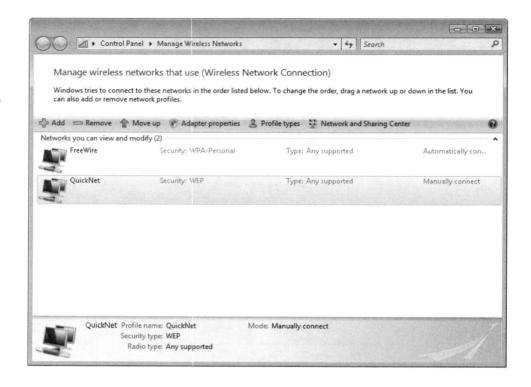

From the Manage Wireless Networks window, you can also remove networks to which you no
longer want to connect.

Now you can surf the Internet—and maybe even do some work—from the comfort
of the living-room couch.

Create an Ad Hoc Wireless Network

What You'll Need

- Hardware: A wireless network adapter in each PC
- Software: Your existing copy of Windows Vista
- Cost: Free to $150 U.S.

In Project 17, you learned how to set up an infrastructure wireless network, one based around a wireless access point that keeps running all the time, manages the wireless connections, and shares resources, such as an Internet connection.

If you'll be using a wireless network consistently, an infrastructure wireless network is almost always the best choice. However, you may sometimes want to set up a wireless network for just a short time so that two or more computers can communicate temporarily or so that you can share your computer's Internet connection easily with another computer—for example, when a friend visits with their laptop in tow. In this case, you can create an ad hoc wireless network, as described in this project, instead of setting up an infrastructure wireless network.

Step 1: Add Wireless Network Adapters if Necessary

The first step in setting up your ad hoc wireless network is to add a wireless network adapter to any PC that you want to use in the network and that doesn't already have an adapter. Most recent and current laptops include a wireless network adapter, so you may not need to add one.

Look back to Step 3 in Project 17 for a discussion of your options. For example, you can add a PCI adapter to a desktop PC, a PC Card or ExpressCard adapter to a laptop PC, or a USB adapter to either.

Step 2: Plan Your Wireless Network

Once each PC that will join the network has a wireless network adapter, you can plan the network. Planning will take hardly any time, especially if the network will consist of only a few PCs, as in the example network shown in Figure 18-1.

Figure 18-1

An ad hoc wireless network lets you temporarily share essentials such as your Internet connection with another PC.

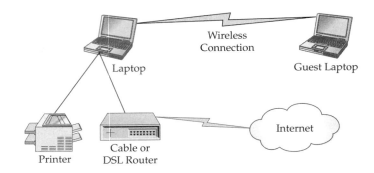

Keep these considerations in mind:

● **Location**   Most wireless network adapters can't manage the same distances that wireless access points cover, so you'll get the most consistent results—and higher data transfer speeds—if the PCs are within spitting distance of each other and without obstacles in the way. That said, wireless signals travel well through floors and ceilings—often better than through walls, especially if the walls are solid rather than cavity.

● **Encryption method**   All the PCs must use the same type of encryption—for example, WPA or WEP.

note   *Windows XP is limited to using WEP for ad hoc networks, so if your network will include one or more PCs running Windows XP, you will not be able to implement tight security—but WEP should be adequate for temporary use. If all your PCs run Windows Vista, you should be able to use WPA—but some people find that WPA causes problems with ad hoc networks and have to drop back to WEP.*

● **Sharing resources**   Any PC that is sharing resources with the other PCs on the network needs to be running all the time that the other PCs need access to those resources.

Step 3: Add PCs to the Network

Setting up a wireless network is largely a matter of telling all the PCs involved in the network to use the same network name (the SSID) and the same encryption method. This section shows you how to set up the network in Windows Vista.

Set Up the First PC on the Wireless Network

When you set up the first PC that connects to the network, you are creating the net-work. Follow these steps:

1. Choose Start | Connect To. Windows launches the Connect To A Network Wizard, which displays the Select A Network To Connect To screen. This screen lists the available networks, if any.

2. Click the Set Up A Connection Or Network link in the lower-left corner to display the Choose A Connection Option screen.

3. Select the Set Up A Wireless Ad Hoc (Computer-To-Computer) Network item.

4. Click the Next button to display the Set Up A Wireless Ad Hoc Network screen, which presents information about ad hoc networks.

note *The Set Up A Wireless Ad Hoc Network screen claims that computers and devices in ad hoc networks "must be within 30 feet of each other." This isn't strictly true. Unless there are thick walls or floors in the way, you should be able to achieve greater distances if necessary.*

5. Click the Next button to display the Give Your Network A Name And Choose Security Options screen, shown here with settings chosen:

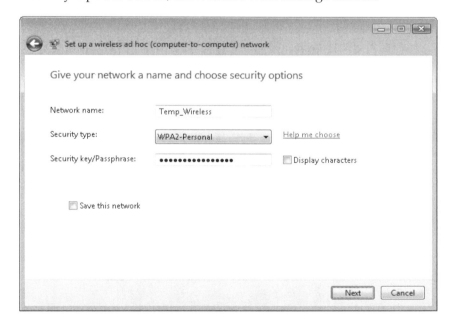

6. In the Network Name text box, type the name you want to use for the network.

7. In the Security Type drop-down list, choose the type of security you want:

   ● **No Authentication (Open)** This setting lets any computer in range connect to the network without authenticating itself. This setting is never a good idea.

● **WEP**   This setting uses Wired Equivalent Privacy, which provides moderate protection. Use WEP if you need to be able to connect Windows XP PCs to the network.

● **WPA2-Personal**   This setting uses Wi-Fi Protected Access, which provides good privacy. Use WPA2-Personal if all the PCs that will connect to the network are running Windows Vista.

8. In the Security Key/Passphrase text box, type the password for the network, making sure that you follow the rules listed next for the type of security you chose in Step 7. Select the Display Characters check box if you want to be sure of what you're typing, and you're confident that nobody is observing you.

● **WEP**   The key must be either 5 ASCII (regular) characters or 13 ASCII characters—for example, **wire0** or **w1relessnet99**. A 5-character key provides 40-bit encryption, and a 13-character key provides 104-bit encryption.

note   *Alternatively, you can enter the WEP key as 10 hexadecimal characters (to produce 40-bit encryption) or 26 hexadecimal characters (to produce 104-bit encryption). Using ASCII characters is easier.*

● **WPA2-Personal**   You can use a password of 8–63 ASCII characters or 64 hexadecimal characters.

9. Select the Save This Network check box if you want Windows to save this network for future use. If you're planning to use the network only once, leave this check box cleared.

10. Click the Next button. Windows sets up the network, and then displays a screen (shown next) telling you that the network is ready for use.

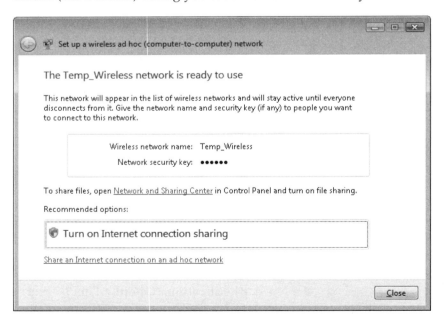

11. If you want to share this PC's Internet connection through the wireless network, click the Turn On Internet Connection Sharing button, go through User Account Control for the Adhoc Wireless Network program (unless you've turned off User Account Control), and then follow through the remaining steps of this list. If you don't want to share the Internet connection, click the Close button, and then skip the remaining steps.

12. The wizard displays the Select The Internet Connection You Want To Share screen.

13. In the Available drop-down list, select the Internet connection, and then click the Next button. The wizard sets up sharing, and then displays the Internet Connection Sharing Is Enabled screen.

14. Click the Close button to close the wizard.

Your ad hoc wireless network is now set up, and other PCs can connect to it.

Add a PC to an Existing Wireless Network

Once you've set up one PC offering the wireless network, you can connect further PCs to the network by using a different technique. Follow these steps:

1. Choose Start | Connect To. Windows launches the Connect To A Network Wizard, which displays the Select A Network To Connect To screen. This screen lists the available networks, as shown here:

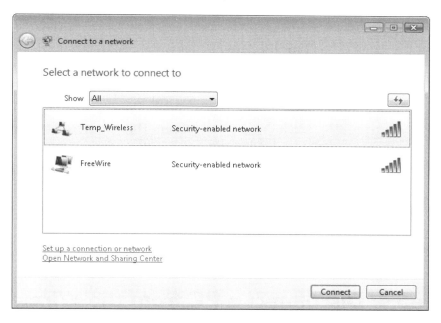

tip *The icon at the left end of each network's row shows the network type. The icon for an ad hoc network shows three computers linked together. If the network list is full of many types of networks, choose Wireless in the Show drop-down list to make the list show only wireless networks.*

2. Click the network you want to connect to, and then click the Connect button. The wizard displays the Type The Network Security Key Or Passphrase screen, shown here.

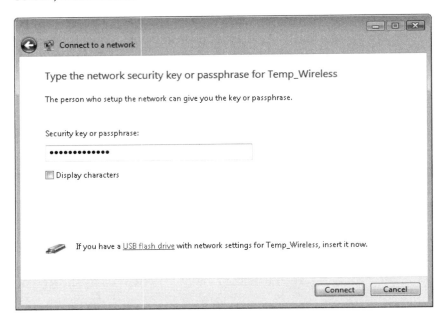

3. Type the network key in the Security Key Or Passphrase text box. If nobody is looking over your shoulder, you can safely select the Display Characters check box to suppress the dots that the wizard displays by default (for your security).

4. Click the Connect button. The wizard connects your PC to the network, and then displays the Successfully Connected screen.

5. If you want to be able to use this network easily in the future, select the Save This Network check box. For temporary ad hoc networks, however, you will probably want to leave this check box cleared.

6. Click the Close button to close the wizard. Your PC is now connected to the network.

Step 4: Disconnect a PC from the Wireless Network

When you want to stop a PC from being part of the wireless network, you disconnect the PC from the network.

To disconnect, right-click the Network Connection icon in the notification area, click or highlight the Disconnect From item on the context menu, and then click the network's name on the submenu. Windows disconnects from the network.

Step 5: Shut Down the Ad Hoc Network

When you've finished using the wireless network, you can shut it down by disconnecting all the PCs on it, as discussed in the previous section.

As you saw earlier in this project, Windows Vista lets you decide whether to save the network for future use. Provided that you did not select the Save This Network check box while setting up the network, Windows Vista automatically discards the details of the network when you disconnect the PC from the network.

Next up: How to streamline your life by digitizing your paper documents. Turn the page.

Digitize Your Paper Documents

What You'll Need

- Hardware: Scanner (required), shredder (optional)
- Software: Microsoft Office 2003 or 2007 (optional), other optical character recognition software (optional), Perforce Server and Perforce Client (optional)
- Cost: $100–200 U.S.

These days, you can manage almost all your information on your PC—manage your correspondence via e-mail or PC-based faxing, handle all your banking online, and even make most of your major purchases (and some minor ones) over the Internet. This doesn't cover the paper documents that show up every day— through the mail, on your desk at work, on your car when you overstay your welcome in a parking bay, or simply the receipts that are the result of any successful shopping expedition.

Bills, invoices, receipts, checks… chances are, you need to deal with them all. Maybe you have a hefty filing cabinet full of such pieces of paper, or maybe you simply throw each year's papers in shoeboxes when they drift into your life, and then truck the boxes to your accountant in the run-up to April 15.

If you want to reduce the amount of paper in your life, you can digitize your paper documents by scanning them into your PC. This project shows you how to scan your documents and how to set up a means of tracking which scanned document is which, so that you can hunt down exactly the document you need in seconds rather than minutes.

caution *Consult your lawyer and accountant if you're not sure which documents you must keep the original hard copies of. For example, I'm not suggesting you scan your passport and then present your laptop at passport control.*

Step 1: Get a Scanner and Install It

If you don't already have a scanner, you'll need to buy or borrow one. The good news is that pretty much any scanner will do for digitizing paper documents, as long as your PC's operating system has a driver for the scanner.

Choose a Scanner

For this project, you don't need a scanner with incredibly high resolution or extra features such as scanning 35mm negatives (although you may want the high resolution and extra features for your other projects, such as creating a family photo album). Standard resolution (such as 300 dots per inch, or dpi) is plenty.

Desktop sheet-fed scanners (like a rolling pin on a mount) were popular in the late 1990s until their habit of tearing documents fed into them ruined their reputation. These days, a flatbed scanner is probably your best bet. If you find yourself scanning scores of documents, you can upgrade in due course to a scanner with a feeder mechanism.

note *Instead of buying a scanner, you may want to buy a multifunction device—a device that incorporates a printer, scanner, fax, and perhaps other features. Having such a device might be easier than having several different devices connected to your PC; and if you're looking to add several types of functionality at once, buying such a device may also be less expensive than buying several different devices. Again, make sure that the device's manufacturer provides a driver for the version of Windows that you're using.*

Understand Hardware Resolution and Software Resolution

If you have a digital camera, you're probably familiar with the difference between optical zoom and digital zoom: *Optical zoom* is the zooming that the camera effects by using its zoom lens, and *digital zoom* is the zoom the camera achieves by using computation to process the data it's seeing and (if necessary) to add extra data synthetically to make the image appear larger. Optical zoom looks much better than digital zoom, because it shows you what's actually there, and in full quality.

Similarly, each scanner has a maximum hardware resolution, which is the highest level of detail that the scanner's "eye" can "see" what it's looking at. Typically, you want to use either this resolution or a lower resolution. Many scanners also offer software-enhanced resolutions that use computation to achieve a resolution higher than the scanner's hardware resolution can provide. Normally, you will not want to use these resolutions, because they include data that is not actually present in the image that you're scanning.

Install Your Scanner

Install your scanner following the instructions that come with it. Typically, for a USB-connected scanner, you install the software from CD, and then connect the scanner. If you don't have instructions or software, connect the scanner anyway. When Windows prompts you about the driver software, choose the recommended option for locating and installing the driver software, and then go through User Account Control for the Device Driver Software Installation program (unless you have turned off User Account Control).

Even if you download the driver software from the scanner manufacturer's web site, you may find that Windows Security objects to it, as in the example shown in Figure 19-1. Provided that the driver software comes directly from a major manufacturer, you should be safe; but if you've downloaded it from elsewhere, you should probably cancel the installation.

Figure 19-1

If your scanner's manufacturer has left the driver software unsigned, you will need to decide whether to install it anyway.

Once you've finished the installation, your scanner should be ready to use.

Step 2: Scan Your Documents

If your scanner includes custom scanning software, read the documentation and experiment with the software to see if you get along with it. If the scanner doesn't include scanning software, you can simply use the scanning capabilities built into Windows, as described here.

To scan a document on Windows Vista, follow these steps:

1. Turn the scanner on if it's currently turned off.

2. Insert the document and align it along the scanner's guides.

3. Choose Start | All Programs | Windows Photo Gallery to open a Windows Photo Gallery window.

4. Choose File | Import From Camera Or Scanner. Windows Photo Gallery displays the Import Pictures And Videos dialog box.

tip *If you have a networked scanner (for example, a multifunction printer that includes scanning capabilities), Windows Photo Gallery may not be able to detect the scanner. In this case, look at solutions such as SANE (www.sane-project.org) or RemoteScan (www.remote-scan.com) to make the scanner visible to Windows Photo Gallery across the network.*

5. In the Scanners And Cameras list, click your scanner, and then click the Import button. Windows Photo Gallery displays the New Scan dialog box (see Figure 19-2).

Figure 19-2

Use the options in the New Scan dialog box to tell Windows which kind of document you're scanning and to make sure the preview looks correct.

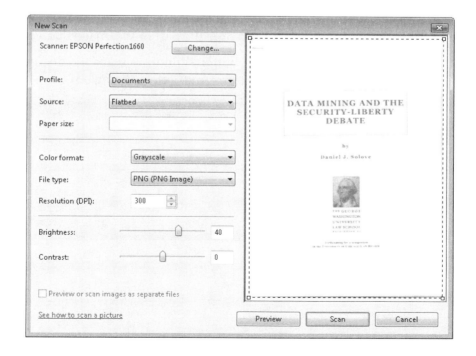

6. The Scanner readout at the top of the dialog box shows the scanner you've chosen. You shouldn't need to change this.

7. In the Profile drop-down list, select Documents if the item you're scanning is a document rather than a photo. Otherwise, choose Photos, the default item.

8. If your scanner has multiple scanning surfaces, make sure the Source drop-down list shows the right one—for example, Flatbed. If the scanner has only one scanning surface, you shouldn't need to change this setting.

9. If the Paper Size drop-down list offers you a choice of settings, choose the correct one for the document.

10. In the Color Format drop-down list, choose Color, Grayscale, or Black And White, as appropriate. For a "black and white" document that includes photos, you will normally get a better result by choosing Grayscale than by choosing Black And White, which changes each shade of gray to either black or white.

11. In the File Type drop-down list, choose the type of file you want to create. See the sidebar "Choose the Best Graphics File Format for Saving Your Documents" for advice.

12. In the Resolution text box, choose the resolution you want to use. Windows suggests 300 dpi for many scanners, which is plenty for documents. (Photos may need higher resolution.)

13. Click the Preview button to make the New Scan dialog box display a preview of the document on the right side.

14. If necessary, adjust the Brightness slider or Contrast slider, and then click the Preview button again to update the preview and see if the changes result in an improvement.

15. If you need to crop the image, drag the handles on the preview box to reduce the selection to only the part of the image that you want to keep.

16. Click the Scan button. Windows scans the document, and then displays the Importing Pictures And Videos dialog box.

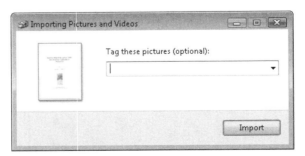

Choose the Best Graphics File Format for Saving Your Documents

Windows offers you a choice of four file formats for saving your documents. Here's what you need to know about them:

- **BMP (Bitmap Image)**   The BMP image format uses no compression, so it produces full-quality images with large file sizes.

- **JPG (JPEG Image)**   The JPEG file format uses lossy compression to produce reasonable-quality images with moderate file sizes. JPEG files are fine for photos that you plan to use on web sites or for other low-resolution purposes, but your documents deserve a more faithful file format than this.

- **PNG (PNG Image)**   The PNG file format uses lossless compression to produce high-quality images with moderate file sizes. PNG is usually the best choice for storing your documents.

- **TIFF (TIFF Image)**   The TIFF file format can use either lossless compression, producing full-quality images with moderate file sizes, or no compression, giving full-quality images with large file sizes. TIFF is widely used for professional image editing.

17. To apply a tag to the picture, type the tag in the Tag These Pictures text box, or choose a tag you've used previously from the drop-down list.

18. Click the Import button. Windows imports the picture, adds it to the Recently Imported category in Windows Photo Gallery, and selects the picture.

19. You can now add another tag to the picture by clicking the Add Tags picture in the right pane of Windows Photo Gallery, typing a tag you want to assign, and then pressing ENTER. Repeat this process to add further tags.

Perform Optical Character Recognition Using Microsoft Office

If you have Microsoft Office 2007 or 2003, you can use its built-in optical character recognition (OCR) features to get the text from a document in a format that you can search (or otherwise manipulate). Entering text via OCR should be faster than entering it manually—but you must proofread the text carefully after scanning it to root out any errors that creep in. This section shows you how to perform OCR using Office 2007, but the process is almost exactly the same for Office 2003.

(Continued)

To scan a document and use OCR to turn it into text, connect your scanner if it's not already connected, and then follow these steps:

1. Choose Start | All Programs | Microsoft Office | Microsoft Office Tools | Microsoft Office Document Scanning. Windows displays the Scan New Document dialog box (shown here). Choose Black And White if you're scanning a monochrome document. If you're scanning a color text document, choose Black And White From Color Page.

2. Choose settings for scanning, and then click the Scan button.

   ● Select the Original Is Double Sided check box if the document is printed on both sides.

   ● Select the Prompt For Additional Pages check box if the document has multiple pages.

   ● Select the View File After Scanning check box to make Microsoft Office Document Scanning open automatically.

3. Click the Scanner button. Microsoft Office Document Scanning scans the document, and then opens a Microsoft Office Document Imaging window displaying the scanned document.

4. Select the part of the document you want to recognize, and then choose Tools | Recognize Text Using OCR. Microsoft Office Document Imaging recognizes the text and then highlights it.

5. Choose Tools | Send Text To Word. Windows displays the Send Text To Word dialog box.

6. In the upper part of the dialog box, specify which text to send to Word:

- **Current Selection** If you've selected part of the document, Microsoft Office Document Imaging normally selects this option button automatically. If there's no selection, this option button is unavailable.

- **Selected Pages** If you've selected one or more complete pages in the left pane, Microsoft Office Document Imaging normally selects this option button automatically. If you haven't selected pages, this option button is unavailable.

- **All Pages** Microsoft Office Document Imaging selects this option button automatically if you haven't selected a selection or pages. You can also select this option button even if one of the other option buttons is selected.

7. If you want to include any pictures from the document, select the Maintain Pictures In Output check box. If you want only the document's text, clear this check box.

8. Click the OK button. Microsoft Office Document Imaging opens a new Word document, places the text in it, and displays the document so that you can start working in it.

In Word, run a spelling check on the new document and take care of any recognition errors. After that, proofread the text quickly against the original in case any whole words have been substituted during the recognition process. Any wrong words will be correctly spelled, so the spell checker will have no quarrel with them, but they will change the meaning of the text.

Step 3: Organize Your Scanned Documents

As you've seen, scanning is easy. The tricky part is keeping your scanned documents in order so that you know where to find them when you need them. The following sections discuss several methods for doing so. Briefly, the methods are as follows:

- Tag the individual picture files in Windows, and then use Windows' search features to search for the ones you need. This solution is adequate if you scan few documents or if you're blessed with plenty of patience.

note *You can also organize your documents into an elaborate system of folders, but this doesn't work so well when you have documents that fit into multiple categories. To make it easier to find the files you need, you can create shortcuts to a file that belongs to multiple categories, and then place those shortcuts in other folders.*

• Create a tracking file, such as a Microsoft Excel workbook, in which you enter details of each document. This solution works well if you scan only moderate numbers of documents (you get to set your own level of "moderate" here) and if you typically use only a single PC.

• Use a professional document-tracking system. This is the best solution if you scan many documents or if you want to use two or more PCs for scanning or managing your documents.

note   *If you have Microsoft Office OneNote, you can organize your scanned documents into different notebooks, sections, and pages. OneNote offers you the choice of either placing the scans in your notebooks or linking to other documents in the manner described shortly for Microsoft Excel.*

Track Your Scanned Documents Using Tags

As you saw earlier in this project, after you scan a document from Windows Vista, Windows Photo Gallery lets you tag the picture with various items of information. This information lets you locate a particular picture or set of pictures in Windows Photo Gallery.

Track Your Scanned Documents Using Excel

If you have Microsoft Office Excel (pretty much any recent version) or another spreadsheet program with similar capabilities, you can create a spreadsheet that helps you track your scanned documents. The following illustration shows an example:

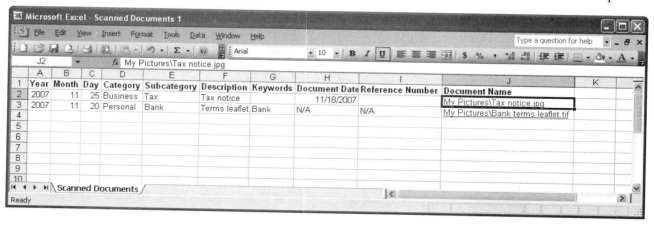

Create a spreadsheet that contains a column for each item of information you want to store about each picture. Here is an example, but you will almost certainly want to keep a different set of data in your spreadsheet:

• **Year**   The year in which you scanned and filed the document.

• **Month**   The month in which you scanned and filed the document.

• **Day**   The day of the month on which you scanned and filed the document.

• **Category**   For example, Household, Personal, or Business.

- **Subcategory**   For each category, create subcategories, such as Bank, Utilities, Essential Documents, or Tax.

- **Description**   Add a short description of the document—for example, "Electric bill."

- **Keywords**   To make the document easier to find, add keywords—for example, "1040" or "W-2."

- **Document Date**   If the document bears a date, enter it here.

- **Document Reference Number**   If the document has a reference number associated with it, enter it here. You may also want to have a separate column for account numbers.

- **Document Name**   Enter the document's name as a hyperlink to the document's location (use the Insert | Hyperlink command).

note   *Another approach is to divide your content logically into separate categories and devote a separate spreadsheet page to each of them. For example, you might choose to keep business documents, household documents, and personal documents separate from each other.*

Once you've created the list in your spreadsheet, you can manipulate its contents using standard Excel commands. For example:

- Use the Data Form command to display a data-form dialog box for the list, as shown here. This dialog box lets you enter information quickly in the columns of the list, but you will need to enter the hyperlink to the document itself manually.

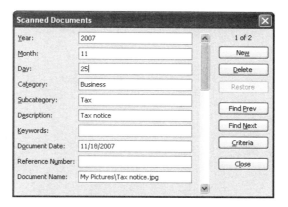

- Use the Sort command to sort the rows of data so that you can see related items. For example, you might sort by category, by subcategory, and by year to pull related items together.

- Use the Find command to locate a particular item by using a string of text or data (for example, an account number or reference number).

Once you've located the document, click the hyperlink to open it in your picture editor.

Track Your Scanned Documents Using a Professional Solution

If you need a heavier-duty solution for tracking your scanned documents, you can develop a database of your own (for example, if you have Microsoft Access) or use an existing software package for document control.

If you're interested in creating a serious—but personal-scale—tracking solution for scanned documents, take a look at the Perforce Software Configuration Management System. Perforce (www.perforce.com/) provides its client software for free, and the Perforce Server software is free for unlicensed use by up to two users and five client workspaces. Better yet, you don't need to run the Perforce Client on a different computer from the Perforce Server computer—you can install them both on the same PC.

Once you've gotten your scanning-and-storage system up and running, use it for a couple of months—and test it as extensively as possible—before reaching for the shredder and the recycling bin. Remember to back up your scanned documents to keep them safe.

Seal Your Private Data in an Uncrackable Virtual Locker

What You'll Need

- Hardware: PC with Trusted Platform Module (TPM) version 1.2 or later, or USB flash drive
- Software: Windows Vista Ultimate Edition
- Cost: Free to $20 U.S.

Theft, accidents, rainfall, floods, fire, or simply an act of God…if you have a laptop PC, you should be prepared to lose it and all its contents at any point. Even a desktop PC suffers plenty of threats, ranging from the mundane curse of gravity to the rigors of daily life (children in the home, cleaners in the office), from the ever-present threats of Internet viruses to the danger of an electrical storm reaching far enough along the cables to damage the PC.

But if the contents of your PC are sensitive or valuable—commercially, politically, or personally—perhaps the worst threat is of someone else accessing your private data. You can protect your PC against intrusion to some extent by applying a strong password to your user account, locking your office, and using a firewall to prevent remote access, but there remains the possibility that a malefactor will find another way in. For example, as you saw in Project 10, someone can use a live Linux distribution such as Knoppix to bypass conventional protection systems such as login names and passwords.

The solution to this problem is to seal your private data in an uncrackable virtual locker by encrypting it using the powerful encryption built into the Ultimate Edition of Windows Vista. This encryption is called BitLocker, and it prevents other people from reading your files even if they manage to access them.

tip *If you're not sure which version of Windows your PC is running, press* WINDOWS KEY–BREAK. *In the System window on Windows Vista, look at the Windows Edition readout.*

If you don't have Windows Vista Ultimate Edition, see the sidebar "An Alternative to BitLocker for Other Versions of Windows" at the end of this project for an alternative means of encryption.

 Windows Vista Enterprise Edition also includes BitLocker. However, this version of Windows Vista is only available to large corporations for bulk purchases. If you're using Windows Vista Enterprise Edition and need to use BitLocker, a system administrator will probably set up BitLocker for you.

Step 1: Understand What Encryption Does—and Why You Must Be Careful

If you've ever played with a code—even a simple one, such as one that involves shifting each letter just a couple of places down the alphabet (A changes to C, B changes to D, and so on)—you know what encryption is: Using a key to transform information from being readable plaintext to unreadable ciphertext. Decryption is the reverse: Using a key to transform the ciphertext back into plaintext.

In the example, the key is knowing that you shift each letter two places forward to encrypt the data and two places backward to decrypt the ciphertext back to plaintext, something anyone can do with some paper or some practice. Encryption in your PC works in the same way but with a much more complex key—one complex enough that the files in practice cannot be decrypted without it.

Because BitLocker uses strong encryption, losing your cryptographic key locks you out of your data just as effectively as it locks out other people. So you must take active steps to ensure that you don't lose your cryptographic key.

BitLocker Is Strong Enough for Serious Use

No encryption is truly unbreakable, but BitLocker provides strong enough encryption for most civilian uses—and perhaps some government and military uses. The strength of encryption depends on the length of the encryption key used. BitLocker uses a 128-bit key and the AES (Advanced Encryption Standard) encryption algorithm. So you can be sure that nobody can crack it easily unless they can determine (by guessing or by brute force) your login password.

Equally, you can be pretty sure that any security professionals will be able to break the encryption eventually. For example, don't expect BitLocker to hold out against the decryption resources of a government agency. (But if these are the people against whom you're trying to protect your secrets, you've got bigger problems than this book can cover.)

That said, modern encryption is hard enough to crack that some governments have resorted to other means of deciphering it. For example, UK law officers can compel UK citizens to disclose cryptographic keys under the threat of five years' jail if they fail to do so.

BitLocker stores the encryption key either in a special chip on your PC's motherboard or on a USB flash drive that you connect to your PC. The special chip is called a Trusted Platform Module (TPM); BitLocker requires TPM version 1.2 or later. You can dig through your PC's specs to find out whether it has a suitable TPM or not, but what's easier is to try to set up BitLocker and see if Windows Vista warns you that your PC doesn't have a suitable TPM.

There's also one technical thing you need to know about BitLocker: It requires two partitions rather than the one partition that Windows normally uses. Both partitions, explained next, use the NTFS format that Windows Vista uses automatically for formatting internal hard drives:

- **System partition** The system partition contains Windows Vista and all your files. This partition is encrypted, but otherwise it acts much like a normal system partition.

- **Active partition** The active partition is an unencrypted partition of at least 1.5GB that allows BitLocker to start Windows and to encrypt data to, and decrypt data from, the encrypted system partition.

You can choose to set up an active partition manually, but there's an easier way. You can download the BitLocker Drive Preparation Tool, which can create the active partition automatically for you by carving out a chunk of your existing system partition.

caution *Encrypting your data requires your PC to work harder to get the same amount of work done, so it will degrade performance. If your PC is powerful enough to handle its regular tasks without breaking a sweat, having to deal with encryption as well may not slow it down enough for you to notice. But if your PC is struggling to run Windows, encryption may be the last straw that brings it to its knees.*

To encrypt your PC's hard drive with BitLocker, you must perform these three actions:

1. Download and install the BitLocker Drive Preparation Tool.

2. Run the BitLocker Drive Preparation Tool and create an active partition for BitLocker.

3. Start BitLocker.

If you want to use a USB key instead of a TPM, you also need to set BitLocker up to use the USB key.

Step 2: Download and Install the BitLocker Drive Preparation Tool

The BitLocker Drive Preparation Tool is one of the Windows Vista Ultimate Extras; extra programs that Microsoft makes available for free only to users of Windows Vista

Ultimate Edition. To download and install the BitLocker Drive Preparation Tool, follow these steps:

1. Choose Start | All Programs | Windows Update to open a Windows Update window.

2. Click the View Available Extras link to open a View Available Extras window.

3. Select the BitLocker And EFS Enhancements check box in the Windows Ultimate Extras section of the list. If you want, you can also select the check box for any other Ultimate Extra you want to install.

4. Click the Install button, and then go through User Account Control for the Windows Update program (unless you've turned off User Account Control). Windows Update downloads the BitLocker and EFS Enhancements package, along with any other Extras (or other updates) you chose to install, and then installs them.

5. When the Windows Update window shows the message "The updates were successfully installed," click the Close button (the × button) to close the window.

Step 3: Create the Active Partition for BitLocker

To create the active partition for BitLocker, follow these steps:

1. Choose Start | All Programs | Accessories | System Tools | BitLocker | BitLocker Drive Preparation Tool, and then go through User Account Control for the BitLocker Drive Preparation Tool program (unless you've turned off User Account Control). Windows opens the first BitLocker Drive Encryption dialog box, which contains a license agreement.

2. Read the license agreement. If you can accept its terms, click the I Accept button to reach the second BitLocker Drive Encryption dialog box (see Figure 20-1). (If you click the I Decline button, you won't be able to use BitLocker.)

3. Read the details of what the BitLocker Drive Preparation Tool is planning to do to your hard drive—for example, create a new active drive from free space on one of your PC's existing drives.

4. If you want to proceed, click the Continue button. The BitLocker Drive Preparation Tool shrinks the PC's existing drive, creates a new active drive, and then prepares the new drive for BitLocker. The BitLocker Drive Encryption dialog box shows you the progress.

5. When the BitLocker Drive Preparation Tool has finished creating and preparing the new drive, click the Finish button to close the BitLocker Drive Encryption dialog box. Another BitLocker Drive Encryption dialog box then tells you that you must restart your computer to apply the changes.

Figure 20-1

The BitLocker Drive Encryption dialog box starts you off with three warnings. Don't worry—things get better soon.

6. Save any unsaved documents you want to keep, close your programs, and then click the Restart Now button to restart Windows.

7. Log on to Windows as normal. Windows then displays the BitLocker Drive Encryption window (see Figure 20-2).

Figure 20-2

If the BitLocker Drive Encryption window tells you that a TPM was not found, you must use a USB key drive for storing the encryption key.

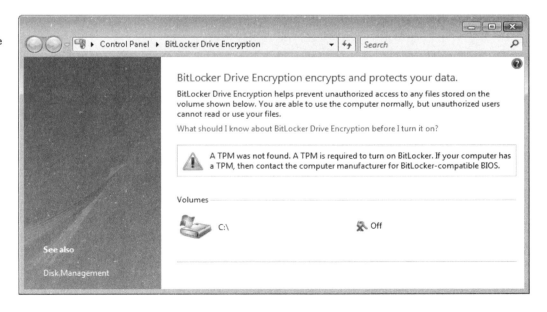

If the BitLocker Drive Encryption window contains a yellow bar telling you that a TPM was not found, follow the instructions in Step 4 for using a USB key drive to store the encryption key. If this yellow bar does not appear, all is well. Go to Step 5 to turn on BitLocker.

Step 4: Use a USB Key Drive Instead of a TPM

If you've just found that your PC doesn't have the TPM required for BitLocker, follow these steps to use a USB drive instead:

1. Minimize or close the BitLocker Drive Encryption window to get it out of the way.

2. Press WINDOWS KEY–R to display the Run dialog box.

3. Type **gpedit.msc** in the Open text box, press ENTER or click the OK button, and then go through User Account Control for the Microsoft Management Console program (unless you've turned off User Account Control). Once you've done that, Windows displays a Group Policy Object Editor window (shown in Figure 20-3 with the tree expanded to show the BitLocker Drive Encryption settings).

Figure 20-3

Use the Group Policy Object Editor window to tell Windows Vista to store the BitLocker encryption key on a USB key drive.

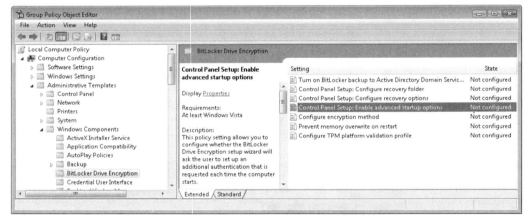

4. Expand the Computer Configuration object, the Administrative Templates folder, and the Windows Components folder. (You can simply double-click each of these in turn.)

5. In the Windows Components folder, click the BitLocker Drive Encryption item to show its contents in the right pane.

6. In the right pane, double-click the Control Panel Setup: Enable Advanced Startup Options setting to display the Control Panel Setup: Enable Advanced Startup Options Properties dialog box (shown in Figure 20-4 with settings chosen).

Figure 20-4

The Control Panel
Setup: Enable Advanced
Startup Options
Properties dialog box
lets you choose where
to store the BitLocker
encryption key.

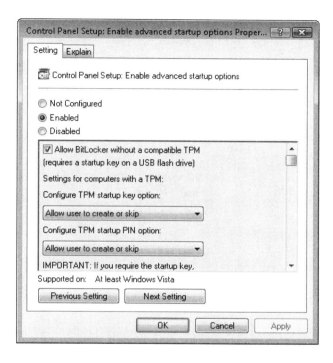

7. Select the Enabled option button.

8. Make sure that Windows has selected the Allow BitLocker Without A Compatible TPM check box.

9. Click the OK button to close the Properties dialog box, and then click the Close button (the × button) in the Group Policy Object Editor window.

10. Press WINDOWS KEY–R to display the Run dialog box again.

11. In the Open text box, type **gpupdate /force**, and then press ENTER (or click the OK button) to force Windows Vista to update the group policy with the change you've just made. Windows runs the command in a Command Prompt window, which it then closes automatically.

12. Choose Start | Control Panel to display a Control Panel window.

13. If the Control Panel window is in Control Panel Home view (showing a list of major and minor headings), click the Classic View link in the upper-left corner to switch to Classic view.

14. Double-click the BitLocker Drive Encryption icon to open a BitLocker Drive Encryption window.

15. Connect your USB key drive to your PC. If Windows opens an AutoPlay dialog box, click the Close button to close it.

Now that BitLocker is ready to store the BitLocker encryption key on a USB key drive, you can turn BitLocker on.

Step 5: Turn On BitLocker

To turn on BitLocker, follow these steps from the BitLocker Drive Encryption window:

1. Click the Turn On BitLocker link to start the BitLocker Drive Encryption Wizard. The wizard displays the Set BitLocker Startup Preferences screen (see Figure 20-5).

Figure 20-5

If your PC doesn't have a TPM, only the Require Startup USB Key At Every Startup button is available on the Set BitLocker Startup Preferences screen.

2. Choose which BitLocker implementation you want to use by clicking a button:

   ● **Use BitLocker Without Additional Keys**   This option uses the BitLocker encryption key stored on your PC's TPM for encryption. This is the standard option, but it's not available if you're using a USB key.

   ● **Require PIN At Every Startup**   This option adds security by making the user enter a personal identification number (PIN) each time the PC is started. Once the user enters the correct PIN, BitLocker uses the key stored on the TPM. If you're using a USB key, this option is not available.

   ● **Require Startup USB Key At Every Startup**   This option lets you store the BitLocker encryption key on a USB drive. Use this option if your PC doesn't have a TPM or if you want to be able to carry the BitLocker key with you.

3. If you're using a USB drive (as in this example), the wizard displays the Save Your Startup Key screen when you click the Require Startup USB Key At Every Startup button. Make sure the wizard has selected the correct drive, and then click the Save button. (If you're not using a USB drive, skip this step.)

4. On the Save The Recovery Password screen (see Figure 20-6), click the Save The Password On A USB Drive button, the Save The Password In A Folder button, or the Print The Password button to save or print the password.

Figure 20-6

Losing your BitLocker recovery password will cost you all your data, so you will probably want to save your password in two or more places.

caution   *Saving the BitLocker recovery password on your encrypted hard drive will not help you recover from forgetting the password.*

5. Click the Next button. The wizard displays the Encrypt The Volume screen (see Figure 20-7).

6. Check that the wizard is planning to encrypt the right drive and that it has selected the Run BitLocker System Check check box.

7. Click the Continue button. The wizard displays the Computer Must Be Restarted dialog box.

8. If you're using a USB key to store the BitLocker encryption key, leave it connected to the PC. Whether you're using a USB key or not, remove any disc from your PC's optical drive.

Figure 20-7

On the Encrypt The Volume screen, make sure that the wizard has chosen the drive you want to encrypt.

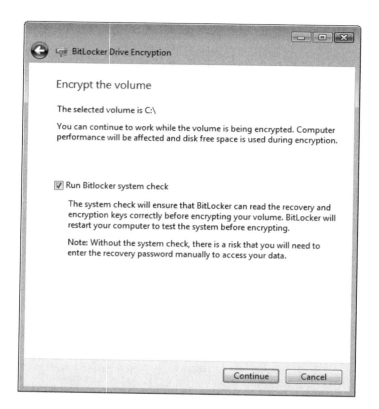

9. Click the Restart Now button. Windows restarts your PC.

10. After you log on, BitLocker runs automatically and encrypts your hard disk volume, displaying a notification-area icon that you can hover the mouse pointer over to get a progress readout, as shown here. (You can also click the icon to display a progress dialog box.) To get the encryption finished as fast as possible, avoid using your PC until the encryption is complete.

11. When BitLocker tells you that it has finished encryption, click the Close button. You can then use Windows as normal.

Step 6: Start Your PC When BitLocker Is On

After you've set up BitLocker to protect your PC, BitLocker verifies the encryption key each time you start the PC:

- If you're using a TPM, BitLocker verifies that the TPM contains the encryption key. As long as it does, you don't have to take any action yourself.

- If you're using a TPM plus a PIN, BitLocker prompts you for the PIN during startup.

- If you're using a USB key, BitLocker prompts you for the USB key during startup. Figure 20-8 shows an example of the prompt.

Figure 20-8

If you're using a USB key with BitLocker, you must have the USB key connected in order to boot the PC.

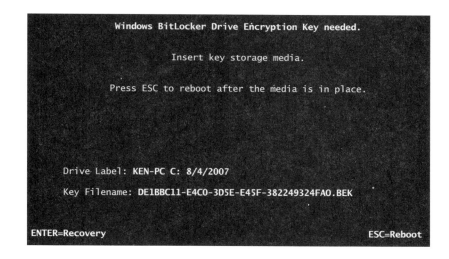

If you've lost or damaged your USB key, but you have the BitLocker password (for example, on a sheet of paper), press ENTER. Windows displays the Windows BitLocker Drive Encryption Password Entry screen (see Figure 20-9). Type the password, noting the instructions to use the F1–F9 function keys for the numbers 1 through 9, and the F10 key for 0, and then press ENTER.

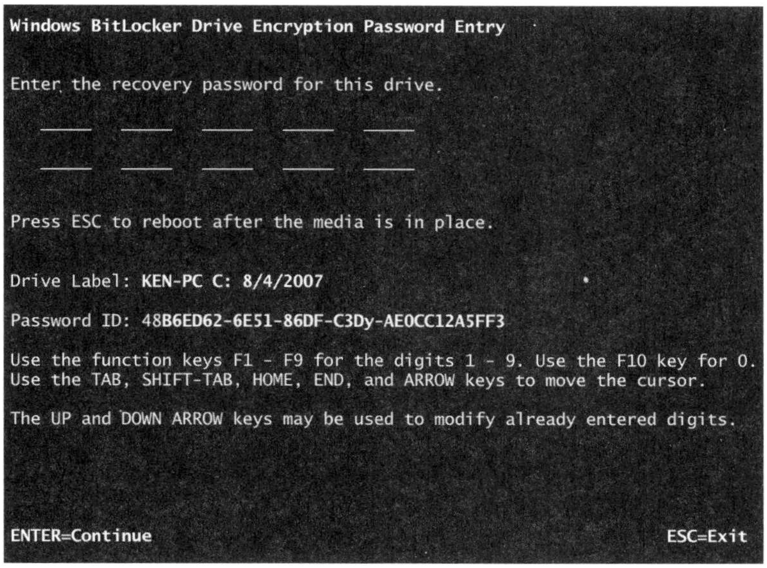

Figure 20-9

You can use the BitLocker password if you've lost your USB key.

Create a New USB Key to Replace a Lost Key

If your USB key is permanently lost (rather than having been, say, left at home or at work), you can create another key. Follow these steps:

1. Choose Start | Control Panel to display a Control Panel window.

2. If the Control Panel window is in Control Panel Home view (showing a list of major and minor headings), click the Classic View link in the upper-left corner to switch to Classic view.

3. Double-click the BitLocker Drive Encryption icon, and then go through User Account Control for the BitLocker Drive Encryption program (unless you've turned off User Account Control) to open a BitLocker Drive Encryption window.

4. Click the Manage BitLocker Keys link to display the Select Keys To Manage window.

5. Click the Duplicate The Startup Key link to display the Copy Startup Key screen.

6. Insert the USB key you want to use, select it in the list box, and then click the Save button.

Step 7: Decrypt a Disk That's Encrypted with BitLocker

If you decide that BitLocker is overkill for your protection needs, you can decrypt your hard disk again. To decrypt a disk, follow these steps:

1. Choose Start | Control Panel to display a Control Panel window.

2. If the Control Panel window is in Control Panel Home view (showing a list of major and minor headings), click the Classic View link in the upper-left corner to switch to Classic view.

3. Double-click the BitLocker Drive Encryption icon, and then go through User Account Control for the BitLocker Drive Encryption program (unless you've turned off User Account Control) to open a BitLocker Drive Encryption window.

4. Click the Turn Off BitLocker link to launch the BitLocker Drive Encryption Wizard, which displays the What Level Of Decryption Do You Want? screen shown next.

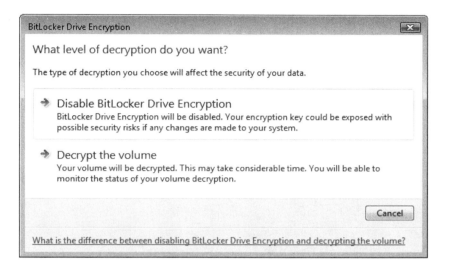

5. Click the Decrypt The Volume button to start the decryption. As with the encryption, decryption can take a while (for example, up to several hours). BitLocker displays a progress icon in the notification area to keep you informed.

 The other option, Disable BitLocker Drive Encryption, turns BitLocker off temporarily but does not decrypt the drive. The normal reason for using this option is to update your PC's BIOS. After updating, you would turn BitLocker on again.

6. When decryption is complete, BitLocker displays a message box telling you so. Click the Close button, and Windows is back to its normal, unencrypted self.

An Alternative to BitLocker and EFS for Other Versions of Windows

If you don't have Windows Vista Ultimate Edition (or Enterprise Edition), you can't use BitLocker. One alternative worth considering is TrueCrypt (www .truecrypt.org), which is free, open source software for encrypting disks. TrueCrypt works on Windows Vista, Windows XP, and Windows 2000.

Stream TV to Your PC or Handheld Device Anywhere

What You'll Need

- Hardware: Slingbox, broadband Internet connection or network with router
- Software: SlingPlayer (included with Slingbox)
- Cost: $200 U.S.

If you pay for cable TV or satellite TV, you'll probably want to make the most of it, especially if you have a digital video recorder (DVR) that makes it easy to record shows when the timing doesn't suit you. But making the most of TV usually means you have to be home at the time—unless you have a device that can grab the TV output and send it out across the Internet to wherever you happen to be.

This project shows you how to stream your TV to your PC or handheld computer using a Slingbox. You can still watch TV as usual after you connect the Slingbox, but you also have the option of watching it remotely. To see the full details of what the Slingbox can do, visit the Sling Media web site (www.slingmedia.com).

In addition to a Slingbox, you need a broadband Internet connection if you want to watch across the Internet (if you don't already have a broadband Internet connection, see Project 2 for a discussion of your options). If you're stuck with a slow connection, you can watch across your own network instead—for example, you can use your PC to watch a TV show being received by the TV or digital box downstairs.

Step I: Get and Connect the Slingbox

First, you need to buy, beg, or borrow a Slingbox. You've got a great chance of finding a Slingbox at your local electronics paradise, but you may prefer to take the easy way out and buy a Slingbox online. Once you have your Slingbox, connect it to your TV source following the instructions in the documentation that comes with the Slingbox. This documentation shows you all the possible configurations, but these are the main two:

- **Cable TV or satellite TV** Connect the Slingbox to the cable outlet to the set-top box, and then connect the TV to the Slingbox. Position the infrared emitter above or below the infrared sensor on your set-top box, and then connect the cable to the Slingbox. If your Slingbox has two infrared emitters rather than one, position one above the infrared sensor and one below it.

tip *Unless you're sure where the infrared sensor is on your set-top box, don't use the sticky strips on the infrared emitter or emitters to stick it (or them) down yet, because it will be hard to shift if you've chosen the wrong place. Instead, stick the infrared emitter down lightly with tape or with sticky tack, or just wedge it in place for the time being.*

- **Aerial** If you receive your TV signal via an aerial, connect the aerial to the Slingbox, and then connect the TV to the Slingbox.

Either way, the incoming signal goes through the Slingbox, so that it can process the signal and "sling" it out across your network or Internet connection. The Slingbox also passes the signal through to the TV, so that you can watch TV as usual.

You then connect the Slingbox to your home network. Ideally, you connect the Slingbox to your network's router or switch directly using an Ethernet cable. But if the router is in a separate room from the TV and Slingbox, you can use another technology, such as a wireless bridge or power-line networking. If you opt for power-line networking, consider buying a SlingLink or SlingLink Turbo kit, which are designed to work with the Slingbox.

Last, you plug the Slingbox's power adapter into the Slingbox and into an electrical socket.

Step 2: Install the SlingPlayer Software

When you've connected all the hardware, it's time to install the SlingPlayer software:

1. Insert the Slingbox CD in your PC's optical drive. Windows displays an AutoPlay dialog box.

note *If Windows doesn't display an AutoPlay dialog box, choose Start | Computer. Double-click the icon for the PC's optical drive to display the CD's contents, and then double-click the Launch item on the CD.*

2. Click the Run Launch.exe button. The Setup Wizard's opening screen appears.

3. Click the Install SlingPlayer button, and then to go through User Account Control for the SlingPlayerSetup program (unless you've turned off User Account Control). The wizard displays the Choose Setup Language dialog box.

4. Choose your language—for example, English (United States)—in the drop-down list, and then follow through the installation process. There's a license agreement that you must accept in order to proceed, and the wizard lets you choose where to install the software. Normally, the default destination folder (a Sling Media\SlingPlayer folder inside your PC's Program Files folder) is fine. If for some reason you want to use a different folder, click the Browse button, select the folder in the Choose Folder dialog box, and then click the OK button.

5. At the end of the installation process, the wizard offers to launch the Sling-Player program for you. If you haven't yet set up the Slingbox (as will be the case if you've just installed SlingPlayer on your first PC), decline this invitation, because you need to set up the Slingbox. But if you've installed SlingPlayer on a second or subsequent PC, accept this invitation, and move right along to Step 6.

Dealing with the "SlingPlayer Is Incompatible with This Version of Windows" Message

At this writing, some Slingbox models ship with a version of the SlingPlayer software that's compatible with Windows XP and Windows 2000 but incompatible with Windows Vista. If you install this older version of SlingPlayer on Windows Vista, you'll see a Program Compatibility Assistant dialog box the first time you try to run SlingPlayer (or when the Setup Wizard tries to run SlingPlayer for you):

Click the Cancel button, launch your web browser, and go to the Sling Media web site (www.slingmedia.com), where you can download a Windows Vista–compatible version of SlingPlayer. Install this version, and the problem should go away.

Step 3: Set Up the Slingbox

If you just completed Step 2, you should already be seeing the Slingbox Setup Wizard's first screen. If not, choose Start | All Programs | Sling Media | Slingbox Setup Wizard to launch the wizard.

Once you've got the wizard running, follow these steps to set up the Slingbox:

1. Make sure you've connected the hardware as described in Step 1. Verify that the two lights at the right end of the front of the Slingbox are on steadily rather than blinking.

2. Click the Next button. The wizard grabs the settings and displays the TV picture, as shown in Figure 21-1.

Figure 21-1

By the second screen of the wizard, you should be seeing a picture from your aerial or set-top box.

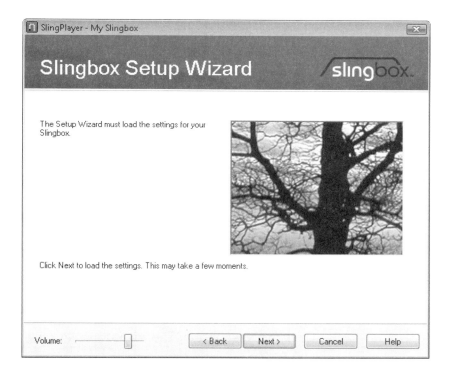

3. If necessary, adjust the volume by dragging the Volume slider. Then click the Next button.

4. If you see the Slingbox Update screen (see Figure 21-2), click the Next button, and wait while the wizard updates the Slingbox with new firmware. The update process may take several minutes, depending on the speed of your Internet connection. If the Slingbox fails to restart after a few minutes, click the Cancel button to close the Setup Wizard, and then choose Start | All Programs | Sling Media | Slingbox Setup Wizard to launch the wizard again.

Figure 21-2

The wizard tells you
if you need to update
your Slingbox with new
firmware.

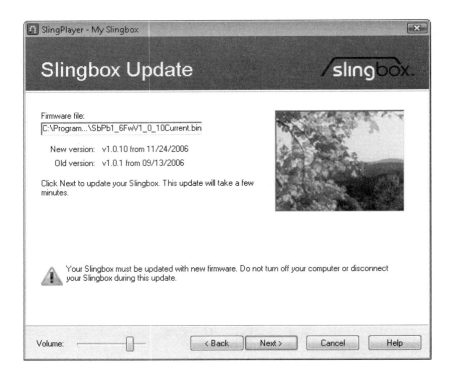

5. The Slingbox displays the Location Of Your Slingbox screen. Select your country in the Where Is Your Slingbox Located? list box, and then click the Next button. The wizard displays the Connection To Your Slingbox screen (see Figure 21-3), which shows the input the Slingbox is currently using.

6. If you're getting a TV picture on the installation screens, you shouldn't need to change the input (unless you have connected multiple inputs and are getting the picture from the wrong input). If you do need to change the input, click the appropriate jack, and make sure you get a picture.

7. Click the Next button. The wizard displays the Television Source screen (see Figure 21-4).

8. Select the type of device you're using, and then click the Next button. Unless you chose a noncontrollable device, the wizard displays the Device Brand screen.

9. Select the brand of device (or select Other if your device is not listed), and then click the Next button. If the wizard displays the Device Model screen, select the model (select Other if the model is not listed), and then click the Next button. The wizard displays the Control Code Setup screen (see Figure 21-5).

Figure 21-3

Tell the wizard which input you've connected the cable to.

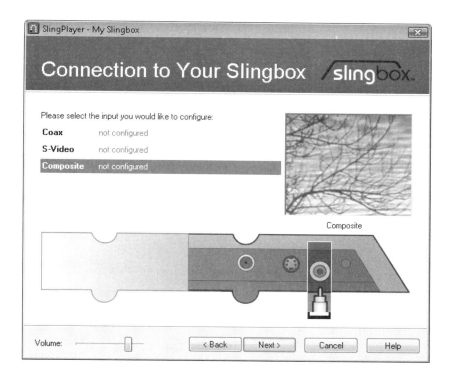

Figure 21-4

On the Television Source screen, tell the wizard what type of device the input is coming from.

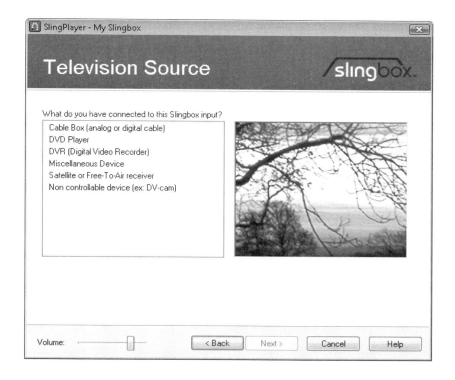

Figure 21-5

On the Control Code Setup screen, test that the device is receiving input from the Slingbox.

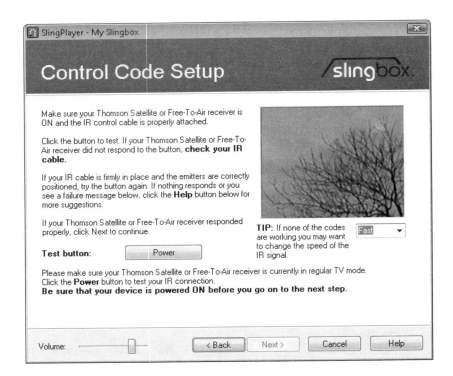

10. Verify that the infrared emitters are positioned over the infrared receiver, and then click the Power button on the Control Code Setup screen.

- If all is well, the device turns off, and you lose the signal; if so, click the Power button to turn the device on again.

- If the device doesn't respond to the signal, verify that the infrared cable is plugged firmly into the Slingbox. The easiest way to check is to unplug it, and then plug it in again.

- If the device still doesn't respond, try changing the IR (infrared) signal speed in the drop-down list on the right side of the Control Code Setup screen. The choices are Fast, Medium, and Slow.

- If changing the speed doesn't help, reposition the infrared emitters, and then try again.

tip *If you're not sure whether the emitter is sending a signal, you can check by using a digital camera that has a screen. Turn on the camera, aim its lens at the emitter so that you can see the emitter on the screen, and then give the command again via the Slingbox software. If the emitter is working, you will see a pulse of white light on the camera screen. (This pulse is invisible when viewed directly with the eye.)*

11. When the device is receiving input from the Slingbox, click the Next button. The wizard displays the Device Setup Complete screen.

note *From the Device Setup Complete screen, you can select the I Want To Set Up Another Device check box if you want to configure another device that you've connected to your Slingbox. Normally, you won't need to do this—at least, not the first time you set up the Slingbox.*

12. Click the Next button. The wizard displays the Name Your Slingbox screen.

13. Type a descriptive name for your Slingbox (making the name descriptive is especially important if you have more than one Slingbox), and then click the Next button. The wizard displays the Set Your Password screen.

14. In the Enter A Password For Your Slingbox area, type a password in both the Password text box and the Verify text box. This password is used to allow access to the Slingbox. You will share this password with anyone whom you allow to view content from the Slingbox.

15. In the Enter An Administrator Password area, type a password in both the Password text box and the Verify text box. This is the password you will need to enter to change the settings of the Slingbox, so make it a strong password and keep it to yourself.

The installation procedure continues in the next section, letting you set up remote viewing.

Step 4: Set Up Remote Viewing

Next, the Slingbox Setup Wizard lets you choose whether to set up remote viewing. You'll need to set up remote viewing if you want to use the Slingbox across your Internet connection. To set up remote viewing, follow these steps:

1. Click the Next button. The wizard displays the Remote Viewing screen (see Figure 21-6).

Figure 21-6

The Remote Viewing screen of the wizard lets you decide whether you want to set up a remote device now. Normally, you will want to do this.

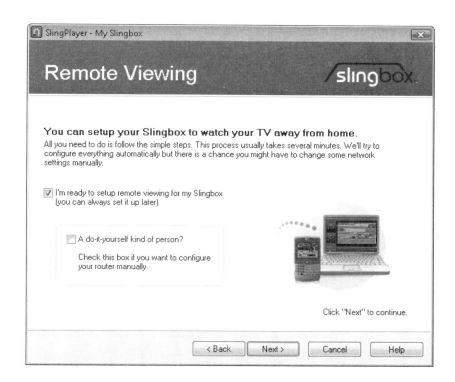

2. Make sure the I'm Ready To Setup Remote Viewing For My Slingbox check box is selected and that the A Do-It-Yourself Kind Of Person? check box is cleared. (If you prefer to use manual configuration, select the A Do-It-Yourself Kind Of Person? check box, and then go directly to Step 5.)

3. Click the Next button. The wizard attempts to detect your router, and then downloads any updates that are needed for configuring it.

4. If the wizard displays the Router/Modem Password dialog box, prompting you to enter the username and password for the router or modem, type them, and then click the OK button.

5. If the wizard announces it has configured your router automatically, you're all set. Skip the next step, and go right to Step 6. If the wizard displays the Remote Viewing – Manual Configuration screen, telling you that your router cannot be automatically configured, go to the next step.

Step 5: Configure Your Router Manually

If the wizard wasn't able to configure your router automatically, you need to configure it manually:

1. Select the Manually Configure Your Router option button, and then click the Next button. The wizard displays the second Remote Viewing – Manual Configuration screen, which is shown in Figure 21-7.

Figure 21-7

The second Remote Viewing – Manual Configuration screen lets you get a tutorial on your router. When you're ready, you can access the Slingbox network settings to change them manually.

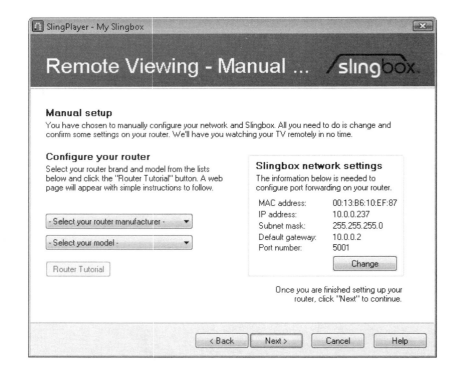

2. To get a tutorial on configuring your router, choose the manufacturer and model in the two drop-down lists on the left side of the screen, and then click the Router Tutorial button. The wizard opens the tutorial in a browser window.

 If the Setup Wizard doesn't offer a configuration tutorial for your router model, consult the router's documentation.

3. When you've learned how to configure the router, click the Change button in the Slingbox Network Settings group box. The wizard displays the third Remote Viewing – Manual Configuration screen, shown in Figure 21-8.

Figure 21-8

On the third Remote Viewing – Manual Configuration screen, apply the network settings required to get the Slingbox working with your router.

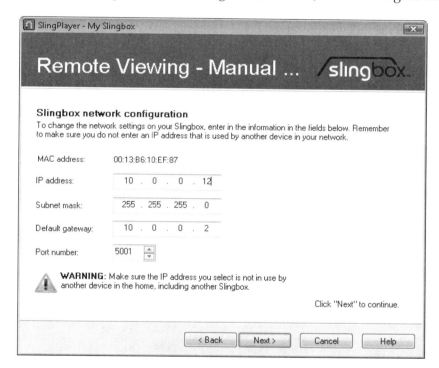

4. Type the IP address for the Slingbox in the IP Address text box. The IP address needs to be unique on your network—each computer, Slingbox, or other device must have its own IP address. In a typical network configuration, this is the item of information that you will need to change.

5. Enter the subnet mask in the Subnet Mask text box. The subnet mask will be the same for each device on the network. For most home networks, the subnet mask is 255.255.255.0. The Slingbox normally detects the subnet mask correctly.

6. Enter the IP address of your router in the Default Gateway text box. This is the internal IP address of your router, the one that is part of your local network. (The router also has an external IP address for its connection to the Internet.)

7. In the Port Number text box, enter the port number that the Slingbox should use.

8. Click the Next button. The wizard applies the settings to the Slingbox and returns you to the second Remote Viewing – Manual Configuration screen.

9. Click the Next button. The wizard displays the fourth Remote Viewing – Manual Configuration screen, on which you confirm the router configuration.

10. Make sure the Yes! My Router Is Now Configured option button is selected, and then click the Next button. The wizard displays the Setup Confirmation screen.

11. Click the Next button. The wizard saves your settings and then tests the remote connection.

12. If you see the Activate Remote Viewing screen shown in Figure 21-9, telling you that "The Slingbox can not be reached from the Internet," follow these steps:

    ● Select the Try Again option button, and then click the Next button. The wizard tries the connection again. If it establishes the connection, you're done.

    ● If the wizard displays the "The Slingbox can not be reached from the Internet" screen again, select the Change Network/Router Settings option button, click the Next button, and go back to step 1 in this list. Change the router settings, and then apply them. Again, if the wizard establishes the connection, you're done.

Figure 21-9

If you see this screen, use the Try Again option button to try the connection again. If that doesn't work, select the Change Network/ Router Settings button, and then change the router settings.

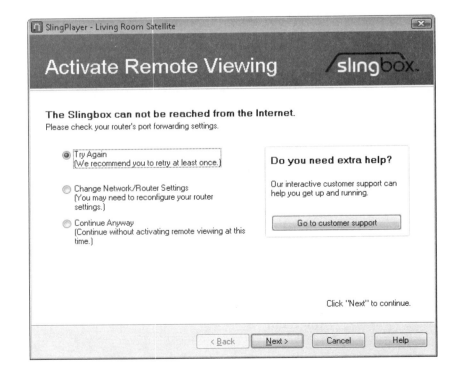

● If the wizard displays the "The Slingbox can not be reached from the Internet" screen a third time, try the Try Again option button once more. If that doesn't work, select the Continue Anyway option button, and then click the Next button to reach the end of the wizard.

Step 6: Watch TV on Your PC via the Slingbox

Finally, you're ready to watch TV on your PC via the Slingbox. Follow these steps:

1. Choose Start | All Programs | Sling Media | Launch SlingPlayer. SlingPlayer opens and automatically displays the Slingbox Directory dialog box, which lists the available Slingboxes, as shown here.

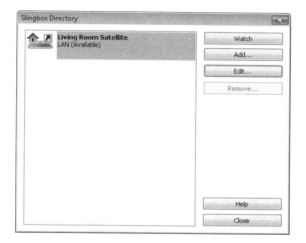

2. Select the Slingbox you want to watch (if there's only one, SlingPlayer will have selected it for you automatically), and then click the Watch button. SlingPlayer displays the Password dialog box, shown here.

3. Type the password in the Please Enter The Password Below text box.

note *Select the Log In As Administrator check box only if you want to log on to the Slingbox to change its configuration rather than to watch its output.*

4. If you want to save the password so that you don't need to enter it in future, select the Save This Password In My Profile check box.

5. Click the Connect button. SlingPlayer connects to the Slingbox and displays its current channel in a window, together with a remote control (see Figure 21-10).

Figure 21-10

SlingPlayer displays a window with a remote control that you can click to control playback.

Minimize   Maximize

Dock Left   Dock Right   Close

6. To reposition or resize the SlingPlayer window, click the Dock Left button, the Dock Right button, or the Maximize button.

7. Click the buttons on the remote control to control playback.

8. When you have finished watching, click the Close button or choose Player | Exit.

note *If you have multiple Slingboxes, you can connect to another Slingbox by choosing Slingbox | Slingbox Directory (or pressing ALT-D), choosing the Slingbox in the Slingbox Directory dialog box, and then clicking the Watch button.*

Project 22

Silence Your PC or Build an Ultra-Quiet PC

What You'll Need

- Hardware: Assorted PC components (each optional, depending on your PC), digital camera (optional)
- Software: None
- Cost: $100–1500 U.S.

Silence is golden. Eloquence is silver. (Some people assert that duct tape is silver too, because it can produce that golden silence.) And trying to concentrate and perform complex work in a noisy environment can be the trigger for the reddest of rages.

This project explains which components in your PC tend to make the noise and shows you how to deal with each of them in turn. What exactly you can do to hush your PC depends on what type of PC it is and how much time, effort, and money you're prepared to put into it.

You know the old saw about "I have my grandfather's ax. My father replaced the handle, and I replaced the blade"? Well, quieting your PC can be like that. It's probably not worth your while to replace every single noise-making component in your PC. So you'll most likely want to listen to the noise coming from your PC, decide which of the silencing operations described in this project will make the most difference, and then work through the steps for those operations.

The end of the project looks briefly at the quick and easy—but expensive—solution: buying a fully silenced PC from a specialist manufacturer. That silence will cost you gold, but you may decide it's a price worth paying.

note *The focus of this project is mostly desktop PCs. If your laptop PC is noisy, there's usually not much you can do about it besides replacing the hard drive with a quieter model; connecting an external keyboard, mouse, and monitor; and placing the laptop as far from you as possible. See Project 7 for instructions on replacing the hard drive in a laptop.*

Step 1: Understand Which PC Components Make the Noise—and Which You Can Silence

In any group of people, you'll usually find several movers and shakers, and it's much the same inside your PC. Here's a quick summary of the usual culprits:

- **Power supply**   Most power supplies have noisy cooling fans that run constantly.

- **Processor fan**   This is the fan that sits on top of the processor and keeps it from melting. Almost all current PC processors run so hot that they need cooling all the time.

- **Fans**   Most PCs have one or more fans to expel warm air from the case and bring in cooler air from outside it.

- **Hard drive**   The hard drive spins at several thousand revolutions per minute all the time you're using the PC. But there is an alternative, described later in this project.

- **Graphics card**   Many higher-powered graphics cards include a cooling fan. Some include two fans. These fans are usually small—and small fans tend to be noisier, because they need to spin faster than larger fans to shift a worthwhile volume of air. To make matters worse, some high-performance PCs have two of these noisy graphics cards.

- **Case**   Normally, your PC's case should be lessening the noise the PC makes. But some cases vibrate noisily because of all the vibrating components in them.

Finding Ultra-Quiet, Silent, and Silencing Components for Your PC

Here are three web sites to consult when you're looking for ultra-quiet, silent, and silencing components for your PC:

- **Quiet PC (www.quietpc.com)**   Sells a wide variety of parts, together with full explanations of what they do and what they're good for. You can also visit the forums to find installation instructions.

- **EndPCNoise.com (www.endpcnoise.com)**   Sells a wide array of quiet PC parts.

- **Silent PC Review (www.silentpcreview.com)**   Reviews silent and ultra-quiet components and is a great source of information. This web site doesn't sell products, but it does link to manufacturer and affiliate sites, pointing you in the right direction for finding the components you need.

Step 2: Identify the Culprits and Open Your PC

Now that you know which components may be rowdy, examine your PC and try to identify the culprits. The PC must be running to make its noises, so start by seeing what you can determine with the case closed:

- You'll be able to tell immediately if the power supply is noisy by placing your ear close to it. The same goes for the case fan or fans.

- You'll definitely be able to tell if the optical drive is noisy, because there will be a whooshing noise when you start running a program or opening a document from a CD or DVD.

- If the case is vibrating, that should be pretty obvious too—especially if you can stop the noise by putting your fingers or hand against the case.

- The hard drive will be spinning all the time the PC is running (unless you've configured the hard drive to go to sleep after a period of inactivity), so it will normally make a constant noise.

- A whining or buzzing when you play demanding games may indicate that the graphics card gets loud when you work it hard—but as the processor will probably be working hard, you may not easily be able to tell which of the two is the offender.

- Much of the remaining noise will come from the processor fan.

Now open your PC (as discussed next) to work out what's making the noise inside the case. (If your PC won't run while the case is open, see the Note.)

note *Some PCs check their case integrity on bootup and refuse to boot if the case is open. This can be a good security measure, but it's a menace when you're trying to reduce the noise your PC makes. If your PC performs this integrity check, look in the BIOS for instructions on disabling it temporarily while you work on silencing the PC. (See Project 6 for instructions on accessing your PC's BIOS.) If you are not able to disable the integrity check in the BIOS, you may need to work component by component—replace the power supply if you think it is noisy, and then see how much the noise level has dropped; change the processor fan if that seems loud, and then check the noise level again; and so on. This is not a great way to proceed, so you may want to explore alternatives, such as removing the cover for an unused drive bay and poking in a microphone on a stick or straightened clothes-hanger to determine how much noise an individual component is making. If you choose to do this, use a flashlight to see what you're doing, and make sure not to touch any component.*

Open Your PC

For most of the remaining steps in this project, you need to open your PC's case. To do so, follow these general steps. The specifics will vary depending on your PC's case and configuration.

1. Shut down Windows, turn off your PC, and disconnect all the cables.

2. Put your PC on a table or other suitable surface.

3. Open the side opposite the motherboard. For example, you may need to undo a latch, unscrew a couple of thumb-screws (the knurled kind you turn with your fingers), or unscrew case screws with a screwdriver.

4. Touch a metal part of the PC's case to discharge any static electricity from your body before you touch any of the electro-sensitive components (that's most of them).

You're now ready to work on the PC's internals.

Step 3: Silence Your PC's Power Supply

The power supply is one area where laptops, with their external power bricks that cool themselves by convection, score over desktop PCs. Many desktop PCs come with noisy power supplies. That's because the power supply is one of the less exciting components of a PC. Provided it can deliver the required wattage, many manufacturers use as inexpensive a power supply as possible to help keep costs down. After all, they're involved in an ongoing price war. (Think back…when you ordered your last PC, did you have a choice of power supply? Chances are that you didn't. If you did, you were dealing with a quality PC manufacturer—and you may want to use them again.) If the power supply hums, whines, or buzzes, too bad—even if the customers whine even louder.

If your PC's power supply is noisy, there's good news: There are plenty of ultra-quiet power supplies on the market. Better news: There are even some silent power supplies (but they cost a bit more). Better news still: Replacing a power supply is far easier than most people think.

Buy a Quiet or Silent Power Supply

First, buy the power supply—or maybe scavenge an old power supply from that ancient PC you retired a couple of years back that used to run so quietly.

Next, check the wattage your PC's current power supply delivers. The easiest way to get the right wattage is to get a replacement power supply with the same wattage. If you're lucky, you'll find the wattage written on the part of the power supply that shows through the case or shows when the case is open; if not, you may need to remove the power supply to find the wattage written on a surface that was hidden.

The following list shows typical wattages for different types of PC:

PC Type	Wattage Range
Conventional PC	250–400W
Performance PC	500W or more
Economical PC	200W or less

The wattage on a power supply is the maximum amount of power it can supply; it doesn't draw that amount of power all the time. So if you put a higher-wattage power supply in your PC, the PC won't suddenly start using more electricity than it used to—it will just have the capacity to use more electricity if you add more power-hungry components.

You have two main options when looking to bring down the amount of noise your PC's power supply makes:

- **Quieter power supply** Look for a power supply described as "quiet" or "semi-fanless" (or both). Quiet power supplies are ones designed to make less noise, usually by using a larger, slower-moving fan rather than a smaller, faster-moving fan. "Semi-fanless" power supplies run their fans only when necessary rather than running them the whole time (as standard power supplies do). Look for a noise level of 30 decibels or less.

- **Silent power supply** If you're prepared to pay a bit more, you can get not just a "semi-fanless" power supply but one that is actually fanless and contains no moving parts. A silent power supply typically has a *heat sink* that projects beyond your PC's case and transfers the heat to the outside, like a miniature radiator. Most such power supplies are rated at 0 decibels—they produce no noise at all. (In truth, some may hum a bit as they get warm. But so may you.) Figure 22-1 shows a fanless power supply.

Figure 22-1

Unlike fanless rock bands, fanless power supplies make no noise. The heat sink protrudes beyond the PC's case and transfers heat to the outside.

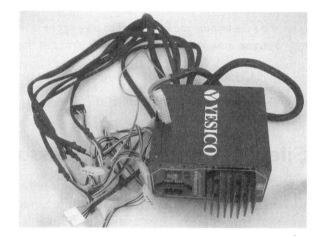

Replace the Power Supply

To replace the power supply in your PC, follow these steps:

1. Shut down Windows, and then open your PC as discussed in Step 2.

2. Optionally, take pictures of how the power cables are connected, to make it easier to connect the cables afterward. Alternatively, make a list or draw a diagram.

3. Unplug each connector in turn. Remember to release any retaining clips and to use patience rather than force for any stubborn connector.

caution *There may be connectors that you can't see—or can see but can't unplug—as long as the power supply is in place. For example, the connector that delivers power to the motherboard is often obscured or made unreachable by the power supply. Be prepared to have to unplug another connector while you're removing the power supply. If the cables are short, having an assistant to provide an extra pair of hands is helpful.*

4. Unscrew the screws that hold the power supply in place:

   ● Start with the screws that are farthest down, judging from the way the PC is lying or standing. For example, in a tower PC that's lying on its left side (seen from the back), the screws on the right side of the power supply are at the top—so start with the ones on the left side.

   ● The power supply is heavy enough to damage any component it lands on, so be sure to support it as soon as it's loose.

   ● If, when you start to move the power supply, you see another connector that's still connected, either park the power supply somewhere safe, or have someone help you juggle the power supply and the cable.

5. Remove the power supply, and then set it aside.

6. Insert the new power supply, and then screw it firmly into place.

note *Depending on the PC's layout, you may need to plug in one or more cables before you insert the power supply, because otherwise the power supply obscures the connections.*

7. Connect the power cables, using your photo, diagram, or list for reference.

8. Close the PC, reconnect the cables, and fire it up.

Step 4: Silence Your PC's Processor Fan

The power supply at least has the common decency to throw most of the heat it produces out of the PC's case. But the cooling fan for your PC's processor simply removes the heat from the processor and distributes it around the inside of the case—which probably already has more than enough heat of its own, thank you. (Additionally, if your PC has two processors, it will produce that much more heat.)

If you've determined that the processor fan makes more noise than you're prepared to tolerate, replace it. Various types of quiet processor coolers and silent coolers are available:

● **Quiet processor coolers** These coolers typically use a heat sink combined with a large-diameter, variable-speed fan and are powerful enough to cool even the hottest processors. Figure 22-2 shows an example of a quiet processor cooler.

Figure 22-2

Quiet processor coolers normally combine a heat-sink with a large-bladed fan that can run at variable speeds. Many quiet processor coolers are large, like the one in the middle of this picture.

Processor cooler's fan   Processor cooler

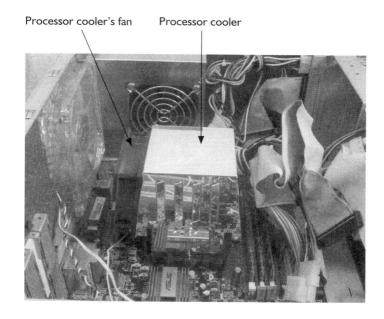

● **Silent processor coolers** These coolers typically use either a heat sink cooled by convection or a liquid-cooled heat sink. Convection-cooled heat sinks can be large, like the Scythe Ninja Plus model shown in Figure 22-3, but usually do not deliver enough cooling capacity to cool the hottest processors.

Figure 22-3

For silent cooling, it's hard to beat a convection-cooled heat sink—provided there's enough space in your PC, and that its processor doesn't run too hot.

caution *Water-cooling systems are complex and are best left to enthusiasts. As you can imagine, a leak in a water-cooling system can hose your PC in two senses.*

The best way to find a cooler is to check what type of CPU your PC has, and then use a site such as Quiet PC or EndPCNoise.com to see which coolers will fit. You can find the CPU type in the PC's documentation or from the BIOS, but you may find it more convenient to use CPU-Z (see Step 1 of Project 1). The CPU tab of CPU-Z shows the processor's name and package type near the top of the Processor group box (see Figure 22-4).

Figure 22-4

CPU-Z provides an easy
way to check which
processor and package
type your PC has.

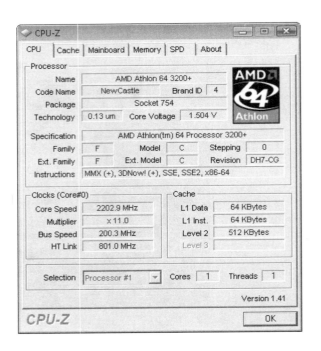

caution   *Most replacement processor fans come with comprehensive instructions; if not, you can find ad-*
vice online. However, replacing the processor fan is one task for which you might want to involve
a hardware professional. If you get the replacement operation wrong, not only may the new fan
get wrecked, but the processor may overheat and ruin itself and your PC's motherboard.

After installing the processor cooler (or, preferably, having it installed profes-
sionally), check the processor's temperature periodically to make sure the cooler is
cooling it enough. If the cooler has an adjustable-speed fan, set it to a moderately
high speed at first, let your PC run for a while, and then check the temperature. If
the processor is remaining cool, turn the fan down a bit, let the PC run again, and
then check the temperature once more. Continue this cycle to establish the lowest fan
speed at which you can safely run the PC without the processor nearing the top of its
temperature range.

There are two main ways to check the processor's temperature. Ideally, your PC
includes a Windows utility like that shown in Figure 22-5, which allows you to keep
an eye on measurements such as the CPU temperature, motherboard temperature,
CPU fan speed, power fan speed, chassis fan speed, and more. Failing that, you may
have to restart your PC, access the BIOS, and find the information there, which is
far less convenient. For example, in an AMIBIOS, you can typically go to the Power
tab, select the Hardware Monitor item, and then press ENTER to display the Hardware
Monitor screen.

Figure 22-5

Your PC may include a monitoring utility that enables you to keep an eye on the CPU temperature easily and warns you when it exceeds the thresholds.

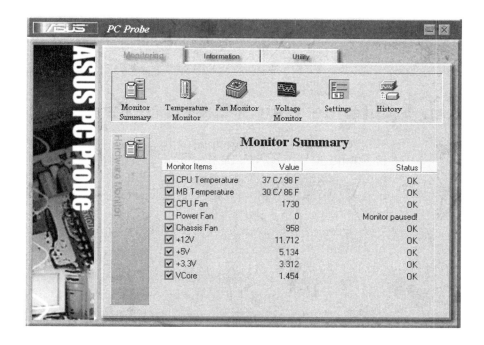

Step 5: Silence Your PC's Cooling Fans

The next source of noise you should consider tackling is your PC's cooling fan or fans. Your PC may have one fan, two, or more. Usually, you'll find one mounted on the back of the PC to pull warm air out of the case. Many tower PCs also have a cooling fan on the front to draw cool air into the case and create a better airflow.

Take a look at your PC's fans, and listen to try to pick out the amount of noise they're making. If they're audible, grab a ruler and measure them. Your PC needs to draw plenty of air from outside the case to keep its inside cool, and the best way to provide this air quietly is by using larger fans that can shift plenty of air at a lower rotational speed. But the chances are that your PC has smaller fans that need to run at a high speed to shift enough air, thus making a good deal of noise.

A 120mm fan (about five inches—roughly the size of a regular CD) at the front and back of the case should provide plenty of cooling for a conventional PC. If your PC is loaded with everything but the kitchen sink, you might need even more cooling than that.

note *To fit larger cooling fans, you may need to cut holes in your PC's case. See Project 11 for information on which tools to use and instructions on installing a fan.*

If your case won't accommodate 120mm fans (even with modifications), look to use multiple 80mm fans running at low speeds. Quiet-component sites offer low-noise fans that cost a little more than regular fans but provide such a reduction in noise that paying extra is a no-brainer. Such sites also sell variable-speed fan controllers that let you adjust the fan's speed by turning a knob on the outside of the PC.

Whichever type of fan you buy, also buy nonvibration mounts that help prevent the fan from transferring its vibrations to the PC's case, even when the fan is running at higher speeds.

Step 6: Silence Your PC's Hard Drive

Next on the list of noisy components is your PC's hard drive (or drives—if your PC has multiple drives, it'll be that much louder). Conventional hard drives rotate continuously unless the PC remains unused long enough for the drive to go to sleep. That means you hear the noise all the time when you're using the PC, plus some when you're not.

If you use a conventional hard drive in your PC, you can do two main things to make it quieter:

- **Dampen the drive's noise**   To reduce the amount of noise the drive makes, you can encase it in a silencing jacket (see Figure 22-6). And to make sure that the drive's vibration doesn't make the case vibrate as well, you can put vibration-absorbing mounts between the drive and the PC's case.

Figure 22-6

A silencing jacket can make a dramatic difference to even a noisy, high-performance drive. The noise of a quiet drive will almost disappear—which is great.

- **Use a quiet drive**   Just as some power supplies are quieter than others, so are some hard drives quieter than others—some by accident, but the best by design. The quietest hard drives tend to use fluid bearings rather than metal bearings and tend to spin at 7200 RPM rather than at a faster speed. You'll find recommendations for quiet hard drives at the quiet-PC sites mentioned earlier in this project. At this writing, the Samsung Spinpoint T series and the Seagate Barracuda 7200.10 series are widely available quiet drives.

Making Your PC's Hard Drive Completely Silent

All hard drives that use spinning magnetic platters make some noise. But there's another type of hard drive that doesn't have moving parts, and thus is silent. This type of drive is a solid-state device based on flash memory. You'll see these drives referred to as *flash hard drives, solid state drives (SSDs),* or *flash SSDs.* These drives are much more shock-resistant than regular hard drives, provide better performance, require less power to run, and should last for a long time. However, they are far more expensive than conventional hard drives, so their use has historically been confined to high-end ultra-portable laptops. Major manufacturers including Dell, Sony, and Apple now offer flash SSDs in some laptop models—at a hefty price premium.

SSDs are relatively new, and until now their capacities have been far smaller than those of comparable conventional drives. However, the technology is evolving fast. At this writing, 64GB flash hard drives are available in the 2.5-inch form factor used in most laptops, and drives of 256GB or more are available in the 3.5-inch form factor used by most desktops. Desktop drives of 512GB and larger should be available in the first quarter of 2008—and with luck, prices will begin to descend to affordable levels.

If the money is burning its way through your pocket, you can find some flash SSDs at online computer stores such as CDW Corp. (www.cdw.com). To find a wider variety, news, and evangelical enthusiasm, visit a specialist site such as DVNation (www.dvnation.com).

Step 7: Silence Your PC's Graphics Card

When the vendor promised your PC would deliver screaming graphics, you probably thought more in terms of getting a higher frame rate in BioShock than in terms of having a shrill whine assailing your ears the whole time…but you got both. If the graphics card is making noise that bothers you, do something about it. You may be able to replace the graphics card's existing fan with a quieter model. But if you really want to bring the noise level down, look for a graphics card that uses a heat pipe rather than a fan for cooling. Figure 22-7 shows an example.

You may have to sacrifice some performance and pay a little more, but you will probably be surprised at the powerful but silent graphics cards that are available from the silence-specialist sites.

Once you've bought your replacement graphics card, replace it by following these general steps:

1. Shut down Windows, and then open your PC as discussed in Step 2.

2. Unscrew the retaining screw holding the graphics card in place.

3. Remove the card. You may need to wiggle it gently from side to side to loosen it.

Figure 22-7

A graphics card cooled
by a heat pipe eliminates
the noise made by a fan.

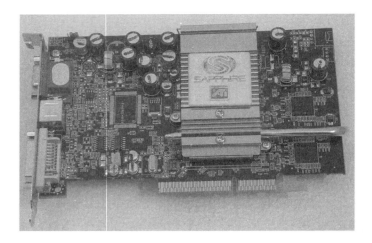

4. Insert the new card, making sure that there's enough room for its heat pipe or other cooling equipment. (In some PCs, you may have to move an existing card to a different slot to make room for the graphics card.)

5. Screw in the retaining screw.

6. Close the PC, reconnect the cables, and then start it.

Step 8: Replace the Optical Drive with a Quieter Model

If your PC's optical drive is noisy, and you need to use it often, you can almost certainly find a quieter replacement from one of the sources mentioned in the sidebar near the start of this project. Technology is constantly marching onward, so look for a drive with similar or better features than your current drive has—but buy behind the cutting edge to get value for your money.

note *This step is near the end of the project because it typically offers less bang reduction for the buck than the other steps. Unless your PC's optical drive is absurdly noisy, or you use it frequently, replacing it with a quieter model probably won't make financial sense. But if you're considering buying a new optical drive for your PC anyway, or if you're buying components for a new PC, you should definitely shop around to find a quiet model.*

To replace the optical drive, follow these general steps. The specifics will depend on your model of PC and optical drive.

1. Shut down Windows, and then open your PC as discussed in Step 2.

2. Disconnect the drive cable and the power cable from the optical drive. For some models, you may need to disconnect an audio cable as well.

3. Unscrew the retaining screws, and then slide the drive out of the PC.

4. Slide the new drive in, and then screw in the retaining screws.

5. Connect the cables you disconnected from the old drive.

6. Close the PC, reconnect the cables, and then start it.

Step 9: Bring Down the Noise Level with a Sound-Absorbing Case or Foam

Unless you've gone the whole hog (with cheese fries) by choosing silenced and fanless components throughout your PC, it is still making some noise. Most likely, the hard drive is grumbling mutedly within its full-metal straitjacket, and the processor fan is sighing gently like a fresh breeze in the lilacs toward the end of a spring day. But that still adds up to some noise that you don't want in your workplace, so you need a sound-absorbing case that confines the noise within the case as much as possible. (If you haven't worked through several of the steps in this project and are stuck with a loud hard drive that makes your PC's case buzz, a sound-absorbing case will probably seem a great idea.)

You have two main choices for keeping the sound within the case and muffling it as much as possible:

- Line your existing case with acoustic foam.

- Move your whole PC to a new, sound-absorbing case.

Let's look at the easier alternative first.

Line Your PC's Case with Acoustic Foam

PC-quietening sites such as those mentioned near the beginning of this project sell acoustic foam kits for silencing PCs. You stick sheets of foam to the case sides, floor, and roof—avoiding the components—and stuff acoustic foam blocks into empty drive bays. Figure 22-8 shows part of a case side with acoustic foam applied to it.

Figure 22-8

Lining your PC's case with acoustic foam helps absorb noise. Unless you buy a precut kit designed for your PC's case, you need to cut around latches (as shown here) and other obstacles.

Cutting the foam sheets to the size you need and sticking them down neatly can take an hour or so, but it typically makes a big difference in the amount of noise that comes out through the case.

You may also want to add antivibration feet to the PC's underside to prevent it from transmitting vibrations to your desk, which can act as a sounding board.

Choose a Sound-Absorbing Case

If you're planning a new PC, you can save some time and effort by buying a case that comes with a custom kit of acoustic foam pieces that are cut to fit it. For example, you can buy a quiet case such as the Antec Sonata II (which comes with a quiet power supply and quiet case fan) with a custom AcoustiPack kit from retailers such as EndPCNoise.com. Or you can go for one of the AcoustiCase line of cases from Quiet PC.

If you want a totally silent PC rather than a very quiet PC, you need to step up your budget to the next level and buy a silenced case such as one in the Zalman TNN series. TNN stands for Totally No Noise, and the cases live up to this by being built as large radiators. Each heat-producing component is cooled with a heat sink, and the heat is conducted to the outside of the case, where it is dissipated through fins.

The TNN cases are heavy—one model weighs 57 lb even before you add a motherboard and hard drive—and work best with specific motherboards and graphics cards (Zalman provides a list). They are also very expensive. But if you need a silent PC, a TNN case can be a great solution. Figure 22-9 shows a TNN 500AF case, which retails for around $1500.

Figure 22-9

The Zalman TNN series of cases uses advanced cooling techniques to keep your PC silent.

Move Your PC to the New Case

How exactly you move your existing PC's components to the new case depends on the model of case you buy and what components your PC consists of. If you're not comfortable working with your PC's motherboard, consider bribing a geek friend or paying for a technician to do the work for you. Even if their hourly rates are painful, they'll probably be less so than the cost of replacing expensive components that you wreck by accident.

Step 10: Buy an Ultra-Quiet or Silenced PC

As you've seen in the previous steps, you can spend a bunch of money and effort in silencing your PC. But if you have money rather than effort to spare, you can—as usual in this world of ours—have someone else do the heavy lifting for you by simply buying an ultra-quiet PC or a fully silenced PC. Here are two manufacturers of ultra-quiet PCs:

- **Hush Technologies** Hush Technologies (www.hushtechnologies.com) builds several ranges of silent PCs designed for various purposes, including entertainment, business, and medical. The Hush PCs use technologies such as those discussed earlier in this project to keep noise down to a minimum. For example, most of the PCs use heat pipes rather than fans to cool the processor and the graphics card, enclose the hard drive in an antivibration chassis, and use fanless power supplies. In addition, the entire case is designed to cool the PC by convection, much like the Zalman TNN case that you saw earlier in this project.

- **EndPCNoise.com** In addition to selling quiet PC components, EndPC-Noise.com also sells a range of completely quiet PC systems, ranging from value PCs to gaming PCs, "Powerhouse" PCs, and digital audio workstations. EndPCNoise.com uses quiet components throughout—quiet hard drives, quiet processor coolers, fanless video cards, and so on—together with a variety of muffled and silenced cases.

The prices of ultra-quiet or silenced PCs are high compared to those of normal, noisy PCs, but if you can afford the price, you will be repaid by tranquility and—with luck and diligence—increased productivity.

Run Other Operating Systems on Top of Windows

What You'll Need

- Hardware: Nothing except your existing PC
- Software: Microsoft Virtual PC, other OSes
- Cost: Free to $300 U.S.

So far, this book has largely assumed that you're running Windows on your PC— either Windows Vista (which is gearing up to celebrate its first birthday at this writing) or Windows XP (which is still celebrating the fact that Windows Vista has so far failed to displace it on many PCs). As you know, Windows is your PC's *operating system* or *OS*—the software that makes the hardware do something useful rather than simply sit there as intricate and expensive shapes of silicon, carbon, and steel. And most computers come with Windows, just like yours did. But what if you need to run another OS on your PC? Or simply want to?

This project shows you the possibilities for running another operating system—or several other OSes—on top of Windows. The next project shows you how to install another OS on your PC so that you can run either that OS or Windows (but not both at the same time).

First, though, let's deal with the $64,000 question: Do you need to run another OS at all?

Step I: Decide Which OSes You Need to Run

Maybe you're scratching your head and saying, "But I've got Windows already—and it seems to be working fine. Why ever would I want to run another OS?" The usual reason for running another OS is so that you can run some software that won't run on your main OS. For example, say you have a favorite game from back in the days of

Windows 95, when the underlying software architecture of Windows was substantially different from it its present form. That game might not run on Windows Vista, even if you use the Program Compatibility Assistant to apply supposedly suitable compatibility settings. If so, you're stuck—unless you find a way of running Windows 95.

You may also want to try another OS out of curiosity—or to save money. For example, you've probably heard a lot about Linux, the open source OS that you can download and install for free. Maybe you'd like to try it and find out whether it's suitable for you, either on your main PC or on an old PC, but without wiping out your current OS, which would be more collateral damage than you can accept.

Step 2: Decide How to Run Those OSes

As you know, a PC typically runs a single OS. Unless you buy a Mac or buy a PC from a specialist vendor, chances are that your PC's OS is Windows—and most likely the latest version. So if you buy a new PC at this writing, you're most likely to get Windows Vista as your OS.

That doesn't mean you're stuck with Windows Vista (or whichever version of Windows you got). You have three options (the last of which is the focus of this project):

- **Install another OS on your PC instead** Usually, when you install a new OS, it overwrites or otherwise replaces the existing OS. If you want to do this, typically you simply insert the installation media for the new OS (for example, by putting a DVD in your PC's optical drive), restart the PC, accept the BIOS's invitation to start the PC from the optical drive, and then follow the prompts for installing the OS. However, you more likely want to install a new OS on your PC without preventing the current OS from operating successfully. This is possible with the following options.

- **Create a dual-boot setup on your PC** In a dual-boot setup, you typically create two separate partitions, or areas, on your hard disk, and then install a different OS on each. Using separate partitions keeps the OSes from interfering with each other. In a dual-boot setup, you can run only one OS at a time. Project 24 shows you how to create dual-boot (and multiboot) setups.

- **Run virtual-machine software** Virtual-machine software, also called PC-emulation software, is a program that runs on your existing OS (for example, Windows) like other programs, and through software imitates the behavior of a PC's hardware. You can then run a separate OS on the virtual-machine software. Read on to learn more about this option.

Step 3: Understand What Virtual-Machine Software Is and What It Does

A virtual-machine program installs on Windows much like any other program, except that it puts some deep hooks (that's actually a technical word, but it's descriptive in its normal meaning too) into Windows to allow it to perform the clever tricks that enable it to emulate a PC.

Once you've installed the virtual-machine program, you install an OS on it—just as you would install the OS on actual hardware, except that in the virtual machine, all the hardware is emulated. You then run the OS on the virtual machine. The virtual machine operates largely like a regular PC, except that it's actually running inside a program in Windows—so you can use both Windows and the OS on the virtual machine at the same time.

note *Most virtual-machine programs let you run one or more other OSes at once. Generally speaking, the more OSes you run at once, the slower each of them runs. So unless you need to run multiple OSes at the same time within the virtual machine, it's normally best to run only one at a time.*

As you might guess, virtual machines have some disadvantages:

- Running a virtual machine is almost always slower than running the same OS "natively" (directly) on the same hardware. But if you have a reasonably fast PC with plenty of memory (RAM), performance should be adequate. (More on this in a moment—and look back to Project 1 if your PC needs more RAM.)

- There are some limitations to what you can do with virtual machines. For example, audio and video performance ranges from unacceptable to truly pitiful, so don't plan any demanding multimedia activities such as recording audio, processing video, or watching TV on a virtual machine. However, for less demanding programs, such as word processing or e-mail, virtual machines can be an adequate solution. For example, if you need to run a Linux program on a Windows PC so that you can avoid buying an expensive Windows program, a virtual machine can be a neat way of saving money and working around the problem.

- You can't install OSes designed for other types of computers. For example, you can't install Mac OS X on a virtual machine on a PC, because Mac OS X requires different hardware configurations. (In short, Mac OS X won't run on a PC.) But almost all OSes designed for modern PCs will install and run successfully on most virtual-machine programs described here.

Because this book focuses on the bottom lines of time, effort, and money, we'll look next at the easiest way of installing another OS on your Windows PC: Microsoft Virtual PC. Not only does Virtual PC make the process of installing and running another OS as easy and painless as possible, but the price is right: Virtual PC is free.

tip *If you find you don't like Virtual PC, try the 30-day evaluation versions of VMware Workstation (www.vmware.com) or Parallels Workstation (www.parallels.com).*

Step 3: Download and Install Virtual PC

To download and install Virtual PC, follow these steps:

1. Open your web browser and go to the Microsoft Downloads web site (www.microsoft.com/downloads/).

2. Find a link for downloading Virtual PC, and then click it. Internet Explorer displays the File Download – Security Warning dialog box.

3. Click the Run button. Internet Explorer downloads the file, and then launches the installation. On Windows Vista, you need to go through User Account Control for the Virtual PC 2007 Installer program (Windows XP does not have the User Account Control feature). The Microsoft Virtual PC Wizard then launches and displays its first screen.

4. Click the Next button, and then accept the license agreement on the next screen if you want to proceed. Click the Next button. The wizard displays the Customer Information screen.

5. Type the username you want associated with Virtual PC in the Username text box, and type an organization name in the Organization text box if you want to. The wizard enters your Windows username in the Username text box, but you can change it.

6. In the Install This Application For area, choose whether to make Virtual PC available to all users of the PC (select the Anyone Who Uses This Computer option button) or to keep it to yourself (select the Only For Me option button).

7. Click the Next button. The wizard displays the Ready To Install The Program screen.

8. By default, the wizard installs Virtual PC in a folder named Microsoft Virtual PC within the Program Files folder, Windows' recommended location for programs. Normally, it's best to use this folder, but if you want, you can choose a different folder by clicking the Change button, using the Change Current Destination Folder dialog box, and then clicking the OK button.

9. When you're ready to install Virtual PC, click the Install button, and then leave the wizard in peace for a few minutes. When the wizard displays the Installation Complete screen, click the Finish button.

Step 4: Install an Operating System on Virtual PC

Once you've installed Virtual PC on Windows, you're ready to create a virtual machine and install an OS.

Create a Virtual Machine for the Operating System

First, create a virtual machine—the pretend PC onto which you will install the OS. Follow these steps:

1. Start Virtual PC running. For example, choose Start | All Programs | Microsoft Virtual PC.

2. The first time you run Virtual PC, the program notices that you have no virtual machines, so it starts the Virtual Machine Wizard to walk you through the process of creating a suitable virtual machine for the OS you want to install.

note *If you (or someone else) have already created a virtual machine, Virtual PC displays the Virtual PC Console window. This window lists the virtual machines available and lets you start a virtual machine, change its settings, or delete it. Click the New button to launch the New Virtual Machine Wizard.*

3. Click the Next button. The wizard displays the Options screen.

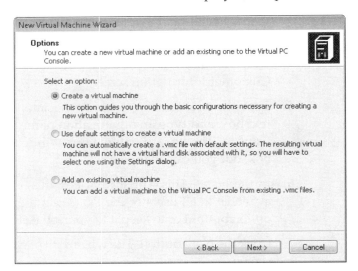

4. Make sure the Create A Virtual Machine option button is selected, and then click the Next button. The wizard displays the Virtual Machine Name And Location screen.

5. In the Name And Location text box, type the name you want to give the virtual machine. For example, you might use the name of the OS you're installing.

6. By default, the wizard creates the virtual machine in the My Virtual Machines folder, which is in your user folder. If your PC's hard drive has plenty of free space, this is as good a place as any. But if you need to create the virtual machine on another hard disk, click the Browse button, use the Existing Virtual Machine Name And Location dialog box to select the folder, and then click the Save button. Table 23-1 shows recommended hard disk

Operating System	Recommended Drive Size	Recommended RAM
Windows Vista	16GB	1GB
Windows XP	4GB	512MB
Windows 2000	2GB	256MB
Windows Me	1GB	128MB
Windows 98	1GB	128MB
Windows 95	1GB	64MB
Linux (most versions)	8GB	512MB

Table 23-1   Recommended Drive Sizes and RAM for Operating Systems on Virtual Machines

sizes and amounts of RAM for virtual machines, leaving enough space to install and run plenty of programs. If you're planning to store many large files on a virtual machine, allow more space.

7. Click the Next button. The wizard displays the Operating System screen, shown here with the Operating System drop-down list open:

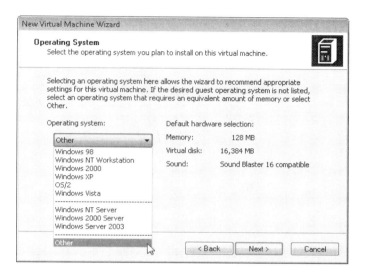

8. Click the Operating System drop-down list, and then choose the OS from the list. If the OS you're installing doesn't appear, choose Other. The Default Hardware Selection area shows the details of the memory, virtual hard disk, and sound hardware that the configuration you've chosen provides.

9. Click the Next button. The wizard displays the Memory screen:

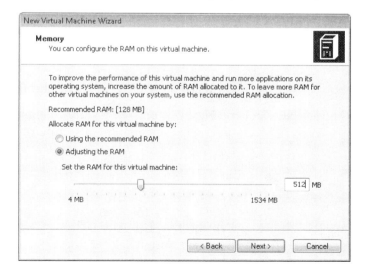

10. If the amount of RAM is adequate (refer to Table 23-1 for recommendations), leave the Using The Recommended RAM option button selected. If you want to increase the RAM (as is normally the case), select the Adjusting The RAM

option button, and then use either the slider or the text box to specify the amount of RAM. The text box is usually the easier means of setting an exact figure.

11. Click the Next button. The wizard displays the Virtual Hard Disk Options screen.

12. In the Do You Want To Use area, select the A New Virtual Hard Disk option button, and then click the Next button. The wizard displays the Virtual Hard Disk Location screen:

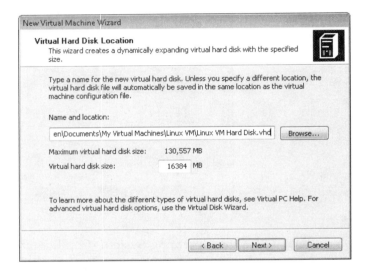

13. The Name And Location text box shows the full path and name of the virtual hard disk that the wizard will create. You can change the name or the location. Normally, the default name and location are fine, but in some cases, you may want to locate the virtual hard disk on a different (real) hard disk for space reasons. In this case, click the Browse button, use the Virtual Hard Disk Location dialog box to select the folder, and then click the Save button.

14. In the Virtual Hard Disk Size text box, set the size for the virtual hard disk. The default size may be adequate, but refer to Table 23-1 for suggested sizes.

15. Click the Next button. The wizard displays the Completing The New Virtual Machine Wizard screen, which summarizes the choices you made.

16. Verify the choices. If necessary, click the Back button to return to an earlier screen and change one of the choices. When you're satisfied, click the Finish button. The wizard closes, and a listing for the virtual machine appears in the Virtual PC Console:

Install the Operating System

With your virtual machine created, you're ready to install the OS. This example uses the Xandros distribution of Linux as the OS, but the steps are similar for other OSes. Follow these steps:

1. In the Virtual PC Console, click the virtual machine you just created (it may be selected already), and then click the Start button.

2. The virtual machine starts, and then tries to boot itself (see Figure 23-1). As yet, there's no OS installed, and no CD or DVD, so it tries to boot from the network. It then fails and gives you the message "Reboot and Select proper Boot device or Insert Boot Media in selected Boot device." Don't worry—this is normal.

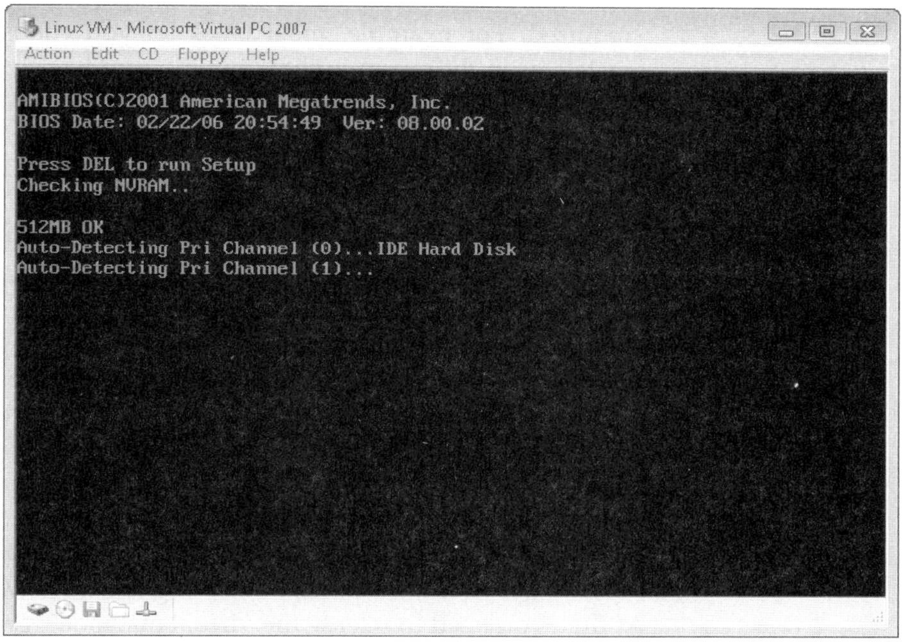

Figure 23-1

The virtual machine starts, looking like a real PC. For technical reasons, the first boot is doomed to failure.

> **note** *If you're quick, you may be able to insert the CD or DVD as soon as the virtual machine starts, and then choose CD | Use Physical Drive Letter (where Letter is the letter assigned to the PC's optical drive) before the virtual machine notices it doesn't have an OS. Generally, though, it's easier to insert the disc at your leisure, and then restart the virtual machine. Another option is to insert the disc before you start the virtual machine—but if you do this, you usually have to deal with an AutoPlay dialog box when Windows reads the disc.*

3. Choose CD | Use Physical Drive *Letter* (where *Letter* is the letter assigned to the PC's optical drive) in Virtual PC.

4. Insert the CD or DVD for the OS in the optical drive.

> **note** *If you have an ISO image (a file containing the image for a CD or DVD) containing the OS, you can use that instead without burning it to disc. Choose CD | Capture ISO Image, navigate to the image in the Select CD Image To Capture dialog box, and then click the Open button.*

5. In Virtual PC, choose Action | Reset. Virtual PC displays a warning dialog box whose title bar shows the name of the virtual machine. The dialog box tells you that resetting the virtual machine will lose all unsaved changes. That's fine, because the virtual machine contains no changes.

6. Click the Reset button. Virtual PC restarts the virtual machine.

7. Depending on the way the CD (or DVD) or ISO image is set up, the virtual PC may prompt you to press SPACEBAR or any key to boot from the disc. If this happens, press SPACEBAR or any key. Other OSes are set up to boot automatically without prompting you. In this case, wait while the OS boots. Depending on the OS, you may then see an installation wizard or a screen of installation options, or the installation process may simply run on its own.

8. Follow through the rest of the installation routine, choosing options where required. For example, most OSes let you choose which components to install, as in the example shown in Figure 23-2.

Moving the Focus Between the Virtual Machine and Other Windows

As you know, the *focus* determines which window receives the keypresses from the keyboard and the clicks from the mouse. Normally, you switch focus by clicking in a different window with the mouse or by pressing either ALT-TAB or WINDOWS KEY–TAB until Windows activates the window you want.

As soon as you start installing an OS with a graphical user interface in a virtual machine, life becomes more complicated. Once you put the focus in the virtual machine, you can switch it from window to window in similar ways (the specifics depend on the OS). For example, once you've clicked inside a virtual machine running Windows, pressing ALT-TAB switches focus among the windows in the virtual machine, not among the windows on your real PC.

At first, you need to release the virtual machine's grip on the focus manually by pressing the right ALT key. But once you've installed the OS on the virtual machine, you can usually install Virtual Machine Additions from within the OS. These Additions enable the virtual machine to grab the mouse pointer as soon as it enters the Virtual PC window and release it when it exits the window. This makes switching between the virtual machine and your real PC much easier.

If Virtual PC prompts you to install the Virtual Machine Additions while you're installing the OS, select the Don't Show This Message Again check box, and then click the OK button. You can't install the Additions until after the end of the installation process. See the section "Install the Virtual Machine Additions," later in this project, for instructions.

Figure 23-2

The installation routines for most OSes let you choose which components to install.

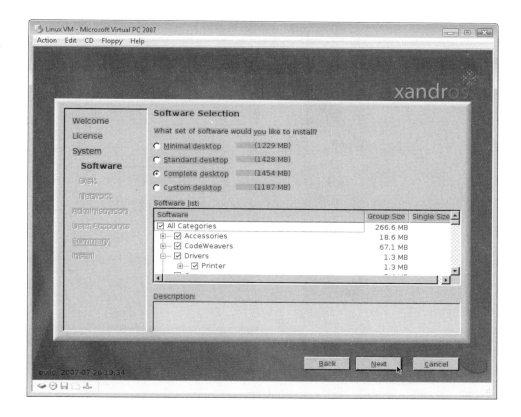

9. At the end of the installation, you usually need to restart the virtual machine so that the OS can finish configuring itself.

10. When the OS has restarted, you can start using it by clicking inside the virtual machine window. Figure 23-3 shows a Linux virtual machine browsing a Windows network.

note *To toggle the virtual machine between a window and full screen, press RIGHT ALT–ENTER. You can also choose Action | Full-Screen Mode to switch from a window to full-screen mode, but not to switch back.*

Step 5: Install the Virtual Machine Additions

To improve graphics performance in the virtual machine, to add mouse pointer integration (which enables the virtual machine to grab and release the mouse pointer), and to add other features such as folder sharing, you must install Virtual Machine

Figure 23-3

Once your OS is
installed, it's ready
for use.

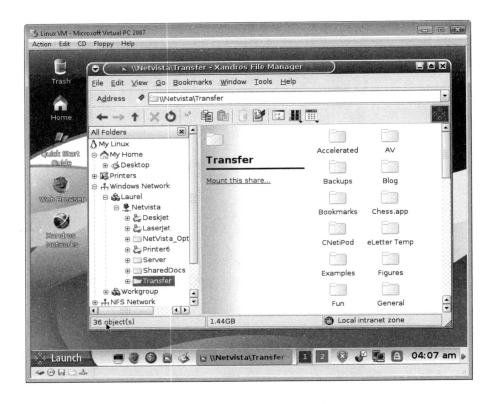

Additions within the virtual machine. The Virtual Machine Additions install using
a setup routine on the OS inside the virtual machine (as opposed to installing from
the PC that's running Virtual PC).

 *Virtual Machine Additions are available for Windows Vista Business, Ultimate, and Enterprise
editions; Windows XP Professional and Tablet PC Edition; Windows 2000 Professional; Windows
98 Second Edition; and several versions of OS/2 Warp, a Windows 95 competitor still grimly
clinging to life in some long-term technologies, such as ATMs.*

Follow these steps to install the Virtual Machine Additions:

1. In Virtual PC, choose Action | Install Or Update Virtual Machine Additions.
    Virtual PC displays the dialog box shown here, with the title bar containing
    the name of the virtual machine that will be affected:

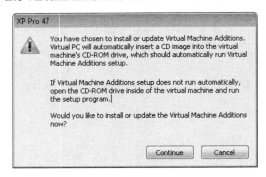

2. Click the Continue button. Virtual PC launches the Virtual Machine Additions setup routine, which displays its first screen.

3. Click the Next button, and then follow through the setup routine. Accept the default settings, because there is no reason to change them.

4. When the setup routine prompts you to restart the virtual machine, click the Yes button.

5. When the virtual machine restarts, you will be able to activate the virtual machine by moving the mouse pointer into its window, and return to the host PC by moving the mouse pointer out of the virtual machine window. You will also be able to drag files from Windows Explorer windows on the host PC and drop them in a Windows Explorer window on the virtual machine to copy them there.

As you've seen in this project, a virtual machine is an easy way to try out another OS, or perform light work on another OS, without removing Windows from your PC. But if you want to run another OS full-bore while still keeping Windows on your PC, you need to create a dual-boot setup. Turn the page.

Install Another Operating System Alongside Windows

What You'll Need

- Hardware: Nothing except your existing PC
- Software: System Commander (optional), other operating systems
- Cost: Free to $300 U.S.

So you need to run another operating system as well as Windows? If you choose not to use a virtual-machine program (as described in Project 23), you can create a dual-boot setup or a multiboot setup—installing two or more operating systems (OSes) on the same computer.

This project describes three ways of creating dual-boot setups using some widely used OSes. Even if none of the combinations is the one you want, these examples should give you an idea of how to proceed with the OSes you want.

 Before you attempt to create a dual-boot setup in any of the ways described in this project, create a fresh, current backup of your existing OS. See Project 16 for instructions for backing up and restoring your PC.

Step 1: Create a Dual-Boot Setup with Windows Vista and Windows XP

This is the easiest dual-boot setup to create—provided that you install Windows XP first and that you have either some unallocated space on your hard disk or another disk or drive on which to install Windows Vista. Because Windows XP was released years before Windows Vista, Windows XP doesn't know the details of Windows Vista's boot process, and tends to overwrite files it shouldn't.

Given that the normal reason for wanting to create this dual-boot setup is that you have a Windows XP PC and want to see how well Windows Vista compares, the first criterion is easy enough to meet. If you need to add another hard disk to a desktop PC, see Project 7.

To create a dual-boot setup with Windows Vista and Windows XP, follow these steps:

1. Install Windows XP if it's not already installed.

2. Insert the Windows Vista DVD in the optical drive.

3. Restart Windows. When your PC prompts you to boot from the CD drive, press SPACEBAR or any other key. The Windows Vista installation routine starts.

note *If your PC doesn't offer to boot from the optical drive, you may need to change the BIOS settings to make it do so. See Project 6 for instructions.*

4. On the first Install Windows screen, choose your language (for example, English), the time and currency format (for example, English [United States]), and your keyboard type (for example, US).

5. Click the Next button. The installation routine displays the second Install Windows screen.

6. Click the Install Now button. The installation routine displays the Type Your Product Key For Activation screen.

7. Type your product key in the box, allowing Windows to enter the hyphens for you at the end of each group of five characters.

8. Clear the Automatically Activate Windows When I'm Online check box unless you're dead certain you want Windows to activate itself automatically at the first possible opportunity. It's usually much better to verify that Windows is running satisfactorily before you activate it, as the activation process ties this copy of Windows to this particular PC.

9. Click the Next button, and then accept the license agreement on the next screen if you want to proceed. The installation routine displays the Which Type Of Installation Do You Want? screen.

10. Click the Custom (Advanced) button. (The Upgrade button will be unavailable unless you have launched the Windows Vista installation routine from

within Windows XP rather than during booting.) The installation routine displays the Where Do You Want To Install Windows? screen:

11. Select the disk or unallocated space that you want to use. If you want to create a new partition in unallocated space, click the New button, enter the partition size in the Size box that appears (as shown here), and then click the Apply button.

12. When you've chosen the disk or space, click the Next button. The rest of the installation routine then runs, and you get to set up Windows Vista.

13. After you log on, you can use Windows Vista.

14. When you want to switch to Windows XP, restart Windows. The Windows Boot Manager screen appears, as shown next. Press UP ARROW or DOWN ARROW to select the Earlier Version Of Windows item (which represents Windows XP), and then press ENTER. Windows XP starts.

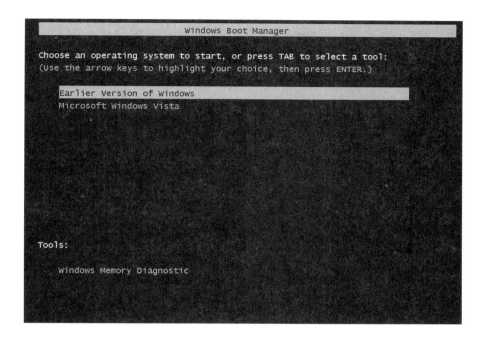

Step 2: Create a Dual-Boot Setup
with Windows and Linux

Some distributions of Linux are smart enough to automatically create a partition on an existing hard disk that has Windows installed. At this writing, the majority of Linux distributions that can manage this trick, work with Windows XP or another earlier version of Windows, such as Windows 2000 Professional, rather than with Windows Vista—but Windows Vista–friendly versions may have arrived by the time you read this.

To create this type of dual-boot setup, you need to have enough space on your hard disk to create a new partition and to install Linux.

note *Before you start, check the compatibility of your PC's hardware with the Linux distribution you're planning to use. Generally speaking, the more mainstream your PC's hardware, the better the chance you have of finding a Linux driver for it. More drivers tend to be available for hardware that has been around for a year or more, as it takes a while for Linux programmers to create drivers for newer hardware.*

To create a dual-boot setup with Windows and Linux, follow these general steps:

1. Set Windows up as usual. (Chances are that Windows came preinstalled on your PC, in which case you're all set to install Linux.)

2. Purchase or download the OS you want to install. This example uses the Xandros distribution of Linux. If you download the OS, burn it to CD or DVD.

3. Start Windows, and then log on as usual.

4. Insert the CD or DVD in your PC's optical drive. Windows automatically launches the installation routine, as in the example shown in Figure 24-1.

Figure 24-1

Some Linux distributions run automatically from Windows, which makes installation easy.

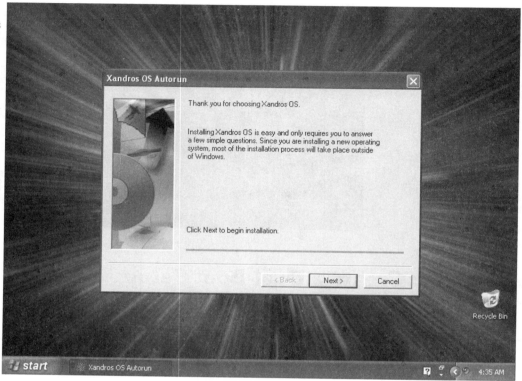

5. Follow the instructions for preparing your PC to boot from the CD or DVD.

6. If the new OS gives you the choice of keeping Windows or getting rid of it, as in Figure 24-2, make sure you choose the option for keeping it.

7. When the installation routine has completed, you usually need to restart your PC so that the new OS can finish configuring itself. When the new OS restarts, you can start using it.

8. To launch Windows, use the other OSes command to restart the PC. When it restarts, you will see a boot menu, such as the example shown here. Press DOWN ARROW to select the Windows item on the menu, and then press ENTER. Windows starts, and you can log on as usual.

Figure 24-2

When installing another OS alongside Windows, be careful to make the right choice (to keep Windows) on screens like this one.

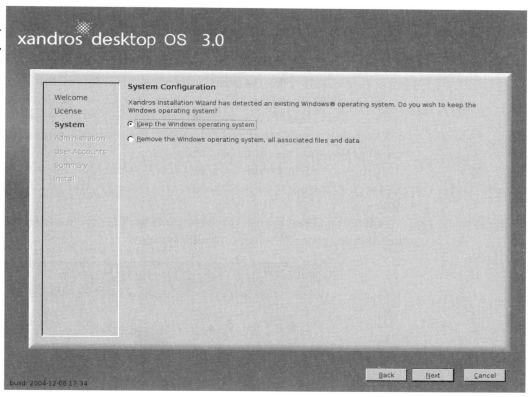

Step 3: Create a Dual-Boot or Multiboot Setup with Other Operating Systems

As you've seen earlier in this project, creating a dual-boot setup is a ticklish process. Get it wrong, and you may find yourself with your main OS wrecked and needing reinstallation. And to add insult to injury, the installation of the destructive new OS may have failed too. If you're prepared to pay to avoid such problems, consider buying software such as System Commander from VCOM (www.v-com.com). System Commander manages the boot process, enabling you to create dual-boot or multiboot setups with little or no fuss.

Get and Install System Commander

To get System Commander, go to www.v-com.com, pay for the latest version, and then download it. You have the option of having a CD of the software shipped for an extra fee, which gives you a bootable CD that you can use to rescue System Commander if you manage to hose it by installing an OS the wrong way. You can also burn the bootable CD yourself, which is cheaper and faster.

To install System Commander, double-click the downloaded file, and then click the Install System Commander button on the System Commander screen.

Follow through the installation process until the Create Diskettes screen, which lets you create a bootable CD containing utilities and recovery tools or create disks containing those tools. These days, most PCs can boot from the optical drive, but you may choose to make disks instead if your PC has a floppy drive. Select the appropriate option button, click the Next button, and then follow the instructions for creating the CD or disks. Label the CD or disks, test the CD or the disks immediately to verify that they work, and then store them safely.

Note the user ID and password that the System Commander Security Settings screen gives, and then finish the installation.

You must restart Windows to allow System Commander to write itself to the boot sector. During the boot process, you'll see the Welcome To System Commander message.

Click the Close button (the × button) to close the message. System Commander then displays the OS Selection Menu window:

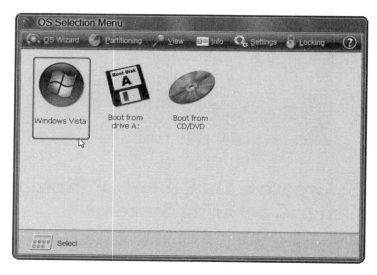

From here, you can click the OS or drive you want to boot. For example, in the previous illustration, you can boot Windows Vista, boot from a floppy, or boot from a CD or DVD. But what you probably want to do at this stage is install another OS.

Install Another Operating System

To install another OS, follow these steps from the OS Selection Menu window:

1. Click the OS Wizard button. System Commander displays the Backup Recommendations screen.

2. Click the OK button. System Commander displays an Operation Tips screen. These tips are worth reading, but once you've done so, you'll probably want to clear the Show This Screen At Start check box so that this screen doesn't appear the next time you install another OS.

3. Click the Next button. The OS Wizard displays the Select The Type Of OS Installation screen.

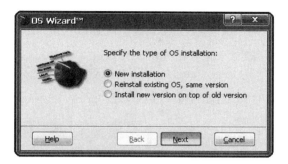

4. Select the New Installation option button. (Your other choices are to reinstall the same version of an OS that's already installed, or to install a new version of an OS on top of the existing version.)

5. Click the Next button. The wizard displays the Select The OS Type You Wish To Install screen.

6. If the category of OS you want is listed, select its option button. Otherwise, select the Show All OSes option button.

7. Click the Next button. The wizard displays a screen that lists the OSes within the category you chose. (If you selected the Show All OSes option button, you see a larger screen with the full list of OSes.)

8. Click the Next button. If the wizard displays another screen with further versions of OSes, pick the one you want, and then click the Next button. The wizard displays a screen confirming you're ready to install the OS.

9. Select the I Have The Necessary Installation Boot CD option button, and then click the Next button. The wizard displays the OS Wizard Action Plan screen:

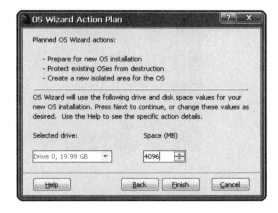

10. In the Selected Drive drop-down list, choose the drive on which you want System Commander to create the new partition. (If your PC has only one drive, you have no choice here.)

11. In the Space text box, enter the size of the partition to create, in megabytes.

12. Click the Finish button. The wizard creates the partition, displaying a Progress screen while it does so.

13. When the OS Wizard Complete screen appears, read the instructions:

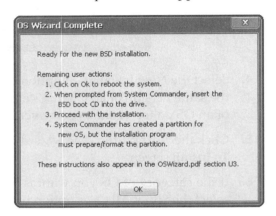

14. Click the OK button. When System Commander prompts you to insert a bootable CD or DVD, insert the disc, and then click the OK button.

15. System Commander starts the installation routine (the next illustration shows an example). Follow through the installation as usual.

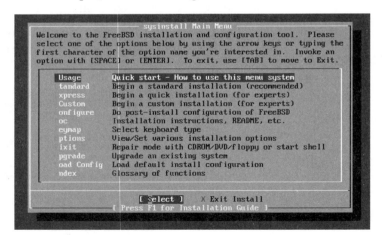

Once you have finished the installation, the new OS appears in the OS Selection Menu when you restart your PC. You can then boot the new OS—or any of the other OSes you have installed.

Index